𝕿𝖍𝖊 𝕾𝖆𝖎𝖓𝖙𝖘 𝖆𝖓𝖉 𝕾𝖊𝖗𝖛𝖆𝖓𝖙𝖘 𝖔𝖋 𝕲𝖔𝖉.

SECOND SERIES.

THE LIVES

OF

S. VERONICA GIULIANI,

CAPUCHIN NUN:

AND OF THE

BLESSED BATTISTA VARANI,

OF THE ORDER OF S. CLARE.

"Gaude Maria Virgo, cunctas hæreses sola interemisti in universo mundo."—*Antiph. Ecclesiæ.*

LONDON:
R. WASHBOURNE, 18 PATERNOSTER ROW.
1874.

Printing Statement:

Due to the very old age and scarcity of this book, many of the pages may be hard to read due to the blurring of the original text, possible missing pages, missing text, dark backgrounds and other issues beyond our control.

Because this is such an important and rare work, we believe it is best to reproduce this book regardless of its original condition.

Thank you for your understanding.

TO

THE NUNS OF ENGLAND,

WHO SHIELD THEIR COUNTRY BY THEIR PRAYERS,

AND BY THEIR MEEK AUSTERITIES MAKE

REPARATION FOR ITS SINS;

AND TO

THE SISTERS OF MERCY,

WHOSE CHARITY IS THEIR INCLOSURE,

WHILE FOR THE LOVE OF THEIR HEAVENLY SPOUSE

IN HIS POOR AND SUFFERING MEMBERS

THEY DENY THEMSELVES

THE PEACE AND PROTECTION OF THE CLOISTER.

Daughters of Mary! in retreats obscure,
Lost to man's thought and eye, amid the trees
And unfrequented fields, on bended knees
Sueing for England's pardon, lives so pure
Mingle in heaven and God's approval share
With that uncloistered love, whose willing feet
Are borne through jeering crowd and gazing street
To scenes of lonely want and pining care.
For you the holy past is now unfurled,
That with its bright examples you may feed
The spirit of devotion. While the world
Honours your goodness with its hatred, you,
Still to your high and calm vocation true,
May win fresh light and strength from what you read.

F. W. FABER.

S. WILFRID'S,
Feast of our Lady of Redemption,
MDCCCXLVII.

PREFACE.

The following Life of S. Veronica Giuliani was written by the Abate Filippo Maria Salvatori, and published in Rome in the year 1839. It was compiled from three lives of the Saint of earlier date, and from the processes of her canonization.

The translation of the Spiritual Life of the Blessed Battista Varani has been made from the French version published at Clermont-Ferrand in 1840. It is founded upon the collection of her revelations, written in Italian by Father Matthew Pascucci, and rendered into Latin by the Bollandists, in the *Acta Sanctorum* for the 31st of May.

The Oratory, London,
May 31st, 1874.

CONTENTS.

S. VERONICA GIULIANI.

BOOK I.

CONTAINING AN ACCOUNT OF HER LIFE IN THE WORLD, AND OF THE MOST IMPORTANT EVENTS IN THE FIRST FIFTEEN YEARS OF HER RELIGIOUS CAREER, TOGETHER WITH A BRIEF SKETCH OF THE OFFICES WHICH SHE FILLED IN THE CONVENT.

CHAPTER		PAGE
I.	The birth of Veronica.—Tokens of her subsequent sanctity and high privileges apparent even in infancy	3
II.	She begins at the age of three years to enjoy familiar intercourse with Jesus and Mary	7
III.	The first proofs of extraordinary virtue which made her childhood remarkable	12
IV.	Her father removes with Ursula and her sisters to Piacenza, where at the age of ten she makes her First Communion.—When twelve years old she begins to practise mental prayer	20
V.	The rich fruit which she gathered from the exercise of meditation.—The first instances of opposition to her religious vocation which she had to encounter at Piacenza	28
VI.	Ursula is sent back to Mercatello, where she resides in the house of her uncle.—New trials of her vocation.—At length her father yields to her influence and repents, ending his life with certain marks of eternal salvation	35
VII.	Having received the desired consent of her father, Ursula procures in an extraordinary way her admission among the Capuchin nuns of Città di Castello	41

CHAPTER		PAGE
VIII.	Her clothing.—Deceits of the devil during her noviciate	46
IX.	Her solemn profession.—Her virtue is strengthened, notwithstanding the assaults of the devil, by special graces which she receives from God during the early years of her religious life	56
X.	The offices which she is called to fill in the convent.—The manner in which she discharged her duties	64

BOOK II.

CONTAINING AN ACCOUNT OF THE EXTRAORDINARY GRACES BY MEANS OF WHICH SHE WAS RAISED DURING THE LAST THIRTY-FIVE YEARS OF HER LIFE TO THE HIGHEST DEGREE OF SANCTITY, AND RENDERED THE LIVING IMAGE OF JESUS CRUCIFIED.

I.	Mysterious vision of a chalice, which prepared her to reproduce in her own person the Passion of our Redeemer	85
II.	Veronica is made to participate in our Blessed Saviour's crowning with thorns.—The severe pains which this caused her, and her sufferings from the remedies to which her superiors required her to submit	92
III.	She is promoted to heavenly espousals.—The manner in which our Lord prepared and conducted them	99
IV.	The gifts and favours which Jesus lavished on His spouse during the two following days.—Her correspondence to them	110
V.	In obedience to a divine command she begins to fast rigorously on bread and water, and continues to do so for several years.—The opposition which she had to encounter from her superiors, as well as from herself, and from the powers of darkness	115
VI.	Further instances of Veronica's fidelity to her divine Spouse.—She receives from Him a wound in the heart.—Four documents written by her with her own blood	127
VII.	Jesus produces in her a still greater resemblance to Himself by imprinting upon her His sacred stigmata	139
VIII.	The stigmata are repeated on various occasions, and attested by new and satisfactory proofs	152

CHAPTER PAGE
IX. Veronica participates in all the other Dolours which constituted the divine Passion.—Wonderful marks imprinted on her heart - - 163
X. The extraordinary graces and favours which accompanied her last illness and holy death - 178

BOOK III.

OF HER HEROIC VIRTUES AND OF THE GIFTS WHICH SHE POSSESSED IN COMMON WITH OTHER SAINTS.

I. Jesus Christ Himself becomes her visible Instructor in Christian and perfect life.—Her constant desire of greater perfection - - - 195
II. Veronica's heroic perfection in the theological virtues - - - - - - 202
III. Her remarkable zeal and charity towards her neighbour - - - - - 211
IV. Her spirit of poverty and mortification, and her angelic purity - - - - - 225
V. Her patience and imperturbable gentleness - 236
VI. Her wonderful humility - - - - 250
VII. Her miraculous obedience - - - 259
VIII. Her tender devotion to the Blessed Virgin, to her guardian angel, and the other saints - - 267
IX. Her gifts of prophecy and miracles during life - 275
NOTE - - - - - - 285

BLESSED BATTISTA VARANI.

HISTORICAL NOTICE - - - - 289
PROLOGUE - - - - - 295
I. Her vow made in childhood relative to the Passion of Jesus Christ.—Her progress in this devotion, and the pious exercises which it suggested to her - - - - - - 298
II. She resists the grace of a religious vocation for a long time, but ends by following it with generosity - - - - - - 304
III. Spiritual favours which followed her entire conversion - - - - - - 312

CHAPTER		PAGE
IV.	What she had to suffer during her noviciate.—Her return to Camerino, where she received great favours from Heaven, and, among others, a visit from S. Clare	326
V.	Other divine favours accorded to Battista: they are followed by new tribulations	337
VI.	Battista addresses to her spiritual father particulars supplementary to the history of her life	349
VII.	First pain.—Sorrow for the sufferings of the lost and the elect	364
	Second pain.—The sorrows of Christ for the sufferings of His Mother, S. Mary Magdalen, and His disciples	370
	Third pain.—The sorrows of Christ for the ingratitude of the Jewish people, and of all creatures; His especial sorrow in the Garden	375

SUPPLEMENT.

I.	Her humility	383
II.	Her charity towards her neighbour, manifested in the warnings she gives her disciple	394
III.	Her virtue is tried by the good and evil fortune of her family.—She establishes a monastery at Fermo, and returns to Camerino, where she is raised to the dignity of abbess	404
IV.	Friendship of Battista with John of Fano.—Beginning of the congregation of Capuchins.—Death of Battista and veneration of her body	406

BOOK I.

CONTAINING AN ACCOUNT OF HER LIFE IN THE WORLD, AND OF THE MOST IMPORTANT EVENTS IN THE FIRST FIFTEEN YEARS OF HER RELIGIOUS CAREER, TOGETHER WITH A BRIEF SKETCH OF THE OFFICES WHICH SHE FILLED IN THE CONVENT.

THE LIFE OF
S. VERONICA GIULIANI.

CHAPTER I.

THE BIRTH OF VERONICA.—TOKENS OF HER SUBSE-QUENT SANCTITY AND HIGH PRIVILEGES APPARENT EVEN IN HER INFANCY.

THE district of Mercatello, which is one of considerable importance in the Pontifical States, being in the diocese of Urbania, part of the Duchy of Urbino, was the favoured birth-place of S. Veronica, whose wonderful life we are about to relate. Her father was Francesco Giuliani, and her mother Benedetta Mancini of S. Angelo in Vado, a diocese united to Urbania; both were of honourable and wealthy families. Their union in holy matrimony was blessed with no male issue, but they had no less than seven daughters, the youngest of whom was our Saint. Even before the birth of this her last child, the mother had reason to foresee that her infant would prove an extraordinary one; for whereas on all previous occasions she had been afflicted with severe sufferings and extreme internal weakness, so that she had been compelled to abstain in consequence from holy Communion, now on the contrary she enjoyed such good health and exemption from the trials usually experienced in her condition, that she was able to perform all her devotions and domestic duties with ease and alacrity, and she declared with astonishment that she had never before spent such calm and joyful days.

At length the day arrived which was to be marked by the nativity of her favoured offspring. It was the 27th of December, which is dedicated to the memory of S. John, the beloved disciple of Jesus Christ; and perhaps it was the special providence of God which appointed this feast for the birthday of S. Veronica, who even in her earliest infancy clearly proved herself to be one of those happy souls on whom God has bestowed the choicest prerogatives of His love. On the following day, being the Feast of the Holy Innocents, 1660, she was regenerated at the baptismal font, in the collegiate church of S. Peter and S. Paul, D. Giovan Antonio Borghese officiating as parish priest. She received the name of Ursula, a presage that she would not only be a virgin Saint, but likewise the guide and mistress of other holy virgins.

The anticipations formed respecting her were quickly realised. Two of her sisters have deposed upon oath that she never uttered a cry nor shed a tear, but was always quiet, serene, and cheerful, without manifesting the least antipathy towards any one, permitting herself to be handled without complaint, and to be nursed at whatever time her mother pleased On three days in the week, Wednesday, Friday, and Saturday, she displayed an aversion from her food, so much so that she would only take a few drops morning and evening; and nothing could induce her to take more on these days. Thus, like S. Nicholas of Bari and other saints, this child early commenced her fasts by way of prelude to those strict ones which she observed afterwards. Many things concur to show that this abstinence was produced by a higher than natural influence; in the first place, she gave no sign of suffering or discomfort, but was bright and calm as usual: secondly, by her mother being compelled on these days to take to her breast some children of the poor, whom she accordingly nursed in the presence of her little daughter, who never showed any symptom of envy or jealousy, as young children so situated are apt to do; on the contrary, it was observed that she seemed to be particularly gratified by the sight of the poor little ones partaking of her own nourishment. Lastly, it is evident, from the above-mentioned days being dedicated in the Christian world to the honour of the Passion of Jesus Christ and to the memory of His most holy Mother, that she was attracted towards both even from her cradle by a peculiar and wonderful devotion. This we shall see confirmed hereafter by those touching communications which were exchanged between Jesus and Mary on the one hand, and our virgin Saint on the other, throughout the entire course of her life.

But something still more astonishing remains to be related. The little Ursula was hardly five months old, when on the Feast of the Most Holy Trinity, which in the year 1661 fell on the 12th of June, she was in the arms of her mother, who had released her from her swaddling clothes, and perceiving a picture whereon that august mystery was represented, she descended of her own accord to the floor, and alone without any assistance advanced with a firm step towards the sacred tablet, before which she made many signs of reverence, and then paused as though enchanted. We can easily conceive the amazement of her mother and of every one present. Her prudent parent, comprehending that it was the work of the Almighty, attempted no interference, but left the child to herself; and henceforward she was wrapped in no swathing bands, but was able to walk alone without meeting with any accident. Another miracle which occurred when she was a year and a half old, is related in the process of her canonization. A servant of the family, called Alexandra, carried her in her arms when she went to purchase some oil at a shop; the man who sold it endeavoured to put her off with short measure, when the little Ursula astounded them all by speaking for the first time, and pronouncing in a distinct voice these words—" Do justice, for God sees you!" A succession of these extraordinary occurrences induced her pious parents to regard her, not only with partiality, but even with devotion, for they had good reason to look forward to the supernatural privileges that were destined for their child. They guarded her as the apple of their eye, and her elder sisters took pains not to annoy her, but on the other hand to foster her natural disposition. The servants followed their example, treating her as though she had been the mistress of the house, as she herself, after she had grown up and become a religious, declared with sentiments of humility and confusion, being herself amazed thereat, for she had the very poorest opinion of herself.

CHAPTER II.

SHE BEGINS AT THE AGE OF THREE YEARS TO ENJOY FAMILIAR INTERCOURSE WITH JESUS AND MARY.

WHEN Ursula had completed her third year, those seeds of devotion which had been implanted in her by heaven began to develop themselves day by day. Even at that tender age, the sports of childhood had no charms for her. Instead of childish toys she chose to entertain herself with a beautiful picture of the Blessed Virgin in the act of nursing her Divine Son, which hung on a wall in the house. Before it she raised a sort of little altar, and all her thoughts and cares were concentrated on the adornment of this her oratory. She would often invite her sisters to assist in her pious work. From what follows it is evident that this was not with her, as is the case with some children, a matter of mere pastime and diversion. The ribbons and corals with which her mother and sisters attempted to decorate the person of Ursula, together with any other ornaments she might receive, were one and all devoted to the furnishing of this cherished spot; for in her holy simplicity she was wont to regard that sacred picture as our Blessed Lord Himself. Hence she would converse familiarly with the Queen of Saints and with the Infant Jesus, as though they were really present before her, and just as if she were addressing her own mother and sisters. She would often deposit her food on this little altar, inviting the Divine Infant to partake thereof; and then she would conceal herself behind the tapestry, and watch to see if the object of her devotion were descending to fulfil her request; and when her wish was not gratified, she would exclaim in her disappointment: "If You will not eat, then neither will I." At other times she would entreat Mary to give her the Divine Infant to caress; and perceiving that her prayer was not heard, she would place one chair upon another in order to mount and take her treasure by force; more than once she had in consequence a fall by which her head was severely bruised. On rising she would reproach the Blessed Virgin for having refused her petition, and claim to have her mishap remedied, which she had no sooner done than she found herself cured.

This simplicity was so pleasing to Mary and her Divine Son, that on several occasions the picture took the form of living persons, and Ursula beheld the Holy Virgin place within her arms the sacred Babe, permitting her to lavish caresses on Him. At other times the Infant Saviour came down from His place in the picture, and partook on the altar of the food she offered, presenting her with a portion of the same, that she might share it with Him. It must have been a wonderful sight to behold the little girl so innocently imploring the favour of Mary, bestowing her small gifts on Jesus, beseeching Him to descend from the picture and to accompany her wherever she went; and then to see the condescension of Mary, and the sacred Hand of her Son stretched forth towards Ursula in token of acceptance, and afterwards rejoicing the heart of His beloved child by the most affecting endearments.

Such interchange of love increased the tender homage of our young Saint towards the two great objects of her devotion, and she was even permitted to hear the voice of Mary addressing her from this picture in accents of love, and giving her frequent and useful directions. One day when she was there in preparation for prayer, the Blessed Virgin said to her: "Daughter, this my Son loves thee exceedingly—prepare thyself, for He will be thy Spouse!" At these words an extraordinary fire of love was kindled in her soul, and she earnestly longed to give herself entirely to Jesus. Whatever she had that was fair and good, she offered Him on her little altar. One day the Divine Infant vouchsafed to acknowledge her generosity by saying to her: "I love thee very much! Take care to expend thy affections on no other than Myself alone." To which Ursula immediately replied: "Dearest Jesus, I love Thee most ardently! teach me what Thou wouldst have me do." The Infant Saviour then turned to His holy Mother and said: "It is My Will that this our beloved child should be guided by thee." On another occasion when she was gathering flowers in the garden for her altar, the Infant Jesus appeared before her, saying: "I am the Flower of the field;" and after these words the vision disappeared. Ursula accordingly ran into the house, thinking that the object of her love had taken refuge there, and full of grief presented herself before her favourite picture, exclaiming: "Thou hast made me run, whilst Thou didst return into the arms of Mary, and I have not been able to overtake Thee," and then she burst into tears. Her loving Lord, Who could not endure to see her thus afflicted, deigned to leave the picture and embrace her, which restored her serenity in a moment.

These facts are taken in part from the deposition of

her sisters, who were careful never to lose sight of her, as also from the testimony of her first confessor, the Canon Ambroni of Mercatello, and in part also from the account which she wrote of herself after she became a religious, in obedience to her directors —her perfect sanctity rendering all idea of deception inadmissible. From these sources we also learn that at the same age, namely, in her third or fourth year, on the return of her mother or her aunt from church, she would know by the perception of a certain celestial fragrance when they had been to holy Communion, and would exclaim, "How sweet the perfume! oh, how sweet!" nor would she leave them for a considerable time. Very frequently when taken into a church, although so young, she beheld the Sacred Host all dazzling and glorious; and sometimes the living form of the Holy Child Jesus was visible to her eyes. We must not omit a remarkable incident which occurred when she was about four years old. Her mother was taken so dangerously ill that the holy Viaticum was conveyed to her. At the moment of the entrance of the Blessed Sacrament, Ursula beheld It resplendent with such heavenly light that she implored the priest to communicate her also. In order to satisfy her, she was told that he had brought with him only one particle of the Blessed Eucharist, to which the child, doubtless enlightened from above, promptly replied that he might break off for her a fragment of that one, for that "as in the case of a mirror, when it is broken into a multitude of pieces, each fragment will still reflect the entire object which the whole originally represented, so each portion of that Sacred Host divided between her mother and herself would contain Jesus as entirely as the whole had done before It was broken." All present were filled with astonishment. As soon as her mother had received holy Communion, the little Ursula exclaimed —" Oh, how lovely is that which you have received!" and springing on the bed and drawing near to her mother's lips, she went on: " Oh, how sweet—how very sweet !" nor could all the scolding addressed to her induce her to tear herself away.

The pious lady had already lost two of her daughters. Being now on the verge of the grave, she called around her the five who still survived, and after bestowing on them all the precious legacy of a parent's dying counsel, she concluded by consigning each of her children to one of the sacred wounds of Jesus Crucified. For Ursula she selected the Side pierced with the spear, which was already the object of that dear child's tender love, besides being the perennial fountain whence throughout her whole life she was accustomed to draw abundance of graces. After this, our Saint's excellent mother breathed her last. The young Ursula, overwhelmed with affliction, could not be persuaded to quit her body night or day ; but there she remained, in that chamber of death, giving vent to her deep affection. There were no means of inducing her to go to bed, for her mother was not there. At last the servants hit on the expedient of placing on her bed an image of the Blessed Virgin with her Divine Infant; the child then gave way, and calmly composed herself to sleep. From that time she kept up the practice of making that sacred image her companion ; and it often seemed to her that the Babe of Bethlehem looked graciously on her and smiled.

CHAPTER III.

THE FIRST PROOFS OF EXTRAORDINARY VIRTUE WHICH MADE HER CHILDHOOD REMARKABLE.

THE wonderful things which we have related serve rather as illustrations of the peculiar favour of heaven towards the little Ursula than as proofs of that supernatural virtue which was so conspicuous even in her earliest years, and to the consideration of which we shall devote the present chapter. Ursula began at a most tender age to manifest an extraordinary compassion towards the poor. She would always reserve a portion of her breakfast, dinner, collation, and supper to bestow on them by way of alms; and this she would present to them with remarkable affection, when she saw them pass along the street. If it happened that she had nothing to give them, she would betake herself to her parents with engaging importunity. On many occasions she impoverished herself to relieve the distressed. Once she saw a little boy almost destitute of clothing, and accordingly took off her apron to cover him with it. At another time she was standing at the window when a pilgrim asked her for a little charitable assistance; having nothing else that she could think of to give him, with holy simplicity she took off one of her new slippers, which she had put on for the first time that day, and gave it him. The poor man said, as he accepted the gift, that one would be of no use to him without the other, which he immediately received from the hand of the generous child. Every one knows how vain children are apt to be of such articles of dress, and how fond they are of displaying them; it may therefore be easily conceived how self-denying was this act of charity on the part of Ursula. Our Lord was pleased to signify His approbation by a twofold miracle. In throwing it over to him the second slipper caught on the arch of the door, but the height of the pilgrim increased to such a degree that he was able to reach it with his hands; presently the most Holy Virgin appeared to Ursula, holding in her hand the gifts which had been bestowed on the pilgrim, now enriched with costly jewels; and the Mother of God explained to Ursula that she had just received them from her in the person of that poor traveller, and that it was her Divine Son who had adorned them with gems. Another time when Ursula had given a piece of rather black bread to a poor man, because she had no better to bestow, she beheld it change in his hands into bread whiter than snow, which the beggar in his wonder showed to every one he met in the street.

This favoured child not only excelled thus early in the grace of charity, but was likewise remarkable for an extraordinary desire of suffering, which was enkindled in the following way. On one occasion while performing her devout exercises before the picture of which we have spoken in the previous chapter, she heard these words from her Infant Saviour: "My Spouse, the Cross awaits thee." The young Saint in her inexperience conceived that she was thus warned to preserve the sacred sign of our redemption from every act of irreverence; and therefore whenever she perceived in the house or garden pieces of straw or thread accidentally laid in the form of a cross, she picked them up with reverence, and put them away in a box, lest any one should inadvertently tread on them. But when she heard the lives of the saints read (for her pious mother was accustomed to make that holy study serve for one of the recreations of her daughters), she very quickly apprehended, by means of the light vouchsafed her from above, the true meaning of those mysterious words, and resolved to obey the injunction they conveyed. She was not more than three years old when, moved by the sufferings of the saints, and especially by those of the martyrs who had encountered flames for the sake of Jesus Christ, her heart burned with such an ardent longing to imitate them that she ran and thrust her hands into a vessel of live coals, nor would she withdraw them till the smell summoned the inmates of the house to her side. In after-life, she thus wrote under obedience of her sensations at the time: "I do not perfectly remember, but it strikes me that at the moment I did not feel the pain of burning; I stood there in a state of temporary abstraction, well pleased to be as I was; afterwards I felt pain in my fingers, which were shrunk up. Everybody wept, but I am not conscious of having shed a tear."

In her fourth year, hearing that S. Rose of Lima was in the constant habit of taking the discipline, and not knowing exactly how to do the same, she made a great many knots in her apron-strings, hid herself behind a door, untied her apron, and struck herself with them. She was one day detected by her mother when thus employed, and sorely was the poor child mortified, because she was aware that her saintly model was wont to hide such practices from the observation of all. Having also heard that S. Rose once by way of mortification crushed her finger beneath the lid of a box, and then, though the pain which ensued was severe, would not consent to have it medically treated, in order that she might suffer the more, Ursula would fain have followed her example, but her heart failed her. Our Lord, however, permitted the occurrence of the following incident. Her hand was accidentally squeezed between the wall and a door which her sister was closing. The innocent cause of the disaster no sooner perceived this than in a paroxysm of self-reproach she cried out that she had killed Ursula, who, on the contrary, without the slightest agitation, implored her to calm herself, for that the hurt was nothing, although it was bleeding copiously; but as she added in her own account of it, "My sister seeing such a quantity of blood uttered still louder exclamations, while I believe that for my part I felt a certain delight in sharing the suffering of S. Rose. But to my grief they insisted on dressing my wound, although I would have much rather endured it without having recourse to any remedies, according to the example of that blessed saint." On another occasion, the scissors with which her mother was cutting a nail of the poor child's foot by some accident inflicted a severe cut. Instead of giving way to tears, Ursula in the most cheerful manner consoled her distressed parent by making light of the injury received; and in this case she succeeded in imitating S. Rose by dispensing with all remedies. The same good motive led her to commit another act of childlike indiscretion, namely, to pile up a number of stones on the top of a little wall, and then give them a push with her head, which brought them tumbling down on her hands which she held stretched out on the ground, thereby occasioning herself considerable pain. At length, having observed that her sisters were in the habit of using certain instruments of penance, she placed herself on the watch, in order to get hold of them; but it was all in vain, for they were kept under lock and key. No one can fail to be struck by such instances of heroism, at an age when the smallest suffering generally draws tears.

The very defects of her childhood were signs of her extraordinary virtue. An evil intention can change an action, in itself good or at least indifferent, into a sin, while either inculpable inadvertence or invincible ignorance excuses from sin. Thus many actions reprehensible in themselves, if done from a good motive, and accompanied by the above-mentioned ignorance or inadvertence, may under certain circumstances become even virtuous, not from their own nature, but from the principle which produces them. Let the reader bear in mind that the actions related of Ursula from her third to her seventh year cannot fail to be marked by much imperfection, because, although she seemed prematurely to anticipate the use of reason, she could not possibly possess at that tender age the light and instruction necessary for observing the exact limits which separate right from wrong, especially in those cases where one may be easily confounded with the other. What may be termed the defects of her childhood are not proposed as matters for imitation, for they are not of a nature to serve as precedents, but simply to illustrate the strength of her virtues, the excess of which, through inculpable ignorance and want of reflection on her part, was wont to carry her to such extremes.

Her father had one day caused two dishes of sweetmeats to be prepared for a relation of his who had arrived at Mercatello. Ursula saw them, and thinking it a great pity that such good things should be wasted on a person who had already a superfluity of comforts, whereas the same provisions would satisfy the hunger of a starving fellow-creature, contrived to break them in pieces, and so obtained leave to dispose of them in alms. It was a laudable practice of hers at the age of five years, when she used to distribute her bounties, to make the objects of her charity begin by reciting some devout prayer or the principal points of Christian doctrine. One day, however, she met with a poor boy who manifested reluctance to repeat his Ave Maria. Her zeal waxed so warm on the occasion that she gave him a push which threw him down the steps, though he was not seriously injured. Certainly it is a virtue to be zealous for the glory of God and the salvation of our neighbour; but for this very reason there is danger of its transgressing due bounds and becoming a fault, unless it be regulated with a degree of prudence that cannot be expected from a young child. She was so excessively fond of adorning the sacred picture of Jesus and Mary, that she seemed to have a holy passion for performing devout festivities there and for decorating the altar which she had placed before it. She was anxious that her sisters should do the same, and if they occasionally appeared unwilling, she would beat time on a box until they complied. One day they were so busy with their bobbins for making lace that they paid no attention whatever to her summons. Ursula felt that it was an affront to Almighty God to prefer their lace-work to assisting in a pious action; so she went and upset their whole apparatus on the floor.

Having heard that a certain potter of the adjacent country led a wicked life, and being aware that trials will sometimes bring back the wanderer into the right path, perceiving, moreover, as she was passing by his shop, a good many of his newly made vessels exposed to the air to harden, she with her small fingers bored holes in a good many of them. It pleased God to overrule this well-meant severity on the part of the child, and to make it instrumental to the conversion of the wretched man.

In her seventh year she noticed that a young man, her cousin, was much attached to the things of the world, so she invited him to play at fencing with her, and for the purpose of rescuing him from the perils to which he was exposed abroad, she gave him a slight wound in the side, which forced him to confine himself to the house for some little time.

One day, being disedified by a certain action of a domestic of the family, her indignation on account of the offence thus committed against God carried her so far as to give the woman a box on the ear; she moreover requested her father to dismiss the servant from his establishment; and her petition being granted, it appeared to her that she had done a very right thing.

Such were the faults of our Saint's childhood, which, however objectionable in themselves, demonstrate the existence in her heart of a large fund of charity, religion, and zeal; and although when we bear in mind her extreme youth, they may attract our admiration as taking their rise in extraordinary virtue, we must not attempt to imitate them. She herself viewed them with far different eyes when she had become a religious, and had attained to maturity in knowledge, and to far greater perfection in virtue; then she was wont to mention them with deep regret and confusion, though in speaking of them to her directors she could not deny that the motives which had prompted them were good. Still later in life, on the morning of the first Sunday in Advent, which fell on the 2nd of December, in the year 1702, our Lord permitted for her purification that she should see the defects of her early childhood under the symbol of a heart of steel; and so painfully was she then made conscious of having failed to correspond with the high favours bestowed on her at that tender age, that in the agony of her self-reproach, she would fain have hidden herself from that harrowing spectacle in the lowest depths of hell. We learn this incident from an entry in the diary of Father Ubaldo Antonio Cappelletti, one of her principal directors. After she had refined her heart in the crucible of intense contrition, it was shown to her again in a state of silver whiteness, and at length as possessing the quality of pure gold, and this was emblematic of her progressive fidelity to grace. The All-Holy sees things far otherwise than shortsighted man! Still it is our duty to bless that Divine liberality which sowed such plenteous seed in the soul of His servant during the spring-time of her life, and assisted her in realising such rich harvests of virtue as those we have been contemplating.

CHAPTER IV.

HER FATHER REMOVES WITH URSULA AND HER SISTERS TO PIACENZA, WHERE AT THE AGE OF TEN SHE MAKES HER FIRST COMMUNION.—WHEN TWELVE YEARS OLD SHE BEGINS TO PRACTISE MENTAL PRAYER.

AFTER the death of Ursula's mother, which was related in our second chapter, when the subject of our history was between four and five years old, her father formed the intention of transferring his residence to Piacenza. Ursulina, as she was familiarly called, remained for a time in her native place with her sisters under the care of one of her uncles. At the age of seven her soul was fortified by receiving the sacrament of Confirmation from the hands of Monsignor Onorati, Bishop of the diocese, within the walls of the same church where she had been baptised. On this occasion, according to the attestation of Sister Florida Ceoli, in the process of S. Veronica's canonization, the sisters and directors of the little girl asserted that her godmother saw her guardian angel visibly standing at her side.

About this time she had other important visions, as we learn from her own writings. "I remember," she says, "that at the age of seven or eight years, Jesus appeared to me on two different occasions in Holy

Week all covered with wounds, and told me that I should be devoted to His most sacred Passion, having said which, He vanished from my sight. I wept excessively, and whenever I heard any mention made of the sufferings of our Lord, I felt in my heart something which I cannot express; and whatever I did I offered up with the intention of honouring His Passion. I was desirous of asking my confessor to give me some penance to perform; but when I found myself with him, my lips were closed on the subject. Out of my own head I managed, however, to practise mortifications without permission from any one (a thing not to be imitated)—such as the use of the discipline, walking on bare knees, pricking myself with pins, kissing some revolting object, or chastising myself with nettles. When I knew of other persons doing penance, I went straightway before the picture of my Saviour, and said to Him, 'Lord, if I had but the instruments which others have, I would do as they do, but as I have not got them, I offer Thee at least this my desire.' Our Lord also permits me to recall such loving communications as the following, which He often condescended to bestow on me at the time of which I am speaking. I had intended to engage in a certain pastime or amusement at a particular hour, and I did not perceive that the time fixed had already arrived. So our Blessed Lord said to me interiorly; 'I am thy true pleasure. What dost thou seek? What dost thou desire?' To which I answered, 'Lord, for Thy love I wish to deprive myself of that promised amusement.' These words were spoken to me, but how I know not. At other times when I looked at the crucifix, it spoke thus to me interiorly: 'I will be thy Guide and thy Spouse;' and then I would open wide my arms and say: 'I am determined to be Thy Spouse, O Lord, and no one shall move me from this purpose. I declare it from my heart. Oh let me never be separated from Thee.'"

She had not quite completed her eighth year when her father, who had obtained the lucrative and honourable post of superintendent of finance at Piacenza, summoned his whole family to join him there. Ursula and her sisters continued to pursue their devout occupations; and the former gave proofs of such uncommon virtue, that in her tenth year she was considered fit to make her first Communion. She had previously manifested the most ardent desire to do so; nor indeed could it be otherwise, considering the rare privileges which she had already enjoyed in connection with this Divine Sacrament. We can easily conceive the fervour with which she approached the sacred banquet for the first time, on the Feast of the Purification of the Blessed Virgin in the year 1670. She felt on this occasion a sensible flame burning within her, which continued even after she had returned home, but imagining that this was one of the ordinary effects of holy Communion, she asked her sisters with holy simplicity how long the warm glow would last. Perceiving their surprise at the question, she inferred that her well-beloved Lord had granted to her a peculiar favour, and accordingly said no more, but took care to obtain permission to communicate as often as possible, receiving the Bread of Heaven with great jubilation and profit.

Her communications with God became likewise more frequent. One day she heard a voice from the picture of our Divine Saviour pronounce these words, "To war! to war!" Ursula being only ten years old, concluded in all simplicity that she was hereby invited literally to take up arms, for at that time the wars in the neighbourhood formed the principal topic of conversation at Piacenza. So she requested one of her cousins who was then staying at the house to teach her the art of fencing. But when she commenced this exercise, the Infant Jesus appeared to her, and reproved her for having so utterly misinterpreted His words; since no other species of warfare had been meant than that which travellers through this life are called upon to wage with the devil, the world, and the flesh. The good damsel turned pale at hearing this rebuke, and resolved to be henceforth on her guard against these foes; nor did she ever shrink from marching courageously to the fight, whence she was wont to return victorious, conquering her deadly enemies in many a mortal encounter, as we shall hereafter see.

As soon as she heard that prayer and meditation were the best arms to have recourse to in such a conflict, she was anxious to avail herself of them. We learn how she commenced the latter of these holy practices, and what fruit she derived from it, in a document which she wrote under obedience to her directors. "When I was about twelve years old," she says, "I remember that I often wished to engage in mental prayer, but I was not acquainted with the proper method. I spoke to my confessor about it, but he knew well the naughtiness of my disposition, and considered that so devout an exercise was only fit for good people, who were thoroughly grounded in virtue. In me he saw nothing but inconstancy and fickleness. It is true that I had paid some attention to dressing my little altars, and while so doing had felt some sort of devotion. When I had finished arranging them, I used to fall on my knees, and continue in that position for a long space of time, but how I employed myself on these occasions, I know not. I seemed to be in a kind of ecstasy, and I enjoyed so great delight, that I cared neither for my food nor anything else. I used to be filled with a desire that all creatures should praise and glorify God. I would then earnestly entreat my sisters to come and sing with me, and when they did so I experienced the greatest consolation. When my father returned home, I called him also, and persuaded him to join in our devotions.

"When Christmas arrived, I could not contain myself for joy, and often when I contemplated the Babe in the stable of the Nativity, I seemed to behold Him surrounded with splendour; and He attracted me to Himself in an indescribable union. I was not in the habit of mentioning these occurrences to any one, nor did I turn them to the account which I ought to have done, but relapsed into my childish ways. On the days when I went to holy Communion, I found my sole delight in my little oratory, and although I had learned nothing of the science of mental prayer, my whole mind used to be recollected in God. I seemed to feel our Lord within my heart in a peculiar manner, and thus I got somewhat into the habit of meditation. The longer I was thus engaged, the sweeter I found it. An interior light represented to me the fleeting nature of earthly things, and this made me desirous to leave all. I felt that none was good but God alone. So much the more was my intention confirmed of becoming a religious. A desire for sufferings appears to have possessed me from infancy as well as in riper years; but strange to say, I profited nothing by all this, for no sooner had I left the spot than I was sure to do something which displeased others."

It is striking to observe, in this her own account, the combination of humility and ingenuity which led her to exaggerate her faults; but still more worthy of our attention and admiration are the various processes by which Almighty God drew her soul by degrees unto Himself, separating her with equal power and sweetness from every obstacle that corrupt nature might oppose to the desired union. It will be interesting to refer once more to our Saint's own narrative, which contains a brief outline of the remainder of her life in the world. "Although," she resumes, "I attempted to recreate my mind with worldly trifles, it was absorbed nevertheless in God alone. As far as I can remember, it was the Passion of Christ which especially moved me, and from time to time excited me to tears. The more I exercised myself in mental prayer, the greater became my aversion from the things of the world. Sometimes I was enlightened in the way of self-knowledge, but of this I said nothing to my confessor. Lights like these caused me to press forward in the path of prayer, and in order to secure leisure for this without being observed, I desired the maid to wake me very early. When she did so I rose promptly, and went on meditating for many hours, but I cannot describe the method which I pursued. I know, however, that when it was over, I experienced a certain fervour, which made me willing to perform all the laborious work of the house; I was not, however, allowed to undertake this. It was seldom that I withdrew from meditation without our Lord having told me interiorly that I was to be His spouse. This strengthened my resolution of becoming a nun, and made me more and more desirous of accomplishing my purpose. Whenever any particular feast occurred, I felt as it were a flame within my heart, which gave new life to my whole being. I could not rest, but ran continually about the house like one deranged, so that I sometimes made those who saw me smile. I found my chief delight in dressing little altars; and though I could not do this so conveniently in my uncle's house, I did not altogether lay aside the practice. For work I had no great genius; notwithstanding which, I managed to get through as much in an hour as another person in a day. I did not regret the circumstance of being taught nothing, for whatever I saw others do, I had courage to attempt myself. I was a perfect cross to every one; and yet I know not how it came to pass, they were all fond of me, and showed great partiality for me. Sometimes I reflected on this treatment, which caused me extreme surprise. No one scolded me, although my delinquencies were numberless. I was by nature passionate; every trifle excited me to irritation, and if it was a serious annoyance which befell me, I stamped on the ground like a horse; all which, believe me, was downright naughtiness, for I had never any sufficient ground for provocation. Frequently I took it into my head to wish earnestly for a thing, being desirous that matters should turn out according to my fancy. I felt interiorly warned to mortify myself, but, alas! I did not listen to this voice. It seemed to me that when I set myself to meditate, our Lord taught me what was His Will concerning me; but I thought this might be merely my imagination; however, I continued to feel what I have described. Much good arose out of this; I began to accustom myself to silence, which I found conducive to recollection; and whereas I had previously paid little attention to mortification, I was now led to practise it habitually. Thus by degrees my thirst after sufferings increased yet more and more. I often rose in the night and made a little meditation. My attention was fixed to a certain degree, but I did not think myself thoroughly recollected. In this manner passed the two last years which I spent in the world; they were the fourteenth and fifteenth of my age. I was subject at that period to many vain things, and they often afforded me a certain sort of satisfaction; but at the very moment of so yielding I felt the reproving whisper of conscience, which left me no peace until I had commenced the task of getting rid of my follies."

Such were the first beginnings of those high gifts of prayer and contemplation to which, as we shall see, she subsequently attained in religion. But let it not be supposed that such exercises were always pleasing and delightful entertainments to her soul. " God only knows what I have endured," she says, while describing the cruel temptations and difficulties, besides the darkness of mind and dryness of affections which she had often to encounter, but which she at length vanquished, triumphing over every obstacle by the force of holy perseverance.

CHAPTER V.

THE RICH FRUIT WHICH SHE GATHERED FROM THE EXERCISE OF MEDITATION.—THE FIRST INSTANCES OF OPPOSITION TO HER RELIGIOUS VOCATION WHICH SHE HAD TO ENCOUNTER AT PIACENZA.

WE have already seen in the account which she gives us of herself some of the advantages which our Saint derived from the practice of mental prayer, but still greater ones will be related in the present chapter. First, we may remark her increased desire for sufferings, a disposition which constitutes the surest foundation for true virtue; and with this was combined still greater fervour at her communions. "The more I persevered in meditation" (it is thus she writes of herself at the age of fourteen) "the greater became my wish to suffer; and as my confessor would not grant me penances, I knew not what to do. However, I renewed my entreaties, and he yielded to my importunity, permitting me to use hair-cloth and the discipline three times a week. This I accordingly did, but it appeared to me a mere nothing. On my communion-days I could not contain myself for joy; it seemed to me that I then heard an interior voice, which said, 'Behold, here I am with thee.' I felt that these were the words of our Lord, for they caused me to pass as it were from a state of death to one of life, and enkindled such a fire within me that I was sometimes asked what was the matter with me. Still I took pains to conceal what passed within me."

But the most satisfactory evidence of her graces is afforded by the uncommon strength of mind by which she was enabled to repel and subdue the attacks of her spiritual enemies on many occasions which were fraught with danger to her innocence. It must be observed that the arrangements of the house were very different during her mother's lifetime, and after her death. Her mother had been to the last so desirous of giving her young daughters a good and careful education, that she always kept them in a kind of monastic seclusion. Their days were passed in retirement, amid industrious occupations and devout exercises. But after her death, though the father of our Ursulina, then in her fifth year, was also pious, the same strict supervision was no longer exercised over the establishment. And unfortunately, when the family removed to Piacenza, the smiles of fortune and the pomp of wealth which his new position enabled him to enjoy in that illustrious city, induced him to desire that his daughters should share in his elevation. It is beautiful to observe the candid and yet humble manner in which Ursula speaks of this event. "As soon as we arrived there," she says, speaking of Piacenza, "my father gave orders that we should be dressed in a style suitable to his rank: he provided us also with men-servants and maid-servants. You can imagine my astonishment at the sight of so much splendour, for we had been accustomed to live in a plain way, and had never been treated like great ladies before. Still it was necessary to acquiesce in this change, and in fact I found it pleasant to do so."

The evil one, however, who is ever on the watch to let no occasion slip of doing us harm, one day laid a snare for Ursula. The young ladies having been left in the charge of thoughtless and mercenary attendants, a maid suggested to our Saint, who was now about fourteen years old, that she should go into a garden close at hand, in order to gather certain herbs for the kitchen. Ursula objected strongly, because there was a narrow lane leading to this place through which she did not like to walk alone. But, as the indiscreet domestic continued to press the matter, promising to keep her eye on her young mistress from the window, Ursula at length made the sign of the cross, and invoking her guardian angel as she was in the habit of doing, left the house. She had scarcely set foot out of doors, when she beheld a profligate youth behaving improperly to a girl no less ill-conducted than himself. The innocent Ursula was shocked, and rebuked them sharply; but they only laughed at her, calling her "a scrupulous fool," and threatening to beat her. She went on, however, to the garden, whence she returned some time after with the herbs, when she saw the same scene being enacted in the same spot; she therefore hurried home, and, as she stood on the threshold, said to herself, "It must surely be the devil." Looking back into the lane, she could see no one, neither had the maid seen any one from the window. Some years after, she was informed by God in a vision, that the wretches she had seen were two demons, who wished, by means of wicked example, to destroy her virtue, which would have failed if her heart had not been armed by the practice of meditation and by special protection from above.

She had to sustain a still severer trial at the hands

of her father, who, through a fond but mistaken affection, had set his heart on seeing her married. He accordingly took all manner of pains to divert her thoughts from the religious life to which she had so often manifested her attachment, wishing to engage her instead in some honourable alliance, her extreme beauty having already caused her to receive proposals from several of the nobility. He took care to supply her with every sort of amusement, and invited to his house young gentlemen of attractive qualities, whose fascinating conversation might instil into her mind desires for the world, and assist in realising his ill-conceived plan. The heart of Ursula had to encounter many violent assaults, but she shielded herself against them by prayer, as we shall see more clearly from her own account. "Our father desired," she writes, "that I should be more richly adorned than the others, and was in the habit of presenting me with various articles of fashionable attire. He was so fond of me that, whenever he was at home, he invariably wished to have me at his side. I was gratified by all this, but I presently began to perceive that it was no wish of his that I should be a nun; he told me that I ought to be married, and that as long as he lived, he wished me never to leave him. I was deeply grieved at this discovery, as my desire to become a religious was ever on the increase. I told him this, but I could get no one to believe me or take my part, least of all my father, who even wept, and absolutely declared that he would not suffer me to do as I proposed; and, in order to divert me from the thought of it, he would frequently bring home with him other gentlemen, and summon me to join them. In their presence he would promise me every sort of excursion and pleasure, and our visitors would unite their voices with his. They painted worldly enjoyments in glowing colours, hoping to make me long for them. But the effect produced was the very opposite of what they wished; I conceived a perfect nausea for the things of the world, and could not bear to hear them spoken of; several times I told them as much, recommending them to spare me such descriptions, because the more I heard of such matters, the less I liked them. It was of no use, however, and I had to go through the same ordeal every day. For a long time I bore it patiently; but at last I declared in the presence of them all, that such conversation was odious to me, and that I could endure it no longer, expressing in conclusion my compassion for the miseries of poor worldlings. I was as quiet as I could, because I knew that my father was delighted to hear me talk: and though I did everything I could against his wishes, it all went for nothing; for he continued to be very fond of me. Sometimes he would come to me and say: 'I wish to please you in everything; only do not become a nun.' At these words he would shed tears of tender affection. I used to reply: 'If you wish to please me, I ask no other favour but that you place me in a convent. All my desires will then be gratified. Grant me this satisfaction: it will fill me with joy, and you will see that it will turn out to be a consolation to yourself also.'"

Her father, continuing as averse from this arrangement as ever, and perceiving that all his artifices and caresses had no power to change the mind of his daughter, thought it time to have recourse to more efficacious measures. He got several devout persons to speak to her, and wean her if possible from the object of her holy desires. But the more they said to her on the subject, the stronger she felt her vocation to be. On retiring to her room to pray before a picture of our Divine Saviour, she seemed to hear sensibly the assurance that she should be His Spouse; and this imparted such vigour to her determination that, laying aside all timidity, she thus courageously replied to their persuasions: "Whatever you may do, I shall really be a nun: it is impossible that my resolution should change; on the contrary, I feel that it gains strength every day." Her father, seeing that this device had failed, conceived the ingenious design of touching a more tender chord. He was aware of the strong mutual affection subsisting between Ursula and her sisters; indeed she seemed to him incapable of living without them. So one day he reminded her that if she entered a cloister, she would not be able to take her sisters with her. But she was not at all alarmed at this suggestion, and frankly replied that to leave father, sisters, and every prospect of temporal advantage, was nothing in her eyes. She then returned to the sacred picture which we have already mentioned, and thus addressed our Saviour: "My Lord, I wish to be entirely Thine; do not forsake me." Again she enjoyed a fresh conviction that she was to be His Spouse; and at that moment a beauty so new and lovely appeared on the adorable countenance represented by the picture, that it could no longer be recognised as the same: Ursula, therefore, always carried it with her, even into the convent, although she was not permitted to keep it in her cell.

Her father, however, would not yet yield the victory, but thought to subdue her constancy by another method. He dropped the subject of marriage, and did not openly contradict her expressed desire of entering religion; but he contrived artfully to insinuate that he wished to keep her with him as long as he lived, and to appoint her mistress of his house. He began accordingly to teach her the mysteries of housekeeping, previously to entrusting her with the charge of his establishment. He suggested from time to time that after all he was her parent, and that a daughter could not refuse the only consolation which he required of her. To these touching entreaties she replied respectfully, but with supernatural firmness: "What must I do if I feel that it is our Lord's Will that I should be His Spouse? God is surely my Father in the highest sense. I must obey Him, and you also. It is necessary for you, therefore, to be resigned to His Will. He wishes to receive this offering at your hands. Will not you present Him with that which was His own gift? In fact, I am no longer yours—I am the property of my Lord alone." Her father was both amazed and softened by this reply. "You are perfectly right," he said; "I consent that you should follow our Lord. I wish to please you, and will even let you be a nun." The holy maiden was rejoiced, believing that the desired victory was now completely gained.

She mentions in her writings a still greater temptation which she had to endure after this at Piacenza. There was a young kinsman of hers whom her father insisted on keeping in close attendance upon her. In

order to excuse her father, Ursula with great humility lays all the blame on her own weakness. This youth, whether prompted by mischievous motives of his own, or at the instigation of our Saint's father, gave her no respite from worldly conversation, and would represent himself as the ambassador of one suitor after another, who aspired to the honour of her hand. But Ursula, faithful to her resolution, manifested a total indifference to these repeated addresses. One day, however, her holy indignation rose so high, that she replied to him with decision :—
" Have the goodness to be silent, or I must leave the room. You ought not to bring me such messages as these. I know nothing of any of these persons, nor do I wish to be acquainted with one of them. Jesus is my Spouse—the Object of my desires—He is mine !" On another occasion the same young man presumed to bring her a bouquet of flowers as an offering from her lovers; but she would not even touch them, and obliged him to throw them out of the window. " All these things," concludes Ursula, " instructed me in the deceits of Satan."

CHAPTER VI.

URSULA IS SENT BACK TO MERCATELLO, WHERE SHE RESIDES IN THE HOUSE OF HER UNCLE. NEW TRIALS OF HER VOCATION. AT LENGTH HER FATHER YIELDS TO HER INFLUENCE AND REPENTS, ENDING HIS LIFE WITH CERTAIN MARKS OF ETERNAL SALVATION.

THEY had now lived at Piacenza for three years, and all the allurements which had been tried by her friends at home, by the servants, and, above all, by her father, having failed to alter the firm determination of the holy maiden, it was resolved that she and her sisters should be placed under the roof of one of her uncles at Mercatello. The hope was not altogether abandoned of subduing her constancy by fresh contrivances at a future day. Her father despatched the necessary instructions to his brother, which either by inspiration, or some other means, came to the knowledge of Ursula, for she mentions them in her writings. It was requested that the whole family should take pains to anticipate all her wishes, and endeavour to please her in all things. It was expressly directed that no one should speak in her presence of nuns or convents; all which injunctions were carefully attended to. Meanwhile two of her elder sisters entered the convent of S. Clare at Mercatello, "which circumstance," she writes, "inflamed my longings, so that I had no peace. It was not so much that I bewailed their departure, but that I feared there was no prospect of my following their example. I recommended my case to our Lord; but as yet the door seemed more than ever closed against my desire. I was deeply afflicted, and became so sad that I expected some great sickness to befall me, as really came to pass."

She was taken ill of a malady so strange that the physicians were unable to understand it, nor could they discover any efficient remedy. This might well be the case, for it was a complaint more of the mind than of the body. Some servants of the establishment, guessing how things were, began one day to talk to her about nuns, at which her spirits immediately rose. She presently relapsed into her usual languid state, and was again revived by means of the same conversation. This happened several times, so that her father came to be informed of it. He, in order to gain time, compromised the matter by consenting that application for her admission should be made at two different religious houses, the names of which are not specified in the process of her canonization. This permission was no sooner obtained, and made known to the holy maiden, the choice between the two convents being left to her own selection, than she rallied as it were from the brink of the grave, rose from her bed, and immediately recovered perfect health.

After this every thought of tormenting her on the subject ought to have been laid aside for ever. Nevertheless one of her two sisters who were about to be clothed in the above-mentioned convent at Mercatello, was instigated by her father to persuade Ursula, if possible, to contemplate marriage. But the latter, with an air of extreme displeasure, reproved her in the following severe words :—" I warn you to say no more on the matter. If you insist on pursuing the subject you will see me no more. And you as a religious should be ashamed to choose such a theme for conversation, and one so contrary to the sentiments of S. Clare, who exhorted her sister to enter religion, not to engage in the vanities of the world." When her father heard this, he seemed at length fully convinced, and again granted his daughter the permission for which she sighed.

In justice to the character of this gentleman, who certainly transgressed legitimate bounds in thus trying the vocation of his child, we may be permitted to make a brief digression for the purpose of mentioning his subsequent contrition for the course he took, which repentance he sealed by a truly Christian death. Our doing so will make our narrative more clear, and be peculiarly acceptable to our Saint, for she was careful to hand down to us the record of it in her writings. It will be seen from the account which is here subjoined that this change in his views must be attributed to the zeal and prayers of his saintly daughter. She had observed the worldliness of his life, and was particularly pained by his disedifying conduct at Piacenza with regard to his daughters. Often she felt moved to venture on some remonstrance, but was restrained by filial respect, so that she never dropped more than a few gentle hints. One day, however, when he was entreating her to give up the idea of being a nun during his lifetime, she felt moved by an extraordinary impulse to reply: "If I become a religious now, you at the moment of death will be spared the thought of having refused me. Since we have time now, let us not count upon it then. The affairs of this life pass like the wind, and at the hour of your departure hence you will enjoy great peace if your soul has been duly provided for, but that is a matter in which my presence could not help you. Now that you have time, consider what is the duty of a faithful Christian, namely, to make a good confession." At these words his countenance changed, and he asked: "Why do you speak to me thus?" Ursula answered: "Because I feel inspired to do so." In fact it was a long time since her father had been to confession. Not long after this conversation he approached the sacred tribunal, and whenever his daughter suggested some holy maxim to his mind, he was evidently touched by a feeling of compunction. On her return to Mercatello she reproached herself severely for not having spoken more plainly than she had done, and she wrote him a letter, in which she declares that she did her best according to her knowledge of his spiritual necessities. Not long afterwards, when she had entered religion, he came from Piacenza to Città di Castello to visit her, and declared that her words had excited him to lead a Christian life, concluding by thus appealing to her: "Dear child, to you I commit the care of my soul; let it be your endeavour to assist me in life and after death!" She gave him the required promise, which she faithfully and fervently fulfilled.

A few years after this interview, Almighty God showed her in a dream by night her father dangerously ill, and this so alarmed the holy daughter that she arose and earnestly recommended him to our Lord. The following night she beheld him in his last agony, shortly after which he expired. When she related these circumstances to the nuns, they advised her to consider it all as a work of the imagination; and she was partly disposed to coincide with their opinion, because she had very lately received letters from him. Still she could not throw off the impression of what she had seen, and from time to time she wept bitterly, feeling, as she truly expressed it, that her heart was bursting with grief; and her visions proved correct, for ere long the news arrived, and it was known that her father had died after a short illness at the precise moment that she had witnessed his decease in her slumbers. She began without delay to offer many prayers for the repose of his soul, and our Lord vouchsafed to hear her. She was first permitted to behold him in a place so dark and fearful that she doubted whether it were not hell itself; but thinking that this idea was suggested by the devil, she prayed for him the more. Then he turned to look at her from the midst of his torments, and seemed to pronounce these words, " It rests with thee to obtain mercy for me !" As may be conceived, she did not spare herself. After performing a number of penances and prayers, she beheld him again, and now his sufferings were greatly alleviated. The pious daughter continuing her suffrages on his behalf, our Lord one day was pleased to say to her, "Take comfort, for on the feast of S. Clare I will deliver thy father's soul from its present abode of pain, but if thou wouldst have it to be so, thou on thy part must suffer much." She willingly offered herself to endure all, and severely did she penance herself to procure him solace. On the feast of S. Clare, she saw that he was still in purgatory, but no longer in the same place of extreme suffering. Her perseverance in prayer at length induced our Lord to assure her that her father should be liberated altogether on the coming festival of the Nativity. It is thus that she relates the event. "On Christmas night I saw him in purgatory, and in a moment an angel seemed to take him thence by the hand; and I beheld my father in the same form and appearance that he had possessed in life, and clothed in white. He accosted me, and thanked me for all the charity I had shown him. Suddenly he appeared to become enveloped in radiance, and his human figure could be distinguished no more. In company with the angel he vanished, and I understood that the most holy Virgin had obtained this favour for me on this sacred night. I was confirmed in this idea the following morning; for after Communion, the soul of my father appeared to me again, all beautiful and resplendent, and informed me that many others had been also released from the pains of purgatory; indeed these newly ransomed prisoners were visible to me in great numbers, and I think that on two or three occasions, I enjoyed a renewal of this blessed assurance. My pen is incapable of expressing the consolation which was thereby conveyed to me."

Behold how wonderful are the privileges which fathers may expect to receive from the hands of holy children! Such instances as these should excite all parents to conduct their families in the ways of God. If Francesco Giuliani had not possessed so saintly a daughter, he would perhaps have been lost for ever; or at all events, the extent of his sufferings in purgatory might have surpassed all conception.

CHAPTER VII.

HAVING RECEIVED THE DESIRED CONSENT OF HER FATHER, URSULA PROCURES IN AN EXTRAORDINARY WAY HER ADMISSION AMONG THE CAPUCHIN NUNS OF CITTÀ DI CASTELLO.

To resume the thread of our narrative. As soon as Ursula had obtained the permission to become a nun, which she so much longed for, she felt ready to go into any convent which her friends might desire for her; still she was excessively anxious that it should be one of the stricter order of religious. Having heard much praise of the monastery of Capuchin nuns at Città di Castello, she informed her family that she wished to make it her choice, although in the house of S. Clare in the city of Mercatello, her birth-place, she had already three sisters in religion, namely Sister Mary Rose, Sister Anna Maria, and Sister Louisa, of whom she was extremely fond. Having written to her father on the subject, she received for answer that in this also she should be gratified. Her uncle accordingly took her to Città di Castello, that she might ask admission into the above-mentioned convent from its ecclesiastical superior the bishop, who was no other than Monsignor Giuseppe Sebastiani, a man of such distinguished sanctity, that to this day his name is never mentioned in the diocese without the title of Venerable being prefixed to it.

When Ursula and her uncle had been presented to his lordship, and when the wishes of the former had been expressed, the bishop informed them that there was no vacancy in that particular convent, the last having been just filled by the admission of a young woman of the city, who was afterwards called in religion Sister Clare Felix. Poor Ursula was disconsolate at this reply, and having no other alternative to propose, she took her departure. But while they were descending the steps of the palace, she felt moved by some influence from above to request her uncle to return with her to the bishop's presence. Being again admitted to an audience, the young girl threw herself on her knees before his lordship, and with the most humble, yet fervent entreaties conjured him to grant her the consolation she implored; and this she did so effectually that the good bishop was persuaded to make an exception in her favour by conceding the boon she asked. He then put several questions to her, inquiring among other things if she could read Latin. Her uncle replied that she could not, but Ursula, incited by some extraordinary impulse, and by a lively confidence in God, took a breviary out of his lordship's hand, and read aloud from it with masterly ease and precision, in a manner which showed that she understood the meaning perfectly. Her uncle exclaimed in astonishment—"This is certainly a miracle!" And such it really was, for she had never learned Latin. The miracle was moreover a permanent one, for from that time she was always able to read the language fluently, and to quote it with intelligence and accuracy. The good prelate being struck by this occurrence, and still more by the rare innocence and virtue apparent in her replies, promised to obtain what she desired, from the nuns; and then dismissed the grateful Ursula. He presently went to the convent, and by his representations of the valuable acquisition which this new postulant would prove to the community, the religious were all induced to accept her, although by so doing they would exceed their p rescribed number.

As soon as the day arrived when the question of her admission was to be formally proposed in chapter, our Saint repaired to their church to await the result. The young person we have already mentioned as having obtained the vacancy a few days before, was likewise there, as the ballot was to decide her lot also on the present occasion. From her statement we learn the following particulars:—Ursula having prostrated herself in prayer, most earnestly supplicated her heavenly Spouse to accomplish her ardent desires. Ere long the news arrived that they were both accepted, and soon the father confessor came to the altar and invested Ursula with the sacred cord, after the custom of the house. We will refer to the testimony which her companion deposed on oath in the process of canonization in order to form an idea of the excess of joy and rapture into which the Saint was thrown on this occasion. "After we had received notice of our acceptance," she declares, "and when the father confessor had given us the cord, we two remained alone in the church to thank our Lord for the grace He had thus bestowed on us; but as I knew that the mother abbess and the religious were waiting for us at the communion grate, I was just going to invite the Signora Ursula to accompany me, when I beheld her ravished in an ecstasy, so that she was utterly unconscious of my presence; and although I attempted several times to shake her, and used force to draw her away, she did not feel it at all. So I fell on my knees at her side, and let her alone." The religious, knowing nothing of this, and being unable to conceive the reason for so long a delay, sent one of the lay sisters who serve outside to inform the postulants that the mother abbess was waiting for them at the grate. Then Ursula came to herself and went with her companion to answer the summons: "and the said Signora," continues the deposition, "manifested such extreme delight at being now accepted as a religious, that it was evident her heart was in a state of jubilation." This happened on the 17th of July, in the year 1677, before she had completed her seventeenth year.

The devil being envious of such happiness as hers lost no time in troubling her peace; and God permitted that it should be so for the purpose of testing the fidelity of His servant, and refining her virtue. At one time the arch-fiend would draw a picture before her eyes of the religious state, which he painted in the blackest colours, representing it as a life of despair; at another time he would recall to her mind the numerous young gentlemen who had desired her in marriage, and the advantageous offers which she had rejected: and then again, he would embitter her delight in prayer by infusing into her soul feelings of insupportable weariness. In short, it seemed, according to her own expression, as though all the powers of hell had been let loose upon her; "but," she continues, "I would yield to none of them. Sometimes when I felt more harassed than usual, I retired to my chamber alone, and relieved myself for awhile with our Lord by laying the matter before Him. I prayed to Him, asked His grace, and implored Him never to leave me. I said to Him in all confidence, 'Lord, Thou knowest that I am Thy Spouse; grant that I may never be separated from Thee. I resign myself now and for ever into Thy hands: behold I am ready for all that it is Thy Will to appoint. I am Thine—I am Thine—and that is enough for me!'" Almighty God, Who permitted these trials for her greater merit, deigned frequently to encourage her by means of an interior voice which said to her: "Be comforted, for thou art Mine. It is My Will that thou shouldst suffer and struggle, but fear not." And thus strengthened by the power of divine grace, the holy maiden resisted the attacks of the tempter.

CHAPTER VIII.

HER CLOTHING. DECEITS OF THE DEVIL DURING HER NOVICIATE.

At length the wished-for day arrived when this saintly virgin was permitted to display her contempt for the world, by enclosing herself in the garden of her heavenly Spouse. It was on the 28th of October, the feast of the holy apostles S. Simon and S. Jude, three months after the ceremony of her formal admission. The bishop, Monsignor Sebastiani, gave her the religious habit, and delivered an interesting and devout address. Throughout the whole of this sacred function the young candidate for the veil appeared absorbed in God; and her entire deportment was characterised by cheerfulness and devotion, together with such an air of heavenly modesty as well became the true spouse of Christ. Every one present was deeply touched; and when the bishop commended her to the abbess, Sister Mary Gertrude Albizzini, he pronounced this prophecy in an undertone: "I particularly recommend to you this new daughter, for she will one day become a great saint." It was on this occasion that, according to custom, her baptismal name was exchanged for that of Veronica, by which appellation we shall henceforward distinguish her: it seemed to be a presage of that tender and especial devotion by which she was hereafter to be attached to the Passion of Jesus. She spent the whole day in an ecstasy of joy, to which she gave utterance by repeating the words, "Now I am happy, now I am happy!"

Sister Teresa Ristori, who was descended from a noble Florentine family, was at that time mistress of the novices; she afterwards became abbess, and was a religious of great virtue. It was under her direction that Veronica commenced her noviciate. This nun had already three of her own sisters as companions in religion—one of whom was the Sister Clare Felix mentioned above, the second was called Sister Diomira, and the third was a lay sister, Giacinta. Our Saint gave herself up from the first to the most scrupulous practice of perfection, and it was remarked that even on the first night, although she was dispensed from attending choir, scarcely had she heard the first stroke of the bell than she sprang out of bed, and repaired with the others to matins. There was no danger that she would ever require more than the first signal for obedience. She was punctual at all the exercises of the noviciate, voluntarily undertaking all the works of the convent, full of the highest devotion and mortification, strict in observing silence, gentle in conversation, humble and pleasant towards all, without being in the least irritated or ruffled by any occurrence, however untoward. And thus the religious began very shortly to agree with the high opinion which the bishop entertained as to her future sanctity.

Among all the virtues practised by the holy novice, that which was peculiarly worthy of admiration at this early stage of her career, as being a sure foundation for religious perfection, was her entire submission to her spiritual directors. This was a point on which she had been defective as a secular; for, as she herself admitted, she had never said one word to her confessor, beyond the avowal of her faults, however slight they may have been, and had made no mention whatever of the supernatural gifts which she so frequently enjoyed, nor of those spiritual troubles with which the devil had done his best to agitate her mind, for she had felt satisfied with the testimony of a good conscience. But she had no sooner entered religion than her soul was illuminated by clearer light, and she became conscious of the various dangers which beset the path of perfection for those who guide themselves therein by their own judgment. Hence she was in the habit of holding long conferences with her directors, in which she disclosed to them with the most scrupulous accuracy and minuteness everything which took place in her interior, whether for good or evil; for she stood as much on her guard against celestial communications and visions as she did against manifest temptations, until she had submitted them to the scrutiny of her spiritual guides.

This practice was particularly displeasing to the evil one, as he perceived that all hope was thus excluded of his being able to influence her by means of deceptive illusions. He accordingly contrived a plan for striking at the root of all. He took advantage of an opportunity which occurred, and assumed the form and appearance of the mistress of the novices, for the purpose of gaining his object. Veronica was alone in her cell when she heard a tap at the door. Thinking that it was the accustomed signal of her mistress's visit, she said immediately, "Come in." As soon as the supposed nun had entered, our Saint began to feel extremely uncomfortable, so much so that she hardly knew how to endure the conversation which followed, finding it wearisome beyond expression, whereas on all former occasions when she had seen and discoursed with the real mistress of the novices, she had felt marvellously refreshed, whatever fatigue she might have been previously undergoing. She was struck by this extraordinary difference, but took care to avoid any expression of what she felt. The artful tempter then addressed her as follows: " There is one thing I wish to say to you, but it is on condition that your amendment be shown in practice, not in words. You must promise me that you will not mention what I am going to say to you, either to our extraordinary confessor who is here at present, or to our ordinary director, or, in fact, to any other creature whatever. I shall speak to you very freely, chiefly because I am anxious for the salvation of your soul, as also for your welfare and that of your confessor, who would not at all like to suffer through you. I shall speak to you therefore with great candour. I had foreseen that remarks would be made about both of you, and this had given me, as it still does, cause for much anxiety. I have thought again and again how to remedy the evil, and have done all I could to defend you by declaring that nothing was the matter. But only think, the affair is now so public that to-morrow we expect to hear that our ordinary confessor is to come here no more, and all this on your account." At these words Veronica felt deeply pained, but assuming an air of perfect indifference, she replied : "Only tell me what the reports are concerning our confessor and myself. I do not mean to allow my peace of mind to be disturbed, because if these charges are true. I will endeavour to correct my conduct, and if they are false, truth will assert its rights. As for me, let them say what they will, it cannot alter the confidence I have in him. Our Lord has given me grace to declare to him whatever passes within me, and this practice I intend to continue for the future." A better reply Veronica could not have given, nor can we imagine one more calculated to confound the devil: in fact the pretended mistress of the novices was evidently perplexed. But as he did not despair of victory in the end, he told her that she must never go to her confessor, not even for the Sacrament of Penance, except in case of necessity, such as when there was anything on her mind which would hinder her from communicating; but that as religious had seldom anything very grave to confess, Veronica might avail herself of the permission which was now given her once for all, to go to holy Communion without approaching the sacred tribunal.

Thus did Satan prolong his discourse, to the extreme distress of the holy novice, to whose mind such subjects were altogether foreign; however she restrained herself, and waited for further explanations. The tempter resumed with a confidential air:—" I must tell you that yesterday evening you were the sole subject of conversation in the infirmary; all the sisters are greatly scandalised; they would never have thought of such a thing. I really am ashamed to mention it to you, but it is said that between you and your confessor there has grown up so close a friendship that from intimacy on spiritual matters you have gone so far as to touch the verge of sin. It is said, moreover, that the case is so flagrant that it may please God to cause you both to be put under severe penance. But as this would be a very great dishonour to religion, I have tried to hush up the matter by saying that I would settle it all with you; and the best remedy that I can think of is that you should have no more interviews: and as to the state of your soul, strive to conduct yourself like ordinary persons, and keep things to yourself. Take care not to mention one word of what I have told you, either to your ordinary or your extraordinary director. I also put you under obedience never again to recur to the subject even with me, for I feel it to be an extremely harassing and disagreeable business. I therefore strictly enjoin you to abstain from any allusions to it in your future intercourse with myself; and if you comply with this request, I shall feel sure that you will obey me in not breathing one syllable of what has passed to your confessor."

"I will say nothing to any one else," replied Veronica; "I will only send for his lordship, and inform him of all that has passed between my confessor and myself. He shall be the judge of what I ought to do, and I will repeat to him everything that you have told me. I am certainly scandalised that the sisters should be capable of conceiving such absurd suspicions against so good a servant of God (meaning her confessor): let them say what they please of me, I more than deserve this trial." The pretended novice-mistress became very angry at this answer, and indignantly exclaimed—"I have told you already, and I tell you again that you are to mention the affair to no one. To the bishop indeed! God forbid that it should reach his ears! Do as I have told you, and live in peace.

Do not go to him, do not converse with him (the confessor) and all will be right." Having said this with an air of displeasure, the speaker departed.

At that moment the bell rang for Compline. Veronica proceeded without delay to the choir, and seeing the real mistress of the novices on the staircase, she wondered how she could have thus got before her: however she did not dare to ask, but felt strongly impelled to go to her extraordinary confessor and relate the occurrence to him. After a long struggle with herself she resolved to do so. When he had heard her account, he thought it over for a time, and suspecting how things were, commanded Veronica to apply to her mistress, and inquire who were the sisters who had made such remarks on herself and her ordinary director. The novice excused herself by reminding him that in the above-mentioned conversation her mistress had forbidden her ever to recur to the subject. But the prudent confessor, in order to fathom the truth, desired Veronica to go to her as usual, and lead the conversation indirectly to the charges in question. The mistress of the novices no sooner heard the first words on the subject than she promptly and seriously replied—"Put all such ideas out of your head; it is impossible that any of the sisters can have said such things. Do not trouble yourself, for I have never heard them say anything of the sort!" Veronica was overjoyed, and returned to her confessor with this intelligence, which convinced him of the diabolical fraud which had been practised on her; and he enjoined her to make known to her directors without fail everything that should pass in her mind.

Her mistress gave her a similar injunction, as soon as she had heard the whole story; and all this strengthened the holy resolution of our Saint to conceal nothing from her spiritual guides.

The prince of darkness was dismayed at this mortifying overthrow of his machinations, which had now recoiled upon himself. As he despaired of being able to take away the dutiful sincerity with which Veronica treated her confessors, he resolved to sow the seeds of discord betwixt herself and her mistress, in whose power it lay to render her very valuable assistance in the interior life. He therefore had recourse to a stratagem worthy of himself. Under the guise of our young novice he entered the cell of a religious, and with a confidential air poured forth many invectives against the excellent novice-mistress, of whom he said all the evil that he possibly could. The religious was astonished, and considered it her duty to inform the calumniated person of what had happened, as well for her own direction as for that of the detractor. The novice-mistress, who had no suspicion of the deception practised upon her, was sincerely grieved, probably not so much for her own sake as for that of the novice herself, of whom she had conceived a very different opinion. While she was deliberating as to the course to be pursued, she maintained a distant air towards the supposed offender, rarely even speaking to her; and this state of things went on for three or four days. Veronica being surprised at this change, and not knowing to what cause to attribute it, adopted the best expedient in similar cases. She went to her mistress when the latter was alone in her cell, and in the most humble manner, with a daughter's confidence requested her to tell her sincerely what were the grounds of her displeasure, for that it was her great desire to be made aware of her faults, in order that she might correct them. The good novice-mistress then told her frankly what had been mentioned to her. Veronica was both astonished and grieved, for she had not only the highest esteem but the most tender affection for this good mother; and she solemnly declared that such calumnies had never entered her mind, and that she had never set foot in the cell of any one of the religious. She begged to be informed of the day and the hour when so slanderous a speech was supposed to have been delivered by her. On comparing notes they both discovered that at the time in question our Saint had been in her mistress's room, conversing about some of her scruples. They were now convinced that the whole affair was neither more nor less than a Satanic deceit; the reputation of the novice was perfectly cleared, and the best understanding once more prevailed between herself and her excellent mistress. The two events above related are taken from her own writings and related very nearly in her own words.

The evil one was dismayed at finding himself thus for the second time overthrown by a simple novice, but he began to attack her again with a multitude of temptations. He took advantage one day of her physical weakness and of the severe labours which her mistress imposed upon her by way of exercise, to suggest to her that all this was more than she could bear, and that she had better declare as much openly or put an end to her life and toils at once. It happened that at this moment she was summoned to draw water for the infirmary;—"I went there very cheerfully," she writes, "and thought as I went of the Passion of our Redeemer; feeling that all these hard works, so far from hindering the application of my soul to God, assisted me on the contrary to rise towards Him. So I was well pleased to undergo this small suffering for the love of God.

"But when I was just at the head of the stairs, I felt myself pushed so roughly that I fell from the top to the bottom, with two pitchers in my hands. I was a good deal hurt, but my pitchers were not broken. I only laughed at these wiles of the devil, who was so anxious that I should not tire myself; and I derived fresh courage from each specimen of his foolish cunning. I even entreated our mother the mistress of the novices that, whenever she had any fatiguing work to be done, she would impose it on me for the love of God, because such employments were good for me."

But while the devil was doing his utmost to discourage her in her noble career, our Lord was pleased to comfort her by means of a celestial vision. Her mistress, in order to gratify her desires, commissioned her on another occasion to provide water for the infirmary. The place whence she had to procure it was in a lower story. Veronica, whose fervour knew no limits, had carried as many as thirty pitchers full, when at length she paused from exhaustion and pain; for the labour of going up and down stairs so many times and with such heavy burdens had caused blood to start from her heels. As she stood in this condition on the landing place, our Divine Redeemer appeared to her, bearing the cross on His shoulder, and thus lovingly addressed her: "Behold the cross which I am carrying—

it is far heavier than thine!" This sight so revived her spirits and strength that she felt nothing of the weariness which she had experienced up to that moment.

CHAPTER IX.

HER SOLEMN PROFESSION.—HER VIRTUE IS STRENGTHENED, NOTWITHSTANDING THE ASSAULTS OF THE DEVIL, BY SPECIAL GRACES WHICH SHE RECEIVES FROM GOD DURING THE EARLY YEARS OF HER RELIGIOUS LIFE.

THROUGHOUT the entire year of her noviciate Veronica had given proofs of such exalted virtue, and the promise of such surpassing excellence, that the religious did not for a moment hesitate to admit her to her solemn profession. She was accordingly professed on the feast of All Saints, in the year 1678, four days after the completion of her twelve months' noviciate. Although, in the process of her canonization, we find no express mention made of the fervour with which she performed this sacred function, whereby she consummated in the most perfect and acceptable manner the sacrifice of her whole being to God, we can easily infer what was her holy ardour on the occasion, not only from the earnest desires which she had cherished from the earliest age to consecrate herself unreservedly to her heavenly Spouse, but also from the saintly dispositions with which she had prepared herself for this great event throughout the entire year of her noviciate, and lastly from the extraordinary devotion with which she was accustomed during each succeeding year of her life to commemorate the two days of her clothing and profession.

For this latter ceremony she endeavoured to prepare herself by prolonging her prayers, and practising severer penances and humiliations, which indeed she carried so far as to appear before the abbess even on the day on which she had made her vows, without the black veil on her head, as though she had been still a novice ; for she wished to be treated as the last and least in the convent.

We may learn from her own written recollections what profit she derived from this exercise. On the day of which we speak, she was recalling to mind the readiness with which Jesus Christ in the garden accepted from the hands of His Divine Father the bitter chalice of His Passion, notwithstanding the repugnance felt by His Sacred Humanity. "Herein," she declares, "I found a lesson so striking, that at that moment I too seemed to become firmly united to the Will of God, and gathered from the mystery sufficient instruction to last the whole of my life ..... From time to time it appeared to me that Jesus turned His eyes on me with love, and said, 'Come to Me, come to Me,' implying that He desired to enrich my soul with all His divine graces. It is impossible to describe the feelings and lights which were granted me on that day. I spent twenty-four hours without knowing whether I was in heaven or on earth." Especially at the time of holy Communion, for which she had taken more than usual pains to prepare herself, a rich supply of graces was conferred upon her ; and she received light and strength wherewith to advance still higher in religious perfection. She writes thus of an anniversary of her profession:—"In holy Communion I found my senses enraptured, and myself absorbed in the sea of divine love." Speaking of another of these anniversaries, she says:—"After holy Communion it suddenly appeared to me that from a state of recollection I passed to one of rapture. In one moment the soul thus favoured becomes united to God in mutual love. It seems as though God deified the soul; I know not how otherwise to express it. I believe that my soul was separated from my body. I am not sure that what I say is intelligible. I do not know if I am talking nonsense; for it is impossible to describe what I then felt. I believe that in that hour my soul was truly espoused to God."

In order that the reader may not suspect any delusion or excitement of the imagination in these accounts, he shall hear how Veronica conducted herself when she was thus exalted in spirit. She writes about the anniversary of her profession in the year 1701:—"This morning, shortly after communicating, I was suddenly in rapture, and beheld a vision of our Lord risen from the dead. It seems to me that I despised it as an invention of the devil, and was firmly resolved to give him no such advantage over me, but rather to die than offend God, desiring nothing but the accomplishment of His holy Will. I prayed to Him to deliver me from such devices of the enemy; protesting at the same time that I did not seek visions or consolations, but only to do the Will of God, and to avoid offending Him. But the vision only presented itself more clearly, producing within me a sense of compunction for my sins against God, throwing fresh light on my faults, and convincing me that it was not the work of Satan, but that of the Almighty, Who was thus pleased to give me new instructions in the path of virtue. I understood in one moment by this communication in what manner each virtue should be practised, how each should be accompanied by detachment from ourselves, by faith and hope in God, by the exercise of the presence of God, by perfect love and purely for God, by holy resignation to the Divine Will, by such entire mortification that the soul enjoys nothing but God alone, by constant diligence, by endeavours to avoid the notice of creatures so as to be known by none but God, by voluntarily embracing all occasions of being treated contemptuously by others, and by going readily where we are likely to be humbled. Whenever we practise any virtue, it should be accompanied by all these things, especially by the grace of holy humility which renders all our actions acceptable to God."

The visions and ecstasies of Veronica were invariably followed by the holy fruits of contrition, horror for sin, love and hope in God, entire resignation to the divine Will, desire for suffering, and a willing endurance of every description of humiliation. It would be absurd to suppose that such admirable dispositions could have been produced by a heated fancy, or by him who is the deadly enemy of all virtue.

But to return to her profession. This event was not with Veronica, as it sometimes is with lukewarm characters, the commencement of a course of relaxation and indulgence; on the contrary she felt herself bound, as indeed she was, to a stricter observance of the rule than ever, in order that by the most perfect rule of life, the union between herself and her heavenly Spouse might be the more strongly cemented. In order to effect this, she not only submitted cheerfully to the custom of the convent, which required her to spend two more years under the direction of the mistress of the novices, in as complete obedience as though she had been a novice of merely a few days' standing, but she would fain have continued in that position all her life if her superiors would have permitted her to do so. All the witnesses who were examined in the preliminary as well as in the apostolic process of her canonization (and they had been for the most part her companions in the cloister), have unanimously deposed as follows; namely, that even from the earliest period of her religious career, she was remarkable for her practice of every kind of virtue, especially for mortification, humility, obedience, and charity, in all which she attained to the heroic degree. One proof of this was the vehement zeal with which she ceased not to thirst for the conversion of sinners, so much that she desired by means of her prayers and sufferings to constitute herself an intercessor between sinners and their God, in order that sin might be destroyed in the world. This was so displeasing to the devil that on these occasions he manifested his special resentment by striking her heavily.

Two instances are mentioned in the account drawn up by her for her directors, which occurred in the early years of her religious life. "I was one day in prayer," she writes, "before the most holy Sacrament, pleading for certain sinners, when I felt my heart bursting with grief, on account of the transgressions which they committed against God. In my anguish I prayed for the salvation of their souls, and presenting myself as an intercessor between them and their Creator, I asked that I might suffer on their behalf. All at once I felt myself struck severely and thrown violently to the ground. I presume it was the devil who did this, as at the same moment I was tempted to cease from offering myself in the capacity of intercessor between God and sinners. But with the divine assistance I took courage, prolonged my prayer, and used the discipline for a considerable space of time. I believe the arch-fiend felt himself defeated, for he made a great disturbance in the church. It seemed as though hell itself had been transferred to where I was; but so far from being afraid, I despised his ridiculous and foolish devices. The blow which I had received on the face left behind it a bruise which did not pass off for several days. I saw nothing, but I heard the clanking of chains and a noise resembling the hissing of serpents.

"On another occasion, when I was at work in my cell, I became sensibly conscious of the presence of God, and I think at the same time God made me aware of the precious nature of suffering. I prayed that He would gratify me with a share in so great a privilege; and I also entreated Him to be pleased to bestow the same light on every soul, to the end that all might be wholly united to Himself through suffering. I particularly recommended all sinners to the Divine Majesty. Suddenly I was made to feel that a heavy blow was aimed at my shoulder, and this was accompanied by so loud a noise in my cell that the sisters came knocking at the door, to desire me to be quiet. However, I only smiled at these insane attacks of the evil one. The pain in my shoulder lasted a good while, so that I could scarcely get through my work; but I cheerfully offered up this little suffering to my God."

While the enemy was thus maddened at beholding this fervent religious making such progress in the path of sanctity, Almighty God failed not to bestow on her most liberally rare proofs of His peculiar favour; He began to communicate Himself to her, and that frequently, by means of an extraordinary elevation of soul, which she called recollection. She was one day at work in the kitchen with three other sisters; they were singing a devout hymn together, when Veronica unexpectedly exclaimed, "My Jesus! my Jesus!" and then fell as one dead on Sister Clare Felix, having lost the use of her senses, and being not only unable to move, but unconscious of the attempts of others to rouse her, and deaf to all their cries. Her countenance meanwhile was fairer than usual and shone like the sun. At length she came to herself and said with a smile, "I have had a little sleep which has affected my heart." These apparent fainting fits were repeated several times, and at first the nuns set them down to epilepsy, and were in great fear lest one of them should prove fatal to her. She was seized in this way one evening in the refectory, so they carried her in their arms into her cell, and having placed her on her bed, called in her confessor Father Cavamazza, of the order of S. Dominic. At first he had his doubts on the subject, and thought proper to wait till she should revive. He then questioned her with great prudence, and became at length fully convinced that these were really supernatural visitations of the Divine Spirit. He accordingly directed the nuns never to disturb her on such occasions.

We learn what took place between God and this favoured soul from her own written account of the first which occurred to her. Her words are as follows: "The first time that I enjoyed one of these raptures, accompanied by a vision, it seemed to me that all at once I beheld our Lord, bearing a heavy cross, and that He invited me to share in that invaluable treasure. This was signified to me rather by some internal communication than through the medium of words. At the same moment I felt an extreme desire for sufferings. Our Lord then transferred that same cross to my heart, and made me aware of the great worth of sufferings. It was thus that He taught me: every kind of suffering was presented to my view, and at the same instant the whole was transformed into most precious jewels, which were all set in the shape of a cross. Meanwhile I was given to understand that our Lord desired from me pure suffering; after which He immediately vanished from my sight. On recovering my senses, I felt a great pain at my heart, which has never left me since; and I retained moreover so ardent a desire of suffering, that I would undergo every conceivable pain and torment. Ever since that time I have been saying to myself that crosses and trials are to be esteemed as precious stones and counted as high privileges."

Veronica adds that it was on this occasion that Jesus Christ engraved on her heart the impression of

His cross, in a visible manner, as was seen by many witnesses in the investigation which was made after her death. The first fruits of this divine favour may be traced in her advances towards perfection; inasmuch as from this early stage of her religious career the sole object of her aspiration was suffering, pure suffering, and the only treasure, the only delight which she prized in this world, was a share in the cross and Passion of Christ.

CHAPTER X.

THE OFFICES WHICH SHE IS CALLED TO FILL IN THE CONVENT. — THE MANNER IN WHICH SHE DISCHARGED HER DUTIES.

WHEN Veronica had passed through her noviciate, she was employed in the various offices of the community, from the lowest to the highest. We shall now give the reader some idea of these, although we shall in so doing anticipate the narrative in this our first book, in order not to break the thread of the more important matters which follow. At different times of her life she had charge of the kitchen, dispensary, linen-room, infirmary, turn, pantry, sacristy, and noviciate; last of all she was appointed abbess. She performed these functions with the most perfect equanimity, and considered herself throughout as the servant of all. Hence she manifested the most scrupulous diligence and exactness in the fulfilment of every duty which she was called upon to discharge. Although her constitution was a peculiarly delicate one, and her appetite liable to be easily affected, she set herself to conquer the repugnance of her nature by heroic actions. One day when she could not help feeling disgusted by the offensive odour of some fish which she was washing, she took one of them to her room and kept it there till it became quite putrid, in which state she would often apply it to her nose and mouth, so that it became quite a treat to her to have fresh fish or what was merely a little stale to dress. In the same way she wished to overcome the repugnance she felt in her service of the infirmary. Her mistress, who was suffering from an ulcer in the mouth, had to keep cotton in it, and Veronica, taking an opportunity of changing this, and conveying what had been used to her cell when no one saw her, proceeded deliberately to chew it.

We can understand how displeasing these actions were to the devil. He accordingly inflicted on her all the annoyances and mortifications that he could; for instance, he would often pour the contents of the vessels in the kitchen, over which department she presided at the time, either into the fire or over the floor; and he would do this on occasions when Veronica's companion in office, Sister Frances, knew that they were so firmly placed that they could not have been upset by natural means. However, Almighty God did not fail to counterbalance these trials by the bestowal of undoubted marks of His favour. Among others, provisions were frequently multiplied under her hands. The same Sister Frances bears witness to the three following facts, which occurred during the time when she assisted the Saint in the office of dispensing the stores. One day Veronica was employing herself in inspecting and cleaning certain moulds of cheese, which were kept in a large jar of earthenware, rather more than half filling it. As soon as she had completed her work, she said to her companion with a smile: "Replace this cheese in its vessel and pack it well in." In doing so, the lay sister found that there was now not only enough to fill the original jar, but that as many as twelve moulds remained over and above; these she put away in a basket, and when she returned presently to the same room, she discovered that they had increased to the number of eighteen. On several occasions, after being accurately counted, the eggs were found multiplied in a similar way to the number of thirty-three, forty, or even a hundred, according to the necessities of the community. A benefactor having sent them some fish which would barely serve them all at the rate of two apiece, Veronica contrived to supply the table for several days, giving them each two or three. The companion to whose joint custody they were consigned was surprised at this, and said to her one day, "How do you contrive, mother, to make these fish last so long?" "Eat away, eat away, and never mind," was the reply. When it was discovered that she possessed this power, those who superintended the stores and kitchen would have recourse to her as often as their stock was accidentally or otherwise diminished. When thus applied to she would only answer, "Have confidence in God," and all deficiencies, whether in quantity or quality, were found to be immediately repaired.

But however great might have been her diligence in the fulfilment of her previous duties, it was surpassed by that which she exhibited when occupying the important post of mistress of the novices. The momentous responsibility of this station must be recognised by all, as it lies with the person so appointed to supply the community with good subjects, who are to constitute its future welfare. For this reason persons of mature age and consummate virtue are generally selected. But such was the conduct of Veronica in her youth that she was chosen for this weighty charge when she was only thirty-four years of age, not more than seventeen of which had been passed in religion. In order to form a correct idea of her success in this charge, it is enough to remark that it was prolonged for twenty-two consecutive years, in fact until she was made abbess. Even then, though it was a thing without precedent, the nuns desired that she should continue to act as mistress of the novices; and to satisfy them she was obliged to do so during the eleven years of her superiorship to the close of her life. It can therefore be no matter of astonishment that under a government so excellent, and of thirty-three years' duration, her convent should have attained to so illustrious a degree of sanctity that it became celebrated through the whole of Italy, we might almost say of Europe. It will be worth while to point out the method she pursued, in order that others may be instructed as to what course they should adopt in similar difficulties.

She considered the young spouses of Christ as her own daughters, and acted towards them on all occasions as a loving mother. She was anxious that they should be deprived of nothing which the rule allowed them, and would subject herself to privations in order that her novices might have less to suffer. One of them having arrived in the middle of summer, and the rule requiring that every one should sleep not merely dressed but covered with a woollen quilt under which even the hands were to be laid, Veronica did what she could to alleviate the trial of her child by changing coverlets with her, taking the new one for herself, and giving her instead her own old one, which was comparatively light; but as soon as the winter came she gave her back the warm counterpane. If one of the novices fell ill, our Saint always laid herself out to assist and comfort her by paying her all the services of charity. She would fain have transferred the malady to herself, that by so doing she might relieve her daughter. Once her wish was miraculously gratified. It is related by Sister Mary Constance Spanaciari, in whose case it occurred, during the time when she was a novice. She had been attacked by a violent fever, accompanied by erysipelas in one of her legs. She received a visit from her holy mistress, who manifested towards her feelings of the most tender compassion, and signed her with a relic of the true Cross. This had no sooner been done than her illness left her, and she arose from her bed perfectly cured. But wonderful to relate, Veronica was at the same time seized by that disorder, and it was ascertained by Father Tassinari, her confessor, that she had asked this as a boon from God.

In like manner when the cells of the novices and indeed those of the whole community became infested with foul and disgusting insects to the grievous annoyance of those servants of God, the saintly mother prayed to our Lord that all the noisome creatures might be congregated together in her cell. Her petition was granted, and her bed, walls, and furniture teemed with them, whereas in all the other apartments there was not one to be found. She was so delighted at having obtained her request, that she danced with joy at the relief which was thus afforded to her daughters and sisters. To reward this heroism, it pleased God, a few days afterwards, to cause the entire pest to disappear from her cell, nor was one of them ever after seen in any part of the monastery. If one of the novices appeared pensive or distressed, Veronica would inquire the cause without delay, and apply the needful remedies. Her cell was open to them at all hours. She always welcomed them with cheerful looks, and dismissed them with kind words. At their recreations in common, she endeavoured to keep them happy in God, taking her share in all they did, and even joining with them in hunting grasshoppers and other mischievous insects from the shrubs in the garden. This was one of the amusements of the novices, and she continued to take part in it during the last years of her life, when she was not only novice mistress but abbess, though her age was advanced, and her sufferings from dropsy considerable.

Having gained the hearts of the novices by these affectionate ways, she set herself to regulate and direct their minds, this being the principal duty of her office. Let no one, however, imagine that she attempted to carry her youthful children with her in her own flight towards perfection. She began by grounding them well in the holy fear of God and in the exact observance of the divine commandments. For this purpose she took pains to make them thoroughly learn and comprehend all that is contained in Christian doctrine. From this she went on to explain the religious rule, teaching them to appreciate its spirit, and doing her best at the same time to render them familiar with the labours and duties of the community. She knew how to put up with such defects and imperfections as proceeded, not from malice or ill-will, but from that weakness which arises from a person being as yet a beginner in the ways of God. Nevertheless she took advantage of every good opportunity to inspire them with that spirit of mortification and total abnegation of self, which is the genuine characteristic of the religious life.

She would often repeat these words—"Whoever wishes to belong to God must first die to herself." Hence she was particularly careful to try them on this point. One day Sister Ursula Ceoli was complaining of the great heat of the dog-days, upon which her holy mistress reminded her how much more violent was the fire of purgatory, and how easy it was to incur its penalties. She also insisted that by way of penance for her murmurs, and as a trial of her obedience and mortification, she should put two additional veils on her head and a cloak on her shoulders, and thus equipped go down into the garden and remain exposed to the burning rays of the sun. The novice obeyed, although she believed that she was going to encounter death. Her wise mistress, however, who was satisfied by this act of self-denial, obtained from our Lord the following miracle: a refreshing breeze lifted the veils into the air, and kept them above the novice's head in the form of an umbrella, causing her thus to enjoy the coolness of spring, until she was ordered back from the garden. But our Saint was more severe with another novice, who grew impatient under the rather peculiar temper of an elderly companion in office, and went so far on one occasion as to call her a whimsical woman. Veronica reproved her very seriously, and obliged her to make five crosses on the ground with her tongue; she also required her to ask pardon on her knees of the injured sister, and to accuse herself of her fault in the public refectory.

But because the acts of evangelical mortification which are most difficult and most pleasing to God, are those whereby we humble ourselves, she dwelt on this virtue with singular emphasis in her instructions. Our Lord Jesus Christ Himself had inspired her to do so by means of a beautiful vision. On Christmas Day she had seen her Saviour, under the form of an Infant, Who recommended her above all other virtues, to train her novices in the path of holy humility: to which Veronica replied, "O my Jesus, how can I do this?—for I do not know what humility is." The Divine Infant gave her this answer: "I am the Master of humility; do not fear therefore, but trust in Me." Now Veronica well knew that the most effective method of inculcating any virtue is to set an example of it. As this rule applies especially to humility, she took particular pains to render her conduct such as might serve for a model to her novices. Not only was she imperturbable and cheerful in the midst of those severe mortifications which she had to endure from others, as we shall see hereafter, but she would frequently humble herself spontaneously before the novices, even in her old age. Sometimes she assembled them together in the chapel and, prostrating herself at their feet on the floor, implored their pardon for the faults she had committed in the execution of her charge, as also for the disedification which she had caused them. Sometimes she would make to them a sort of general confession, exaggerating even the defects of her childhood, and requesting and obliging them under obedience, to set their feet upon her lips and to trample upon her as a being unworthy of taking her place among the servants of God. In so doing, every one of course endeavoured to step on her as lightly as possible, and only for appearance' sake; but Sister Florida Ceoli asserts that she once felt herself forced by some invisible hand to tread so hard on the mouth of her holy mistress, that one of the lips continued dreadfully swollen and injured for several days; this was either a piece of revenge on the part of the devil, who could not bear to witness such extraordinary proofs of humility, or it was a favour granted by God to satisfy the lowly desires of His handmaiden.

She was in the habit of concluding all her instructions with an exhortation to avoid tepidity, which she declared to be the true plague of souls. She was desirous that her daughters should consecrate all the actions of the day to God, and thereby maintain a perpetual exercise of love. In order to keep them to this holy practice, she introduced into the noviciate the custom of thus mutually questioning each other when they met: "Sister So and So, what are you doing?" to which the reply was: "I am loving God!" at least, if the sister addressed could say this with truth. It happened one morning that a novice, meeting her holy mistress and being asked the usual question, failed to give the accustomed answer through fear of saying what was not true. Hereupon Veronica turned pale, as she was in the habit of doing when she suffered great pain, and remonstrated with the novice in so impressive a manner as to draw tears from her eyes, to the great advantage of her soul. Our Saint was more severe to another novice who came out of choir after None, declaring in a laughing way that she had been somewhat distracted during the recital of office. On this, the zeal of her mistress was enkindled, and she exclaimed in a tone of high displeasure: "What can you be thinking of, to say with a smile, 'I have sinned?'" She then placed herself at table with an air of extreme distress, seemingly unconscious of all around her, and eating nothing. The lukewarm novice observed this, and asked her what was the matter, and if she had been the cause of her loss of appetite. "Well," said Veronica, "do you wonder at my displeasure, when you have told me with a smile on your face, that you have sinned?" Then she went on to point out to her in the most striking way the true nature of an offence against God, even though the matter be ever so small, so that the novice was touched to the heart, and burst into tears.

It was thus that she constantly endeavoured to exercise her novices in divine love, by using the greatest diligence to preserve them from the least fault whereby they might displease their Beloved. Although she had been herself led by Almighty God along the sublime path of heavenly communications, raptures, and supernatural favours, to a greater extent than we find to have been the case in the lives of other saints, as the sequel will abundantly prove, Veronica did not attempt to make her disciples follow the same course. On the contrary, she made it her practice to forbid them the study of mystical works, and to keep them to more simple books, such as the "Lives of the Saints," the "Christian Perfection," by F. Rodriguez, and similar treatises. She would tell them that the love of God consists in never offending Him by the smallest deliberate fault, and in doing, as far as possible, whatever is most pleasing in His sight. To promote the attainment of her object, it pleased God to favour her with light from above, whereby she was enabled to read the hearts of her spiritual daughters, so that when she conversed with them, she could put her finger on any thought or inordinate affection which might be causing them uneasiness, without even betraying her knowledge of it. This was attested by Sister Maria Maggi, who had herself experienced the effects of this gift, and had observed its influence on the whole community.

Sometimes, when it was requisite for their good, Veronica would acknowledge that she knew all that was going on in their minds. She did so in the case of Sister Mary Magdalen Boscaini, who, during the first year of her noviciate, was troubled for several days by an affliction of spirit, and made no mention of it to either her confessor or her mistress. The latter perceived it, and asked her several times if she were not labouring under some spiritual trial. The novice always evaded giving a direct reply, so at last our Saint said to her, "Are you not troubled by such and such an affliction?" and she went on to detail minutely the time and cause of the trouble she was suffering from, which however was completely dispelled before the termination of the interview. There was another novice who cherished certain feelings of aversion towards a companion; but although she was successful in concealing what was passing in her mind, she was one day summoned by her saintly mistress, who warned her to watch herself very carefully, lest a great flame should be kindled from a small spark. The novice, thus taken by surprise, inquired the reason of this admonition. Veronica then explained to her the antipathy which had been fermenting within her with such minuteness, that she seemed to have been reading her inmost soul;

and at the same time that she exposed the wound, she effected its cure.

From what has been already said, it is clear that Veronica could not possibly have done more than she did in the fulfilment of the duties entrusted to her. But how true it is that the judgment of God is ever peculiarly strict towards those who rule ! We learn as much from the sixth chapter of Wisdom, which is very applicable to the superiors and directors of religious communities, if through any fault on their part, the standard of spirituality is lowered, or if abuses are suffered to intrude, or if such as have been already introduced are permitted to continue. On the 9th of November, 1707 (that is to say, in the thirteenth year of her superiorship and the forty-seventh of her age), we find it mentioned in the diary of Father Cappelletti, that Veronica, having been taken extremely ill of a malady which had been predicted by our Lord on the 22nd of the preceding October, was to all appearance in her last agony at nine o'clock in the evening. At that hour she had a vision, in which she was borne in spirit to the tribunal of the Divine Judge. She beheld Christ with a severe aspect, seated on a majestic throne in the midst of a multitude of angels. The most holy Mary was on one side, and her patron saints on the other. When her guardian angel presented her at this dread judgment-seat, she expected to receive the sentence of eternal condemnation, so awful were the words of her Judge, and so destitute did she feel of all good works. But so earnest were the intercessions of Mary and those of her patron saints, that at length the Divine Countenance of Christ assumed an expression of mercy, and, after bestowing on her various admonitions, He dismissed her with a loving embrace. We may form some idea of the alarm which she suffered, from the circumstance of her illness being so much increased thereby, that about nine o'clock on the morning of the following day Father Cappelletti, her confessor, thought it right to administer Extreme Unction after communicating her.

As it may conduce to the instruction of others, we will quote from the journal which she wrote in 1717, an account she gives of her vision of the divine tribunal. "The Divinity Itself," she declares, "becomes a Mirror to the soul, wherein she beholds herself exactly as she is: she sees not only the state to which she has been reduced, but also the causes which have brought her to it. Mirrored, as it were, in the Divinity, she sees herself covered with defilement, and is horror-stricken at the sight. What would she not give to be able to hide herself in the earth, and flee away from the Eye of God, which fulminates vengeance! All that she sees of herself impels her to fly; but through the just judgment of God she stands there mute and immovable. . . . I am unable either by words or illustrations to describe this tremendous judgment, owing to the fear and terror which my soul then experienced." The human mind is incapable of imagining such a scene; for although we were to conjure up the most painful and terrific conceptions, we should fall short of the dreadful reality, with which, however, every one will one day be made acquainted.

We may infer the nature of the reprimands which she received during this vision from what we are about to relate. That same morning, having somewhat re-recovered from her illness, she told her confessor that she wished to speak privately to her novices, for that on the preceding day her Divine Judge had made her aware of the faults of each, and also of her own negligence in failing to correct them. F. Cappelletti gave her permission to do so, and added that it should be done in his presence. So she called them to her one by one, and whispered in the ear of each so effectively that every one of them burst into a flood of tears. The confessor did not hear what she said to them individually about their defects, but he heard the following words, which she addressed to them all collectively— "Do not imitate me, for I have been a stone of scandal in my whole life, whether as to my observance of the rule or my practice of obedience, love, and charity —I have been throughout full of pride and destitute of humility." She concluded by desiring them to recommend her to our Lord and the Blessed Virgin, that so her sins might be forgiven, and she might receive grace and mercy. At these words the sighs of her novices increased, and they implored her with sobs to forgive them for not having followed her holy instructions and example. But Veronica replied: "Be careful of small things; for before God these things are reckoned very differently from what we might imagine." When she had closed her conference with the novices, all the other nuns were anxious to visit her; "and to all" (we read in the above-mentioned diary) "she spoke very freely, without human respect; and each individual derived great advantage therefrom."

Let us conclude our account of the offices she successively filled. In March, 1716, in the fifty-sixth year of her age, she was obliged under obedience to accept the dignity of abbess, which she retained till her death. Throughout this period the rule was most strictly observed, and the most perfect harmony prevailed among the religious, as was unanimously attested by them in the process of her canonization, so that "the convent had never before been so well governed and directed. Nor had there ever been a superior more highly esteemed and valued by the religious than she was." Such is the statement of Father Tassinari, who was confessor to the community for forty years, during which time he became thoroughly acquainted with it, and was moreover one of Veronica's particular directors. The spotless tenor of her life, her sanctity and zeal for the observance of the rule, impressed all the nuns with reverential fear; while at the same time her humble deportment, her love and maternal solicitude for them, nourished in their minds a feeling of filial confidence towards her, and they had recourse to her as to an affectionate parent in all their spiritual distresses, certain of being kindly listened to at any hour, and of being succoured as occasion required. If one of them was so constrained by human respect or by temptation from the devil as to attempt to conceal her state, Veronica, being enlightened from above, would go to her assistance of her own accord. Thus it happened one day that a nun, who was labouring under heavy temptations, and had consequently fallen into a condition of profound sadness, shut herself up so that her door could not be opened from without: Veronica, whom no one had informed of this, came to see her, and having obtained admission after a good deal of knocking, made the religious understand in a very gentle way the deception which Satan had been practising on her, and also the danger of falling, to which she had exposed herself by failing to mention the trial she was undergoing.

Sister Mary Rose Gotoloni was ill of a very serious

fever, and being unable to eat in consequence of the nausea which caused her to loathe every kind of food, she felt herself becoming faint without strength to help herself or power to call for assistance. While she was commending herself to God, she beheld her saintly abbess entering the room with some sweetmeats in her hand. "It seems to me," said the latter, "that you need refreshment; eat." Accordingly she ate with considerable appetite, found her strength return, was entirely free from all feeling of sickness, and in a short time completely restored to health.

Veronica was particularly careful to maintain the strict observance of community life, which constitutes the very soul of religious perfection. She would never permit any difference to be made in the treatment of individuals, except in the case of illness. For this purpose she set them an example in her own person; for although she was abbess, she would suffer no distinction to be made in her cell, or clothing, or food, but would join the others in performing the meanest offices, such as washing dishes in the kitchen, &c. Hence her subjects were ashamed of being more fastidious than their abbess, and submitted with a good grace to the punctual fulfilment of community duties.

Experience teaches us that it is in vain for a superior to be zealous for regular observance unless, in addition to the good example of which we have spoken, she is careful to guard against a scarcity of provisions or other necessaries allowed by the institute, which might result from her indolence or negligence. Our excellent abbess was well aware of this, and being not only instigated by a spirit of charity, but likewise impelled by prudence and well-regulated energy, took great pains to have her community well provided with whatever the rule of their profession permitted, in the way of diet, clothes, and medicine. The convent buildings being on an extremely small scale, it was one of her first plans, as soon as she was made abbess, to enlarge the edifice; accordingly she contrived, in the first years of her superiorship, to add to it, by means of voluntary contributions, a long dormitory which may be seen to this day, namely the one on the right hand side of the chapel dedicated to our Blessed Lady of the Rosary. Thus was verified a prediction which had been made twelve years before she became superior by F. Ubaldo Antonio Cappelletti, a worthy Oratorian, at that time confessor to the community. He had caused the above-mentioned chapel to be built with Sister Florida Ceoli's dower; and when it was finished, there is a tradition among the nuns that he said: "Would that I were as certain that the gates of Paradise will be opened for me as that here" (and he marked the spot to the right of the chapel) "a door will be opened, and a long dormitory be constructed." Veronica proved him to be a true prophet.

The way in which she procured a supply of water was by no means less remarkable, nay perhaps even more so. Every one knows how much the want of this commodity is felt in a community, especially in one of nuns. Before Veronica was abbess, all the water used in the establishment had to be drawn and carried round by hand for the kitchen, the infirmary, the garden, &c., to the great inconvenience of the good religious. But when she was raised to this dignity, she obtained from the honourable family of Vitelli a considerable quantity of the water which supplied in abundance the magnificent mansion of that family; and having conveyed it to the convent premises, she made a large fish-pond in the garden to receive it, so that it could be easily used to water the plants and herbs. She likewise furnished the kitchen, the infirmary, and in fact every part of her monastery with this essential element, by means of leaden pipes, which were presented out of devotion by Cosmo III., Grand Duke of Tuscany, so that the appointments of this convent were inferior to those of no other religious house.

It is not surprising to find that an authority at once so wise and holy was profitable and acceptable to all, that the religious, having experienced the blessing of being governed by her, did all they could to prolong the term of her power, and that she continued to be their abbess until death took her from them.

BOOK II.

CONTAINING AN ACCOUNT OF THE EXTRAORDINARY GRACES BY MEANS OF WHICH SHE WAS RAISED DURING THE LAST THIRTY-FIVE YEARS OF HER LIFE TO THE HIGHEST DEGREE OF SANCTITY, AND RENDERED THE LIVING IMAGE OF JESUS CRUCIFIED.

CHAPTER I.

MYSTERIOUS VISION OF A CHALICE, WHICH PREPARED HER TO REPRODUCE IN HER OWN PERSON THE PASSION OF OUR REDEEMER.

WE were able in the last book to catch no more than slight glimpses of the great sanctity of this glorious and heroic soul, for we were only considering the secular portion of her life, and the first fifteen years which she spent in religion, and merely glanced at the latter portion of her mortal career in our mention of the various offices which she successively fulfilled for the community. We now proceed to the last thirty-five years which she passed on earth: which indeed present to our contemplation a new kind of life, which the apostle might have termed the life of Veronica hidden in Christ, or the life of Christ in Veronica: for we shall see that she gloried in nothing save the cross of Christ, and that with Him she was fastened to that cross in the truest and most real manner that is attainable by a human being, whereby she was fashioned after the likeness of Christ, and as it were, transformed into Christ. In describing this new life, we shall have to describe a long series of supernatural gifts of the most extraordinary nature; and if the narration of these should awaken in the mind of the reader any suspicion of exaggerations or fanciful delusions, we would entreat him to weigh well the wonderful effects of heroic virtue, which in her case produced visions and marvellous gifts, such as could not have originated in any other than a divine and supernatural source.

Down to the year 1693, which was the thirty-third of Veronica's age, the events of her life progressed in the manner already described in our first book. It was now the Will of Almighty God to draw her into a more intimate union with Himself, and to raise her to a more sublime degree of sanctity. He accordingly began to bestow on her the rarest graces, in order to mould her into a closer likeness of His only-begotten Son, Who is the Model of all the predestinate, and especially of the saints. At the time to which we have just referred, Veronica was favoured with a vision, wherein she beheld a mysterious chalice, which she recognised as a presage of the divine Passion that was to be re-enacted, so to speak, in her own person. This vision was repeated several times in successive years, with various modifications. At one time this chalice was presented to her view on a bright cloud, surrounded with splendour, at another time unaccompanied by any ornament; sometimes the liquid it contained seemed to be bubbling up within it; at other times it would boil over to a considerable extent, and occasionally it would fall drop by drop. The spirit of our Saint was always ready to drain the chalice to the dregs, but her lower nature shrunk with horror at the sight, as did our divine Redeemer in the garden of Gethsemane. Accordingly she set herself to subdue the resistance of the flesh by means of severe penance, as we shall presently explain. At length her nature ceased to feel repugnance, but she wrote as follows :—" I do not trust it, for I know that it is not as yet dead. I have always found my soul ready, and even anxiously desirous, to share in that bitter draught, in order to accomplish the Will of God. Sometimes," she continues, "I felt such longings that I exclaimed, 'Oh when will the hour come, my God, in which Thou wilt grant me to drink of Thy chalice? I resign myself entirely to Thy Will, but Thou alone seest my thirst. *Sitio*—I thirst—not for consolation, but for sufferings and afflictions.' I seemed incapable of enduring further delay. One night when I was rapt in prayer, our Lord appeared to me with the chalice in His hand, and said to me, 'This is for thee, and I give it thee in order that thou mayest taste of it as much as I have, but not now. Prepare thyself, for in due season thou shalt partake of it.' Immediately after these words He vanished, leaving the chalice so vividly imprinted on my mind that from that hour to this it has never left me."

It was on this occasion that our Lord signified to her the dreadful sufferings which she would have to undergo in mind and body, not only from the insults and temptations which demoniacal malice had in store for her, but likewise from the false accusations, attacks, and contempt of her fellow-creatures, and lastly, from God Himself in the extreme desolation and dryness of spirit which was appointed her. To all this the generous virgin offered herself a willing sacrifice.

Our most Blessed Lady, the Queen of Dolours, together with other saints, assisted in inspiring her with courage to accept her cup of bitterness. During the night of the solemn feast of her Assumption, the Holy Virgin and her divine Son appeared to Veronica. Our Saviour, Who was seated on a majestic throne, in His radiant glory, presented to His Mother a chalice full to overflowing. Mary received it, and, turning to our Saint, said, "My daughter, I make thee this present in the Name of my Son!" At the same time the two sainted virgins, Catherine of Siena and Rose of Lima, who attended in the train of the Queen of Heaven, made signs to Veronica to accept it. Afterwards, on the night of the 28th of August, the feast of S. Augustine, she again beheld Jesus Christ on His throne of glory; and that holy Doctor of the Church, who was there with many other blessed spirits attending our Lord, turned to Veronica, with a chalice in his hand. "This," he said, "is indeed a precious gift, for it is presented to thee by God Himself." At that moment the contents of the chalice began to boil over on every side, and being received by angels into vessels of gold, were presented at the throne of our Lord. Then Veronica asked for an explanation of the vision, and was informed that the rich liquid signified the sufferings to be endured by her for the love of God, and that the golden vessels were meant to denote the precious nature of those sufferings.

But the following vision, which shall be related in her own words, was more touching and efficacious than those we have already mentioned:—"Finding myself overwhelmed with anguish," she says, "so that I felt hardly able to stand, I went to the church, and prostrating myself before the Most Holy, I offered myself once more unreservedly to Him. Suddenly I felt somewhat recollected, that is, rapt out of myself, and our Lord presented Himself to me. I cannot explain how this came to pass. I only know that He said to me, 'Take courage, and fear not; I am here to assist thee; behold Me.' With these words He caused me to see the condition of His Sacred Humanity during the scourging at the pillar. He stood before me all streaming with blood and covered with wounds. The chalice was in His Hand, and He said, 'Look at me, My beloved; behold these Wounds, which are, as it were, so many voices inviting thee to drink of this bitter chalice; I give it to thee, and wish thee to partake of it.' Having said this, He disappeared, leaving me the chalice." Now let us observe the result of all this. "I felt," she continues, "refreshed in spirit, and even recruited in body. I found myself in possession of interior peace, and ardently desirous of accomplishing the Will of God, and of pleasing Him in all things."

We shall now describe one by one the bitter sufferings which corresponded with what was shown her in these visions. In the first place, her human nature recoiled from this chalice, which was constantly before the eyes of her mind; she was daily attacked by violent fever, which kept her at first for about eight days from eating or drinking anything. Sometimes the contents of that mysterious chalice seemed to be poured over her, and then she felt herself consumed with so fiery a heat that the more she drank the more raging did her thirst become. At other times she beheld the same liquid dropping on her food, to which it imparted a most bitter taste, whereby her palate was poisoned for a long time. Then again this draught of sorrow would fall in drops, which were presently changed into so many swords, spears, and arrows, which seemed to wound her body, and transfix her heart. But still more painful were the remedies to which she was called to submit. Her health and strength having suffered the most serious injury in consequence of the trials we have already described, the superior wished to put her into the hands of physicians. She promptly obeyed, not being willing to say anything about the supernatural cause of her maladies. Three different kinds of medicine were administered to her, but they all occasioned her the most dreadful torment, and she had no sooner swallowed one than she was forced to reject it. She writes as follows:—"Every day that these three remedies were tried, seemed likely to be the last of my life . . . so great was the violence which I had to use towards myself in order to take them, that I felt ready to burst asunder." And yet she never manifested the least repugnance; on the contrary, she went on repeating to our Lord from her heart the words: "*Sitio*, I thirst, I thirst:" and her desire was gratified, for her medical attendant happening to enter the room just as she had been forcibly compelled to reject one of these doses, he wished her to take another immediately, which she accordingly did, and it produced the same effect as the preceding one.

The demons meanwhile took care to fulfil the part which Veronica had been warned in the vision to expect. One night they placed her in a bath of icy coldness, and kept her there for two hours. When it was over she was senseless and motionless. The infirmarians having found her in this state, endeavoured during no less than four hours to restore her by means of fire and heated clothes, as well as by restoratives, but this only added to her sufferings. At other times the devils would attack her innocence, by assuming the forms of young men, or would attempt to terrify her by appearing as terrific spectres, or would suggest the most wicked misrepresentations of the religious state, which they portrayed as a sort of hell, accusing the sacred habit she wore as the cause of her eternal condemnation. They went so far as to bind her with chains; they struck her frequently, and expressed their desire to drag her away with them, calling out with infernal merriment, "Thou art ours, thou art ours!" Though so grievously afflicted, this generous soul was invincible; she even invited them to torment her further, and to try her to the very utmost permitted them by God. "Come then," she said, "behold, I am ready to suffer all; and if you are endeavouring to rival each other in inflicting torments upon me, here I am prepared to contend with you. See how you can torture me, and see how I can bear it. Come then; the more you harass me, the better shall I be pleased. Blessed, blessed be the cross! Blessed be suffering!" And then, with more fury than ever, her foes rushed upon her like so many rabid dogs, while she contentedly drank her chalice of bitterness.

But her most severe trial and most bitter chalice was what came to her from God Himself. For the purpose of proving the fortitude and fidelity of her soul, He was pleased to withdraw Himself from her, at least in appearance, for in reality He was nearer to her than ever with His grace, and the eye of His mercy was no less constantly upon her, regarding her with increased satisfaction. She expresses herself on this subject to the following effect: "All my other trials were nothing, compared with that which I suffered interiorly—forsaken, abandoned, and environed with thick darkness; placed moreover at so great a distance from God, that I felt incapable of breathing forth a single aspiration to the Lord. Oh, what intolerable anguish is this to a soul, to find herself deprived of every support, and banished from her highest good!

She sighs, but is not heard; she calls to her Heavenly Spouse, but He comes not; she seeks Him, but He flies from her; she prays to Him, but He will not hear her. . . . Thus was my spirit troubled; it seems to me that the agony of death cannot be worse than what I then endured." Let us here remark the proofs which Almighty God gave of His especial presence: "The only refreshment I had," she continues, "was to behold the chalice drawing constantly nearer to me. . . . I seemed to be filled with abhorrence for everything that the tempter set before me; I despised his artifices, and repeatedly taxed him with his falsehoods; I declared to him that I was misled by none of them; I professed myself content in accomplishing the Will of God, Who is my absolute Master. . . . Blessed be God! Everything seems little that is endured for His love. Blessed be the simple cross. Blessed be pure suffering! Behold, I am ready to bear all, in order to please my dear Lord, and to promote the fulfilment of His divine Will."

CHAPTER II.

VERONICA IS MADE TO PARTICIPATE IN OUR BLESSED SAVIOUR'S CROWNING WITH THORNS.—THE SEVERE PAINS WHICH THIS CAUSED HER, AND HER SUFFERINGS FROM THE REMEDIES TO WHICH HER SUPERIORS REQUIRED HER TO SUBMIT.

WHEN Veronica had been prepared by frequent visions of this bitter chalice to drink it with unreserved generosity, our Lord began to bestow on her a share in the greater sufferings of His most dolorous Passion; a privilege so rare, that it is reserved for the noblest and dearest of the children of God. We find from the memorials in our possession, that it was on the 4th of April in the year 1694, that Jesus appeared to her with the insignia of His Passion, and presented her with His crown of thorns. The following is her own account, written under obedience:—

"On the night of the 4th of April, while I was in prayer, I became rapt in recollection, and beheld an intellectual vision, in which our Lord appeared to me with a large crown of thorns on His Head. Immediately I began to say to Him: 'My divine Spouse, give me those thorns: they are fit for me, and not for Thee, Who art my highest good.' Meanwhile, I felt that our Lord answered me thus: 'I am come to crown thee now, My beloved;' and, in an instant, He took off His crown, and placed it on my head. The pain which it caused was so severe, that I am not conscious of having ever felt anything equal to it. At the same time I was made aware that this my coronation was a sign that I was to be the spouse of Christ, and that, in token of this, He desired that, by participating in His sufferings, I should acquire the title of the Spouse of God Crucified; therefore I was myself to be crucified with my divine Spouse. Every puncture on my head seemed to invite me to this. On the same day our Lord promised me that the grace I had just received should be repeated on different occasions. But the satisfaction which I derived from my sufferings was such that I seemed literally to pine after torments." Surely this was a proof of the truth of the supernatural favour she had received.

She then goes on to relate the sequel of her vision.

"As soon as I came to myself," she writes, "I found that my head was swollen and racked with such excessive pain that I could hardly stand. Feeling utterly incapable of encountering any fatigue, I addressed our Lord thus with the greatest confidence—'I implore this boon of Thee, my God; if it be Thy Will, grant me sufficient strength to go through all my labours and duties, and permit these graces which Thou hast just bestowed on me to be kept secret for ever.' Immediately I felt my strength return, and I could have done anything. But the agony inflicted by the thorns continued, and whenever I bowed my head the torture was so acute that I seemed ready to expire. Let me bear all for the love of God: everything seems little or nothing that is endured for His love."

Her prayer and its immediate effect corroborate our remarks as to the reality of her gifts. In another part of her journal she writes as follows of the repetitions of that painful coronation:—

"Several times when I was engaged in prayer, with some desire for suffering, I suddenly felt the thorns piercing me so violently that I fell to the ground with pain, remaining there for a considerable space of time unconscious and as if dead. By what I suffered I was enabled to conceive the overwhelming torments of our Redeemer when He was crowned with thorns. The thought of this made me still more anxious to suffer, and again I felt as it were an invisible hand pressing the crown upon me. On another occasion, during a sort of ecstasy, the value of suffering was made known to me; and whilst I felt the renewed pressure of the thorns, every wound they inflicted seemed to call aloud for fresh torments. Our Lord was frequently pleased to assure me in visions of the understanding that I was His beloved: and it seemed to me that He would fit the crown on my brow, and for my greater satisfaction, press it vehemently into my flesh. Then ecstasy would be added to recollection, and I received such intimate revelations as to the precious nature of suffering, that I am unable to express them adequately. All this caused me to long so much for sufferings that when my senses returned I gave myself up to the use of the discipline and various descriptions of penance, scarcely conscious of what I did. The utmost pain that I inflicted on myself seemed little or nothing: everything inflamed my desire for suffering. Each cross seemed to invite me to bear another. The Passion of my Redeemer was so deeply engraven on my heart that I frequently fainted away for anguish."

The zeal with which, in the midst of her sufferings, she burned for the glory of God and for the conversion of sinners, furnishes us with an additional proof that the wonders we have been contemplating were the work of God. It is thus that she continues: "The anguish which I endured caused me to feel such compassion for all sinners, that I offered to the Eternal Father for their conversion all the sufferings of Jesus, together with all His merits and those of the most holy Virgin; earnestly praying that I might suffer more, declaring to the Lord that I desired to act as mediatrix between Himself and sinners, and conjuring Him to add to my pains. That very moment I felt a renewal of agony from my crown of thorns, not only round my head, as I had been accustomed to do, but likewise all through it: and thus for several hours I went on rejoicing amid a thousand torments. A few days have elapsed since this occurred to me: but at the time of which I have spoken, I received notice that the whole of this Lent was to be passed by me in perpetual suffering. Praise be to God; all is too little to bear for His love. Meanwhile I unceasingly repeat—Blessed be the Cross! Blessed be suffering! I wish for nothing but the Will of God; I am satisfied with what is His divine pleasure; behold, I am prepared for everything."

It appears from her own accounts and from those of her companions that she continued to enjoy these favours, for such they must indeed be termed, during the entire remainder of her life, that is to say, for thirty-four or thirty-five consecutive years. We may infer from what she wrote twelve years after her first coronation, that the pain and the punctures then inflicted were permanent, and were felt by her more or less acutely. She was accustomed to feel them especially on all Fridays, as well as during the seasons of the carnival and Lent, but still more particularly during Holy Week. And wonderful to relate, notwithstanding the faintness, which rendered her scarcely able to support herself on her feet, she was endowed with such supernatural strength that she was able to transact all her business and to fulfil all her duties, while her desire for fresh torments was so intense that she repeated again and again—"My Lord, if it is Thou Who thus afflictest me, let Thy Hand fall still more heavily upon me, to the end that I may feel more pain."

When her directors were informed of what she had undergone, they commissioned Sister Florida Ceoli to examine her head, and to see if there were any visible marks to indicate the crown of thorns; and the following statement was made upon oath by that religious in the process of our Saint's canonization.

"I went to see her, and perceived that her brow was encircled with a colour approaching to red. Sometimes I observed thereon certain pimples like little buttons, of the size of large pins' heads. On other occasions her forehead was covered with purple marks like thorns, which reached down to her eyes. Then again I saw that one of these apparent thorns came down under her right eye, causing it to shed tears, and they were tears of blood, as I saw from the veil with which she wiped them away. I have witnessed this and similar occurrences, and have mentioned them repeatedly to the confessors who directed me to observe her." Her companions made depositions to the same effect.

Notwithstanding all this, the bishop, Monsignor Luc' Antonio Eustachj, was so anxious to proceed with caution, that he wished our Saint to put herself into the hands of medical practitioners, in order that it might be ascertained beyond all doubt whether these things proceeded from a supernatural cause or from any physical indisposition. This was ordained by God, that His beloved might acquire fresh merit, and that the reality of her gifts might be rendered more than ever unquestionable. Accordingly they began to anoint her with a particular kind of oil, which caused her head to feel a burning pain. At the same time that she felt this external heat, the centre of her brain seemed to be cold as ice, on which account the doctors agreed to apply a hot iron to her head and to one of her legs. All present were astonished at the invincible firmness which she displayed during this painful operation. Not one of the religious had the heart to hold her: she, however, assured the surgeon that he might begin without fear of any movement on her part, and in truth she remained as still as if she had been insensible; so that afterwards Massani, her medical attendant, observed that he seemed to have been operating on a statue. Within a few days it became necessary to close the issue in her head, because it only served to increase her pain to such a degree that she was unable to speak, or to rest her swollen head on her pillow. Another hot iron was applied to her neck instead, but as it caused such violent irritation of the nerves as to preclude the possibility of repose either by night or day, the surgeons were obliged to close that wound also.

The physician then thought it expedient to try the effect of a seton in her neck. This was an operation frequently resorted to in the medical practice of those times, and consisted in perforating the skin with a good-sized needle or some other instrument of steel heated red-hot, by means of which a knot of cotton was introduced and permitted to remain there in order to keep up a species of running wound. One may easily conceive how extremely painful such a process must be. The nuns were so timid that they could not bring themselves to render the least assistance, or even to hand the heated needle to the surgeon, so the patient performed that office herself, although she was well aware that this operation would cost her far more pain than the hot irons had done. She endured it with her usual courage and calmness, and declared when it was over that the only fault she could find with it was its speedy termination. After a short time, the knot having broken, two similar setons were applied to her ears. But as the cold which she felt internally continued undiminshed, and as nothing seemed to relieve the pain of her wounded head, they changed their plans and cauterized her arm. But as this only aggravated her sufferings by occasioning violent convulsions and swellings both in her arm and leg, it was necessary to permit the flesh to heal. The medical professors would not, however, acknowledge themselves defeated; and twice more they tormented her by applying setons to her ears. But discovering at last that no remedy was of any avail, but that their efforts to benefit her had only made matters worse, they protested that their science had no power to cure diseases of that nature. Therefore the bishop and the confessors of Veronica were convinced that it was the Hand of God which had wrought thus on His highly-favoured servant, and they committed her to the power of her Lord, Whose Will it was by means of these privileges to cause her to resemble Himself.

CHAPTER III.

SHE IS PROMOTED TO HEAVENLY ESPOUSALS.—THE MANNER IN WHICH OUR LORD PREPARED AND CONDUCTED THEM.

THAT most intimate union, the result of perfect love, which takes place between the soul and her God, is described in the pages of Holy Writ by the title of Espousals. Throughout the book of Canticles, the divine Spirit represents to us by the mouth of Solomon that burning intercourse of love which is exchanged between a holy soul and her Lord, who are introduced to our contemplation under the figure of a devoted bridegroom and bride. Jesus Christ Himself, moreover, in the Gospel of S. Matthew, sets before us a picture of those wise virgins who are both invited and admitted to the heavenly nuptials. It has sometimes pleased our Lord, in the case of certain noble souls, to celebrate these spiritual nuptials with visible signs, and with external rites analogous to those which are practised by mortals on their bridal day. It happened thus to S. Catherine of Siena, and to a few more saints of the highest rank. Our Veronica was one of these favoured souls. In the preceding chapter we saw from her own account that on the occasion of her being crowned with thorns, our Lord made her understand that it was a token of His desire to espouse her. And truly, when her brows were encircled with His own diadem, she was considered by the divine King of Martyrs worthy to be His bride. Nevertheless, in order to render her still more deserving of a dignity so exalted, He was pleased to prepare her for it by means of many other gracious visions.

"One morning," she declares, "I was assisting at holy Mass, and became suddenly much absorbed. My heart was touched, and inflamed with a great desire to be entirely united to God. All at once it seemed as if God withdrew from me the use of my external senses, and informed me by means of an interior communication that He was about to make me His own by espousing me to Himself. This assurance caused my heart to leap for joy, and I felt as it were on fire. At the same time it was given me to understand the whole process through which I was to pass by way of preparation, and which was to be one of pure suffering. These beautiful tidings increased my longing to suffer."

She then goes on to declare that after this vision the mere repetition of the words, "My most divine Jesus, Spouse of my soul," would throw her into such exuberant joy that her whole frame was wonderfully invigorated. Therefore she frequently repeated the following short sentence in the form of a rosary, reciting instead of each angelical salutation the sweet words, "My Jesus, my Love, Spouse of my soul!" She adds, that Jesus would often invite her to His divine nuptials under the appearance of a beautiful Child; and that on the 1st of January in the year 1694, He appeared to her under this form, and told her that all her preparation would consist in various descriptions of suffering. The heaviest trial of all to her was an overwhelming desolation of spirit, which oppressed her more especially on the 25th and 26th of the following March: she experienced on those days such interior darkness and spiritual dryness that she knew not what to do. However, she repeated with perfect resignation, "Blessed be Thou, my Lord. I am satisfied in accomplishing Thy Will. My God, if it be Thy good pleasure that I continue thus, I desire that it may be so. I wish for nothing but for the absolute fulfilment of Thy desire and Will. Herein my heart, and my will, and my whole being find repose." By such declarations she gave evidence of her lively faith in God, and whenever she addressed Him as her Spouse, she felt the most profound confidence in Him.

The following vision, which occurred on the 27th of the same month, was still more touching. Our Lord manifested in it the satisfaction with which He had accepted her patience and heroic resignation. She thus described it under obedience to her confessor:—

"In this state of faith and confidence I became suddenly absorbed in recollection. I beheld our dear Lord all covered with wounds, but they appeared environed with glory, especially those of His hands and feet. In that of His sacred Side I beheld a most lovely jewel, on which He seemed to look with pleasure. I felt extremely anxious to know who had presented Him with so choice a gift. He turned towards me and inquired if I recognized it. To which I replied, 'I do not know, but I think a loving soul must have offered Thee some particular suffering, for I perceive that it comes from the treasury of sufferings.' I thought that our Lord answered me joyfully, 'Know then, My beloved, that thou hast afforded Me this gratification by thy sufferings of the last two days. Every time that thou didst repeat the declaration that thou hadst no other will but Mine, and every time that thine act of resignation was renewed, thou didst give beauty to My holy Wounds; and of all thy sufferings together I have formed this jewel, which I keep in My Side, and on which I look with the greatest pleasure. Never shall I cease to behold it, and with loving eyes I shall see it grow constantly more and more beautiful. Now thou mayest indeed comprehend how dear to Me is thy suffering!' By these words He enkindled within me a burning desire for every kind of suffering, and I appeared to answer Him thus—'I am ready, O my God, to be sacrificed as a victim on the altar of Thy cross. I wish to be crucified with Thee. Cause me to undergo all that Thou hast endured for me, but in this, as in everything else, I commit myself to Thy holy Will.' Hereupon our Lord seemed to bend down and embrace my soul, bestowing one divine kiss, which raised me to a state of rapture. This occupied only a brief space of time, but it sufficed to unite my soul to God in a manner which I have never before experienced. The communications then vouchsafed to me were various; the principal was a solemn contract of betrothal. I cannot describe what I felt. . . . When we return to ourselves after such communications as these, we are enabled to form a lively idea of the untold treasures which lie concealed beneath crosses, mortifications, humiliations, and the contempt of our fellow-creatures. Such are the lessons which one learns in the school of divine love."

We should not omit to mention that two days before the vision narrated above, on the feast of our Lady's Annunciation, the gracious Virgin was pleased to honour Veronica with her presence, to give her notice of her approaching espousals, and to prepare her for that high dignity. It was by means of an intellectual vision, as our Saint terms it, that she beheld the Queen of Angels on a magnificent throne, attended on one side by S. Catherine of Siena, and on the other by S. Rose of Lima. These two saints were imploring Mary to obtain for her servant the earnestly desired favour of being espoused to her divine Son. To this the Blessed Virgin graciously answered that their petition would shortly be granted. At the same time Veronica perceived that the Mother of God held in her hand a most beautiful ring, saying that it was shortly to be hers, and therefore that she must prepare herself for the celestial union which awaited her.

"And then," adds Veronica, "she turned towards the two saints, and told me that I was to imitate them in the practice of the most heroic virtues, especially in humility, charity, and knowledge of self. And while she thus addressed me, she seemed to bestow on me interiorly those very virtues, and the priceless treasure which is hidden in them. . . . Since that day I have lived as it were out of myself, and have always had an intimate sense of the presence of God."

So time passed on till the tenth of April, which happened that year to be Holy Saturday. During the whole of Lent she had exercised herself in the most cruel austerities, which we shall not relate in this place for fear of interrupting the thread of our narrative. On the morning of Holy Saturday our divine Saviour once more appeared to her in all His glory. He invited her to His heavenly nuptials on the following morning, and at the same time showed her the marriage ring. Mark well the following proofs of the truth of this vision—"I was likewise informed," she writes, "that it was necessary for me to pass through a process of complete renewal. A new rule of life was given me; I was to inflict on myself greater austerities; I was to be more silent; I was to work with more fervour and love, to do everything with a pure intention, to honour Jesus by denying every natural inclination, to embrace all that is opposed to nature, to fly from the praise of man, to cherish contempt and mortification, to be a lover of the cross in everything, to hold it constantly in my hand as a powerful shield, to be crucified to all things, and to attend to all that constitutes the height of perfection."

Veronica followed the example of the wise virgins in the gospel, and in expectation like theirs she passed the whole night which preceded Easter Sunday in prayer, imploring her future divine Spouse to inspire her to do everything which she ought by way of preparation for the solemnity. "I felt," she declares, "from time to time such loving invitations bestowed on me that they seemed to take me out of myself. These were no other than the summons which my divine Spouse addressed to my heart, saying, 'Come to Me, My beloved.' This single sentence had such power to unite my soul to God that I ceased to feel the encumbrance of this material frame; but this passed quickly, though my heart continued to burn. At other times I had a vivid sense of the presence of Jesus within my heart, and it seemed as if He cast from thence whatever was not suitable to a heart of which He was about to take entire possession. He cast out everything that was earthly, or defiled with self-love, as well as everything that was foul, such as human respect; besides all the imperfections which might impede my progress. Our Lord during this process of clearing my heart spoke to me thus: 'My spouse, dost thou see all these things from which I am delivering thy heart? Do thy best to prevent their return. I am come here now to prepare it, and to garnish it for Myself. Endeavour to preserve it free from all these things. I wish to occupy it all alone. Behold, I am entirely thine.'"

After this vision she had two others the same night, in which she saw our Lord Himself in the act of adorning her heart with rich and costly attire; and she was informed that these things were His divine merits, bestowed on her as His spouse by way of dowry.

Thus the night passed away, and at length came the hour of Communion, which was the time fixed for the expected solemnity. As she drew near to receive the sacred Host, her ear caught the notes of an exquisite melody sung by angels; and the words they sang were, "Veni sponsa Christi"—"Come, spouse of Christ." Presently she was rapt from all objects of sense, and permitted to behold two magnificent thrones. The one on the right hand was all of gold, enriched with most beautiful gems; and here our divine Lord was seated in His glory, His Wounds eclipsing in their splendour the rays of the sun. The one on His left was made of the purest alabaster, and likewise enriched with jewels; it was occupied by the Mother of Jesus, in a precious robe of white. Our Blessed Lady was imploring her Son to hasten the espousals. An immense multitude of the heavenly court was in attendance. The holy virgins, Catherine of Siena and Rose of Lima, advanced, and the former approaching Veronica, instructed her as to her part in this august function. She tells us that she was then slowly conducted by both of them towards the thrones, and as they proceeded on their way they arrayed her in various articles of gorgeous attire, each more precious than the preceding, with which they covered her religious habit. Over all was a robe of white, elaborately embroidered. Thus she was brought before the throne of Jesus Christ. His raiment she declares herself unable to describe. In the wounds of His hands and feet the most radiant gems were gleaming. The wound in His divine Side was open, and poured forth a flood of splendour more brilliant than the sun. There it was that she beheld the nuptial ring; and into that sacred haven she would gladly have thrown herself, to dwell therein for ever. Our Lord raised His hand to bless her, and with a benign countenance intoned the words, "Veni sponsa Christi"—"Come, spouse of Christ;" and the most Blessed Virgin with all the court of heaven continued the antiphon, "Accipe coronam, quam tibi Dominus præparavit in æternum"—" Receive the crown, which the Lord has prepared for thee for all eternity." S. Catherine then began to take off her robes, leaving her simply attired in her religious habit. This was probably designed to teach her the dignity of that habit, which was worthy to be worn even before so august an assemblage. We may infer as much from the effect it produced upon her. Religious would do well to take heed to the following words, which are her own:—

"On finding myself in the presence of my divine Spouse, clothed in this habit, I blushed, for at that moment I was enlightened as to the true value of the gift which God confers in calling a person to religion. This light left my mind filled with an affection for all that religious have to practise, and with an anxious desire to fulfil all those observances punctually. Oh how grand is the very name of a religious, and how much does it comprehend! Although it was given me to conceive the extent of what it includes, I am incapable of describing it. Even now I have such confidence in the mere habit of religion, that to imprint a kiss on it gives me pleasure."

But to return to the mysterious ceremonies. Veronica waited for a short time in her religious habit, until our Lord made a sign to His blessed Mother that she should array our Saint in her nuptial attire, which consisted of a magnificent robe woven of different hues, and covered with precious stones. Mary presented it to S. Catherine, who invested Veronica with it, and then placed her between the two thrones. And as she felt more than ever wounded with love, she beheld our Lord draw from His side the nuptial ring, and lay it in the hand of His holy Mother. We will borrow her own description of this:—"The ring shone resplendently; it appeared to me to be made of gold, and enamelled all round, so as to form the Name of our good Jesus. . . . From time to time I looked up lovingly at our Lord; I seemed to speak with Him, and to implore Him to espouse me." Hereupon the Queen of heaven directed her to present her right hand to S. Catherine, after which our Lord took it in His own, "and at that moment," she continues, "I felt myself more intimately united with Him. Together with His most holy Mother, He then placed the ring on my ring-finger, and when He had done so He blessed it."

At the same instant Veronica heard a majestic harmony of the heavenly choirs; and when these ceased, she received from her divine Spouse fresh rules whereby to attain to greater perfection, so as to be entirely obedient, and dead to her own will; to live as though there existed no other being save Jesus and her own soul; to practise all virtues, even those which are most heroic; to observe strict abstinence; to impose on herself more rigorous penances than ever; in short, her whole life was to be one of crucifixion. On these conditions Jesus would be entirely hers.

Thus ended the mysterious function of her espousal, in which, as she informs us, her bodily eyes took no part, but only those of her mind. She adds that the ring remained on her finger, and that on communion days she felt its pressure more than at other times, and that on almost every occasion of receiving the holy Eucharist, she enjoyed a renewal of her espousals. This wondrous ring was more than once seen by her companions in religion, and was described as follows in the process by Sister Mary Spanaciani, who declares herself to have seen it once "with her own eyes and with distinctness" when she was a novice. "It encircled her above-mentioned ring-finger, exactly in the way that ordinary rings do. On the outside there appeared to be a raised stone, as large as a pea, and of a red colour, which inspired me with fear and veneration (as is usual when we see anything supernatural or miraculous); several times I was on the point of asking her what it was, but I never ventured to do so; and meantime the countenance of this servant of God was glowing and radiant, as though she were in a sort of rapture, and this proved to be the case, for though I asked her various questions, she never answered to the point. It was, however, remarkable, that a few hours after, though I looked at her hand carefully, there was no ring nor jewel there; and now that it had disappeared, she was herself again, and able to give connected replies to my inquiries." Mention is made in the processes of two different rings which were given her by our Lord at her espousals, and on the occasion of their renewal, one of which she called the ring of love, and the other the ring of the cross. Veronica speaks, moreover, in her journal, of a third ring which was presented to her by our Lord on the renewal of her espousals at Easter, in the year 1697. This last was enriched with three gems, on one of which were engraven two hearts, so closely united that they appeared but one; on the second stone was a cross, and on the third all the instruments of the Passion. Jesus Himself informed her that the first stone was meant to signify the union subsisting between His heart and hers, and that the second represented the dowry which was appointed her in token of that union, while the third was the remembrance she should have of His sufferings. Our Saviour then asked her by what sign He might recognize her as His spouse, to which she replied, "By Thine own most sacred Wounds which Thou hast imprinted on me, unworthy as I am" (it was in that year that she had received the stigmata). "Yes, it is as thou sayest," rejoined our Lord, "these Wounds I leave thee as a pledge, to put thee constantly in mind of Me; rest on My Will, for I am thine."

CHAPTER IV.

THE GIFTS AND FAVOURS WHICH JESUS LAVISHED ON HIS SPOUSE DURING THE TWO FOLLOWING DAYS.— HER CORRESPONDENCE TO THEM.

THE solemnities connected with these heavenly espousals were not brought to a close on Easter Sunday, which was the feast of their celebration, but were likewise spread in different ways over the following Monday and Tuesday. On the former of these days Jesus introduced Veronica, if I may be allowed the expression, into His treasury, and gave it into her possession. At her Communion on that morning He appeared to her, and marshalled, as it were, before her all the precious actions of His mortal life, and the fearful torments of His Passion, together with His infinite merits, telling her to dispose of them all at her pleasure. Veronica was overwhelmed by such infinite liberality on the part of her divine Spouse, as well as by the consideration of her own nothingness. "It seemed to me," she writes, "that it was an office ill-suited for me to distribute these treasures. At the same time I felt such interior faith that I turned to our Lord and said, 'My God, my divine Spouse, I leave all these infinite treasures in Thy hands. I pray Thee to distribute them; Thou alone should be the Dispenser of them. I beseech Thee to bestow them among all, but especially among those who love Thee from their heart; and grant that by means of these graces they may correspond to Thy love.'" She went on to pray particularly for her director, for all priests, and peculiarly in behalf of confessors, to the end that they might be illuminated by divine faith and inflamed with divine love. But more than all, she prayed for her own convent, saying to Jesus, "By means of these Thy treasures cause that this Thy order may flourish here in the perfection of observance."

In this place we must be permitted to make a brief digression, which will serve to show the efficacy of the prayers of our Saint. When Veronica entered the convent, it possessed a reputation for superior excellence, and it was on this account that she had made choice of it, as we have already explained in the proper place; but from the time of her entrance it began to be considered a community of saints, and in fact more than one of its inmates passed to another life in the odour of sanctity. In this category we may place the choir sisters Mary Teresa Vallemanni, of Fabriano, Mary Constance Spanaciani and Mary Rose Gotoloni, both of Tolentino, Gertrude of Pisa, Angela Mary Moscani, of Castello, Mary Angelica degli Azzi, of Arezzo, Mary Anne Piazzini, of Florence, Florida Ceoli and Mary Magdalen Boscaini, both of Pisa; besides the lay sisters Frances and Giacinta, of Castello, own sister to the former; also Mary Felix, of Florence, and generally speaking all the novices of Veronica, for they were distinguished for their virtue, as were, indeed, nearly all the rest who lived with her. The new annals of the Capuchins contain a brief compendium of the lives of the above-mentioned sisters, each according to the year and day of her happy death. A

112 S. VERONICA GIULIANI.

separate biography has been also published of Sisters Boscaini, Piazzini, and degli Azzi.

. The process of Sister Florida Ceoli's canonization was commenced, but afterwards suspended for want of pecuniary means, though it may possibly be terminated at some future day. It was asserted by some one who confused her with her aunt, that she was once one of the ladies of the court of her Serene Highness Violante, Grand Duchess of Tuscany, but in reality she never was at court, as we have ascertained from authentic documents. Through the same means we have learnt that she once clearly predicted to a very estimable priest well known to us, that he would become an Oratorian, which really came to pass. There are likewise other particulars connected with her and her fellow-religious of that holy community which it would be irrelevant to mention here. With regard to the members of the convent now alive, we are assured by one who is thoroughly competent to do so, in consequence of having been their director, that they are still at all times actuated by the spirit of their saintly sister, and that in due time they will prove to be faithful copies of that holy model.

To return to our history: it was on Easter Monday that Veronica heard a voice within her heart, saying, "My beloved, I am waiting for thee to present Me with a jewel." She recognized the voice of her heavenly Spouse, and understood that His words signified a desire to receive some sacrifice of rare mortification at her hands. As nothing else occurred to her that she could do, she took the brass case of an hour-glass, on which was engraven the most holy Name of Jesus, and having heated it thoroughly at the fire, she used it to imprint on her breast the sacred cypher as a perpetual token of fidelity and homage to her Well-beloved. Not satisfied with this, she inflicted on herself other fearful austerities, until she again heard the same voice pronounce the words, "This is sufficient for Me." And here, lest any weak or ill-regulated minds should presume to cavil, or blaspheme God, as though He cruelly delights to behold the torture of human beings, it may be as well to remark that it is not the torture itself which pleases God, but rather the great benefit which accrues from thence to ourselves, and procuring for us by means of transient pain the enjoyment of unfading and infinite glory. It is for this that He has created us. The rebellion of the flesh places itself in opposition to the accomplishment of this, and therefore it must be subdued by mortification; and the more it is tamed by penance, the more easily will the spirit unite itself with God, and ascend at last together with the body to enjoy the beatific vision in heaven. In order that this end may be attained, God is pleased that we should suffer, and He, therefore, both counsels and enjoins that we should avail ourselves of this necessary means for procuring true and eternal bliss; and He encourages us to do so by giving us the bright example of His only-begotten and divine Son, Who for our sakes resigned Himself to such dreadful torments that He is rightly termed the Man of Sorrows.

On Easter Tuesday also our Lord Jesus deigned to bestow new marks of love on His Spouse. She had no sooner received the Bread of Heaven in holy Communion than she found herself in an ecstasy with her Well-beloved. "Our Lord approached me in a loving way," she writes, "and said to me, 'I am thy peace: I am Who am. Behold Me, tell Me what thou wouldst have.' 'Nothing but Thyself, my divine

Spouse,' I replied. Our Lord made me understand that He was greatly pleased at this, and seemed to stretch out His right hand and embrace my soul. I cannot describe what were my feelings at that moment. I can only tell you that it was an affair of brief duration; if it had been otherwise, I do not know how I could have lived." She then attempts to give some idea of the wonderful delight and enlargement of heart which she experienced in receiving Jesus under the Eucharistic species. "When I went to holy Communion," she says, "it seemed that the door of my heart was thrown wide open, as if for the purpose of receiving a friend; and as soon as He had entered, it was closed. Thus it came to pass that my heart shut itself up alone with its God. It is out of my power to describe all the effects and movements and exultations which His presence produced. If I were to give to you as an illustration every pastime and pleasure which our dearest friends could provide for us, I should say they are nothing in comparison; and if all the joys which the universe can afford were united, I should pronounce them nothing when compared with what my heart enjoys with her God, or rather with what God works in my soul, for it is all His own operation. Love causes the heart to dance and leap for joy, to sing and to be silent according as it pleases; love soothes it to repose, or wakes it to triumphant bliss; love sets it vigorously to work afresh for its God; love possesses it, and it yields to all; love rules it, and it rests."

Presently she continues, "If I were to relate all the effects which are wrought in the heart by love at the time of holy Communion and at other seasons, I should never finish. Suffice it to say that the holy Eucharist is the very palace and sanctuary of love. The heart becomes more than ever inflamed when it sees itself the dwelling-place of the most holy Trinity, and when Jesus comes to me in the Blessed Sacrament, and I hear the words, 'Hail thou temple of the whole Trinity!' then my heart becomes so enlarged and enkindled, that sometimes I seem to hear sweet melodies, and am ravished with heavenly music. When engaged in laborious duties, I find myself ready to do anything. Sometimes I am impelled by such mighty desires to praise and bless God that my heart would fain be converted into tongues, wherewith to invoke and glorify its sole and highest good. As far as I am aware I find no greater satisfaction in anything than in pure suffering. It is then that I seem to behold flowers of unrivalled loveliness encircling my cross; and these cause me to wish for fruit besides, and this fruit is more suffering."

Here we may remark that in the midst of her fairest spiritual delights, she neither esteemed nor desired aught but suffering—pure suffering, without one drop of sweetness—and all this through love for her Beloved. This is a sure proof of the Spirit of God.

CHAPTER V.

IN OBEDIENCE TO A DIVINE COMMAND SHE BEGINS TO FAST RIGOROUSLY ON BREAD AND WATER, AND CONTINUES TO DO SO FOR SEVERAL YEARS.—THE OPPOSITION WHICH SHE HAD TO ENCOUNTER FROM HER SUPERIORS, AS WELL AS FROM HERSELF, AND FROM THE POWERS OF DARKNESS.

AMONG the injunctions which were given to Veronica by Jesus her divine Spouse, on the day of her mystic nuptials, was one which directed her to observe a strict abstinence, as we have already mentioned at the close of the third chapter. She was already so mortified in this respect as to be an object of wonder to the other nuns. But our Lord, Who desired to separate her more and more from earthly things, and to unite her more closely to Himself, inspired, or rather expressly commanded, her to undertake for three consecutive years a strict fast upon bread and water. We find from her own writings that it was on the 26th of March, 1695, that she received this injunction, just a year after the solemnity of her espousals. As she was never in the habit of doing anything without the orders or approval of her confessors and superiors, she informed them of this order from our Lord. But it pleased God to test her obedience to His ministers; and to instruct us through her example as to the dependence which we ought to place on His representatives, even in the holiest practices. He therefore ordained that they should all agree in refusing her the permission which she asked. She offered no resistance, though to comply with their will cost her dear; for from that moment, whatever she ate she was forced instantly to reject, except merely a mouthful of dry bread, which she took in the course of the day when she felt on the point of fainting. Even this slight refreshment she gave up as soon as it was prohibited. In order to try her still more severely, Almighty God ceased not to urge her to keep the appointed fast, and sometimes He reproached her as though she were responsible for not accomplishing His divine Will; however, being enlightened from above, she replied, "Lord, I promise to do it; but I am certain that Thou desirest that I should obey in all things those who stand in Thy place with regard to me; do Thou therefore dispose them whose duty it is to give me the required permission." And then full of confidence she presented her petition afresh, but was put off with a still more obstinate refusal. But as she was guided by the true rules of the spiritual life, she tells us that she was satisfied, because in this way she was compelled to suffer much, though she felt that she had done all in her power. Every time that she sat down to table, she had to undergo a new martyrdom. Every sort of food that she saw stimulated her appetite, but no sooner had she tasted any than it assumed the flavour of the bitterest wormwood, or became so nauseous that she knew of nothing to which she could compare it. The violence with which she was forced to reject it occasioned internal bleeding, and for some days after she abstained from all nourishment. Her directors and superiors, even the bishop himself, were cognizant of these facts, and yet it made no alteration in their opinion.

Veronica confesses that her nature was inclined to revolt under this; and that she found it a grievance to be refused permission to eat a little dry bread by itself, as it had been already ascertained that it was the only kind of food which she could take with impunity. And yet this obedient religious would not venture to eat bread by itself, because she had been told by her superiors to partake of everything there was. Her strength of spirit and resemblance to Jesus Christ are strikingly illustrated by the sentiments which accompanied her docile submission. "I would fain have done," she writes, " what God required of me; but they would not give me leave to do so.

While I sat at table, it seemed to me that at every mouthful I took our Lord reproached me. Sometimes I heard an interior voice saying to me, 'When art thou going to fulfil My injunction, and live entirely on bread and water?' And my soul was consumed with sorrow at not being able to do what our Lord bade me. I offered Him my obedience and the suffering which my food occasioned me : I resigned myself afresh to His sacred Will, but persevered in firm adherence to the practice of holy obedience. I endeavoured to carry out this principle so completely as not to transgress it in the least. I was aware of the great. assistance which the soul derives from living, as it were, in a state of death, and following the direction of the representatives of God. I felt that my desires for suffering were more than ever on the increase. I earnestly longed to drink in good earnest of that bitter chalice which contains every kind of torment; and it often seemed to me that our Lord made me taste its contents. . . .. The mere sight of this chalice surrounded me with pain, but at the same time imparted great strength, for it seemed to me that my spirits became thereby more attuned to suffering and to the love of the cross." Veronica had to endure this agonizing conflict between the commands and reproaches of God on the one hand, and the prohibitions of her superiors on the other, from the 20th of March to the 8th of September in the same year. Meanwhile the resistance of nature continued in the manner we have described, so that she would frequently pass several days without taking the least refreshment. At length our Lord, moved with compassion for this severe trial of her virtue, was pleased to bestow on her a very rare favour, which we do not find to have been vouchsafed on any other, except the holy virgins Lidwine, in Holland, and Gertrude of Oost, in Belgium, according to the testimony of the Bollandists. Veronica being one day thoroughly exhausted, owing to the causes mentioned above, passed into one of her usual raptures, during which our Lord directed her to sustain her life by taking daily five drops of a certain liquid contained in her left breast, but not until she should receive the permission of her confessor, to whom the whole matter was to be referred. "I then returned to myself," she writes, "and found myself like one distracted, not knowing what to do. I felt interiorly a profound sorrow on account of my sins against God : it seemed to me, also, that I was more enlightened than I had been on the subject of virtues, especially on that of humility : I was consumed with desire for the salvation of souls : from time to time I felt my soul so enkindled that it seemed to consume me; I also appeared to feel the effects of the fluid within my bosom. I was not willing to lay any stress on this;* and I did not know how I should explain it to my confessor, owing to the repugnance which I feel on all such occasions. I was frequently reproved for not conquering myself, and received a fresh inspiration to manifest this particular; but I could not tell how to set about it. I went on in this way for about three days. As I could not retain the food which I took, my strength was failing fast, so that I could hardly stand. I did not

* Let the reader mark the caution with which she dealt with visions and extraordinary favours, and how reluctant she was to mention anything which was likely to redound to her own glory : these things prove that the spirit which guided her was good.

venture to taste the liquor in question, because I had not permission to do so, but I felt that it was in my breast. Our Lord rebuked me severely; and I was given to understand that it was His Will that I should triumph over myself, and mention my case to His representative. At last I overcame myself, and related all the circumstances. My confessor would not permit me to taste the liquid for the present, but desired me to continue taking my ordinary food. I did so accordingly. The next morning he told me to eat as usual; but that in case sickness should ensue, I was to take the five drops after a short interval. I did this, and experienced extraordinary effects. Scarcely had I tasted it when I felt myself strengthened and invigorated. . . . This happened on the 2nd of June. To God be all the glory. Blessed be the cross."

The account which Veronica gives tallies exactly with the deposition made in the process, which may be found in the summary of her virtues by Father Carlo Antonio Tassinari, of the order of Servites, who was at that time extraordinary confessor to the convent. He it was who first refused and then gave our Saint permission to avail herself of that mysterious fluid, with the approbation of the bishop, Mgr. Eustachj, with whom he had taken counsel on the subject. The liquor in question was then examined. It was similar in appearance to milk; but so extremely delicious was its odour that wherever it was brought it filled every place with fragrance; it was in a phial which Veronica had been obliged under obedience to fill with it. When it was conveyed to the sick it wrought wonders, as was attested in the process by Sister Florida Ceoli and Sister Mary Magdalen Boscaini, as well as by the lay sister Giacinta. Our virgin

Saint continued to support herself by means of this supernatural liquid during five years of rigorous fasting. Whether it went on till the end of her life we are neither informed by others nor by her own writings. This milk of Veronica was certainly out of the course of nature, as were the circumstances which accompanied it: and this miraculous gift of hers, together with the others which have been already related or which remain to be recounted hereafter, was ably defended in the Congregation of Rites, in the two last treatises on her virtues, printed in the years 1786 and 1796; which, by the variety of illustrations that they present, and the weighty arguments they contain, may well serve in future to support and defend all similar cases. It is certain with regard to the case of Veronica, that notwithstanding the numerous and grave objections made by the promoter of the faith, it received the unanimous approbation of their Eminences, and of the other very reverend consultors, in the general congregation that was held on the 12th of April, 1796, in the presence of Pius VI., who issued his decree of approval on the 24th of the same month. The following words taken from it are peculiarly suitable to the last-mentioned incident in the life of our Saint, as well as to all her various endowments—*The fathers agree in deciding that those other wonderful gifts of hers are clear from all fallacy and machination; neither do they contain anything indecorous or inconsistent with sanctity.*

But to resume the thread of our history. It was on the morning of the 8th of September, 1695, being the Feast of our Blessed Lady's Nativity, after Veronica had endured about six months of opposition, that her confessor saw her, and said to her: " This morning you shall begin to live on bread and water. Our prelate (Mgr. Eustachj) has directed me to enjoin you to do so." We may easily infer with what delight this message would be welcomed by Veronica after all that had passed, and we may conceive with what alacrity she commenced the fast so earnestly desired; though to flesh and blood it was of course a sore trial. She herself relates that she found her whole nature recoil from it. It is, however, true that from this time the nausea from which she had suffered so much was at an end. But feeble humanity cannot but shrink at the idea of taking no other nourishment than bread and water during whole weeks, and months, and years. It is pleasant to contemplate the generosity with which she brought her mind to bear it, as also the magnanimity which led her to make light of, and even jest at, the matter, as is evident from the following ingenuous account which she gave her confessor, beginning from the time of the carnival :. "Mother abbess declared in chapter that, during these four carnival days, we might each take whatever we required for our own needs. Self was delighted, and immediately cried, 'I, too, will take whatever I require.' I began to chide Self, and to tell her that she should not have all that she asked for. As might be expected, she was wanting to eat and to sleep. All at once she desired me to give her, at least, a little bread and water, of which she stood in great need. But I replied, 'Be quiet, for I am going to give you the food you ask for. You know the three penances which I have promised you; well, these are to be your bread and water.' Soon after, I went to the dispensary, and no sooner did Self find herself there, than she wanted to have a morsel of everything.

So I made her lie with her mouth on the ground for a short time, and said to her, 'Eat this dust and dirt, and be satisfied for once.' This plan answered, and she was quiet again, but I could not help smiling within myself. The next morning, directly she entered the dispensary, she began the same course that she had pursued the day before, and said to me, 'It is Sunday morning; even the hermits eat something to-day; and poor I am to have nothing but bread and water.'* In the midst of these murmurs she began to prepare some macaroni for the nuns. I laughed at the quantity she took out, and can assure you that she knows how to be roguish, and has a mischievous tongue in her head. I was not able to penance her then, for my companion was in the room."

She writes as follows on the 30th of September, a twelvemonth of her fast having elapsed: "I can assure my father confessor that I find the matter as great a privation to my natural appetite as I did the first day I began to abstain. I find that Self wishes to have a share of all the food which I provide for the nuns, and grumbles as she divides it into portions. She will have her way, and I cannot accustom her to keep quiet. I endeavour to pass it off with a smile; but this year, as I shall still have to regulate my diet very strictly, I must try to make an impression upon her by inflicting some new mortification. I have promised her the following three: first, that if ever she wishes to eat anything secretly, as temptation, or rather, private gratification, may suggest, she

---

* It was the custom in this convent that the religious, even those who were professed, and held the higher offices in the community, should occasionally work in the kitchen and dispensary.

shall walk into the middle of the refectory, and proclaim this faulty inclination aloud to all the nuns. The bare thought of such a humiliation puts her on her guard. Secondly, if she complains of having nothing but bread and water, she shall be made to pass three days without drinking at all. I find this threat very effective. Thirdly, as she has to cook and carry round the provisions of the other religious, if she continues to accompany this duty with lamentations, as she is accustomed to do, she shall be forced to express what is passing in her mind, in an audible way, to her companion, whoever it may be. For I will not tolerate these murmurs any longer. This last mortification will touch her to the quick."

Veronica's confessor suggested to her another method of conquering her repugnance to this fast, and of quelling the incitements of natural appetite. He recommended her to hold a raw and decayed fish to her lips whenever she felt a craving for food. We will refer again to her own lively narrative. "I took a fish," she says, "which was already in a state of decomposition, and put it aside. Well, after some time had elapsed, you may conceive the condition it was in! Every time that I found nature discontented and rebellious in the matter of diet, I said to myself, 'you know where your food is to be found.' I really cannot stay to relate all the complaints which Self was disposed to lay at the door of the person who had invented this penance, and I will only repeat one thing which she said. It was this: 'The person who thought of such a penance ought first to try the experiment himself, and see whether he is not proposing an impossibility. . . .' However, I made her undergo this trial, and another too, which she did not at all like. I still keep my fish at hand; and whenever she is inclined to bewail the method in which she is fed, or anything else, I make her undergo this particular penance, and very thoroughly, too. Blessings be on the head of him who taught me such a lesson; and to God be all the glory."

Notwithstanding the holy energy with which Veronica engaged in the conflict, she still found it hard work to struggle with the infirmities of nature. This, however, must not be taken as an evidence of feeble virtue in our Saint; on the contrary, she rose from every combat strong and victorious, with her weapons in readiness to maintain possession of the ground she had gained, and to carry her conquests further. It was thus that Christ instructed His apostle. When S. Paul implored deliverance from the "angel of Satan," our Lord refused his petition, and declared, "My grace is sufficient for thee: for power is made perfect in infirmity." It follows, therefore, that so heroic a virgin as Veronica became more and more refined and purified in proportion to the power of the league of the flesh and the devil against her. She gave written accounts to her confessor of the great and frequent temptations by means of which Satan tried hard to make her relax somewhat from the rigour of her fast. Sometimes he would drag her by night into the refectory, when she felt almost famished, and present her with an array of delicacies. Sometimes he would convey these luxuries to her cell. But she was always firm in her generous refusal to partake of them, and was in the habit of making the sign of the cross over all that he set before her, which caused it immediately to disappear, leaving behind it so fearful an odour that it occasioned her to faint away.

The devil, despairing of being able to subdue her, conceived the idea of blackening her reputation, and of making her appear a sacrilegious hypocrite, by the following stratagem. He frequently assumed her form, and contrived to be caught in the act of eating greedily and surreptitiously, at improper hours, sometimes in the kitchen, sometimes in the refectory, and sometimes in the dispensary. The nuns were extremely scandalized at this, especially when they once or twice saw Veronica go to holy Communion after they had witnessed one of these unlawful repasts. But it pleased God to undertake the defence of His servant, by causing the infernal plot to be discovered. One morning, about the time of Communion, some of them found the supposed Veronica engaged in eating, and accordingly ran to the choir to inform the abbess, but there they found their holy sister rapt in prayer.

Amidst all these troubles, she continued her fast on bread and water during three consecutive years, as long as she was permitted to do so. Besides this, during two years more, she lived exclusively on shreds of altar bread, with a few orange pippins, and some of that marvellously potent fluid, of which we have already spoken. Indeed, it may be said that all her religious life was one perpetual fast.

CHAPTER VI.

FURTHER INSTANCES OF VERONICA'S FIDELITY TO HER DIVINE SPOUSE. — SHE RECEIVES FROM HIM A WOUND IN THE HEART.—FOUR DOCUMENTS WRITTEN BY HER WITH HER OWN BLOOD.

It may be easily conceived how the malice of her infernal enemy increased when he found himself so utterly scorned by Veronica, and when he beheld her at the same time so closely united to her divine Spouse. There was no art to which he did not resort for the purpose of rendering her unfaithful. He would present to her the most dreadful images of guilt, and in company with other fiends under the forms of wicked young men, he would enact scenes, the very thought of which is abhorrent to nature. The saintly heroine of whom we write was on several occasions tormented by this fierce ordeal, but never had she to encounter so dire a conflict, or one so protracted, as happened in the year 1696, which was the second after her mystic espousals. But the struggle served only to elicit fresh proofs of her unimpeachable constancy to her heavenly Spouse, as well as new pledges of His love for her. For particulars we will refer to her own narrative, written on the 1st of July in the same year.

"The demons went on with their horrible deeds. They assumed at the same time my form, and declared that I was lost for ever, that in that form I had committed a number of sins, though at present I did not recognize them. They said that they reserved them for the hour of my death, hoping to make me die in despair. Besides all this, I had to endure such sadness and mortal agony that I could do nothing for myself.

It seemed as though for me there were neither God nor saints. I did my utmost to revive my spirits, but it was all in vain.* I said to these infernal monsters, 'Away with you; I belong entirely to my Jesus; I have nothing to do with you; I will not listen to you; I love God with all my heart, and I desire always to do His Will. Do whatever you are permitted to do against me—strike me, afflict me, only let me fulfil the divine Will, which I embrace and love. Here I take my stand. Blessed be the pure Will of my Lord.'" It is thus that faithful spouses speak of their God.

Veronica was attacked in a similar way in the October of the same year, and this furnished a new proof of her fidelity. She wrote as follows on the 17th:—"To my other trials this new one was added. Whilst I was at prayer † such a crowd of sinful thoughts rushed into my mind, that it threw me into a perspiration, after which I became as cold as ice, and experienced within so violent a conflict that I was completely upset by it. I did not mean to allow myself to be disturbed or agitated by it, but I could not help it. I was tormented and plunged into these horrible ideas, and my mind was so darkened that I could apply myself to nothing. Satan tempted me, and I seemed to hear his terrific voice accosting me thus, 'Of what use is it to pray for sinners? All their transgressions recoil upon thee. Do good if

* Let the souls of the just be comforted when they fall into similar temptations and desolation; for these are trials to which God subjects His most beloved servants. Let such learn from our Saint how to act when their turn comes.

† Therefore let others be comforted when they suffer from temptations in the hours of devotion.

thou canst.' And then the tempter seemed to be rejoicing. O my God, what pain this gave me! As well as I could, I entreated our Lord for the salvation of souls, and said to Him, 'My Well-beloved, and Spouse of my soul, I will not offend Thee voluntarily; I detest and execrate all these evil thoughts, and with my will I renounce them for ever. I would a thousand times rather die than consent to anything which might displease Thee.' While I said this with a great effort, the devil endeavoured to suggest worse thoughts, and declared that there was no help for me. I replied, 'False fiend that thou art, I disbelieve thy lies. I will love Jesus, I will serve Jesus, and Jesus shall be my only good.' This combat lasted for several hours, with much dryness and desolation. To God be all glory." Her fidelity towards her heavenly Spouse was accompanied by such zeal for His glory that she was never tired of labouring to promote it by the conversion of those who had wandered from the right way.

On the 13th of the following November Veronica makes mention of another kind of temptation with which the devil assailed her. He endeavoured to inspire her with a feeling of internal vexation against herself, and with sentiments of irritation and contempt towards her companions, inciting her to the utterance of harsh and cutting expressions. But our Saint was ever on her guard, and when thus tried she would say to herself, "Is it possible that there is so much wickedness in thee? Bear in mind that our Lord wishes thee to be all sweetness and peace." She relates with astonishing humility and minuteness the feelings which rebellious nature suggested, all of which she attributes to her own pride, self-love, human respect, and fictitious charity. These sentiments had reference more particularly to her superior and another religious who was connected with herself in the office of dispenser. She carefully avoided any outward expression of what was passing in her mind, and on the contrary manifested the greatest possible satisfaction. She resolved at length to meet this temptation by having more fervent recourse to her divine Spouse in the Blessed Sacrament. When prostrate before Him, she felt, as she informs us, that nature and sense were tranquillized; they dared not speak, and thus her soul resumed its dominion over them. It was our Lord, she adds, Who produced this calm, and gave her strength to fulfil her duties in the dispensary, and to execute everything that was required of her.

In the March of 1696 she went through the spiritual exercises of S. Ignatius, in order that her soul might be more perfectly purified, and strengthened against the attacks of the devil. She gave the following succinct account to her confessor on the 11th:—"I am beginning these holy exercises with the intention of leading a new life, and of being a totally different person to what I have hitherto been. I find nothing but coldness and ingratitude in myself. As I am ordered to do so by holy obedience, I will describe my whole state as well and distinctly as I can. But I am so stupid that I hardly know what to say. If I must speak, it will be of the cross, because I know that it and I are inseparable; and I trust that I shall find it serve me as a book during these days of retreat."

Her humility is indeed worthy of remark, and we may reflect with advantage on her constant efforts to attain to a higher degree of perfection during this sacred retreat. We may observe also that a soul accustomed to the most exalted and intimate communications with God, cares for nothing but to establish herself in the most solid virtue.

"With regard to the resolutions and fruits attributable to these days of retreat," continues Veronica, " I have summed them all up under five heads.—First, resignation to the divine Will; secondly, punctual observance of the rules; thirdly, blind obedience; fourthly, fraternal charity; and lastly, never to excuse myself under any contradiction."

Even at this time the enemy was troubling her with a new temptation. She had begun to make a more minute confession than usual, so he suggested that she had better leave off telling such long stories to her confessor; but perceiving the delusion, she turned to our Lord and said, "My God, I resolve to be obedient to Thy representative, and I will tell him all that passes in my mind." Then it was that the demons endeavoured to frighten her by means of horrible apparitions. "But I took courage," she adds, "and began to invoke the most holy names of Jesus and Mary, making the sign of the cross from time to time, and submitting myself to the entire Will of God concerning me."

She concludes by mentioning various tokens of love which she received at the hand of her divine Spouse. "At length," she says, "I was able to be a little recollected; and whilst I was in prayer, contemplating the immense love of God for our souls, I found myself gently raised from the things of earth, and favoured to behold a vision of our Lord, which was so beautiful that I cannot describe it. He approached me, and I saw the chalice and the cross in His Hand. The latter was adorned with many gems and precious stones. He gave me to understand that it was I who had thus adorned it by means of the confession I had begun to make. He informed me also that it was His Will that I should continue it, and that for the future I should conceal nothing from my confessor, but should tell him everything, in order that the wonders of divine love might be known. I was likewise made to comprehend that, ignorant and ungrateful as I had been, the gifts and graces of our Lord had been lavished upon me."

She goes on to mention an ecstasy in which her soul flew, as it were, to the Infant Jesus, and enjoyed such intimate communications with Him, that she found herself incapable of describing them. She thus concludes: "When I came to myself, I rushed from my cell like one deranged, not knowing what I did. So, for a long time, I took the discipline to blood, and afterwards I went to prime. But my heart could not contain the joy which it felt. And then your reverence came" (her confessor) "and said Mass, during which I made a spiritual communion, and committed myself entirely into the hands of my Jesus. After this, I continued my confession, and experienced great relief and benefit."

But the most tender pledge of love bestowed on her during that year by her divine Spouse was a wound literally inflicted on her heart, from which a stream of blood issued forth. This took place on Christmas day. Before proceeding to give any account of this remarkable event, we will refer to what happened previous to that feast, in order that we may see with what fidelity she merited so great a favour. She writes as follows, under date of the 15th of December, 1696:—

"I had been labouring all night under my accustomed trials and agitation, and had become so tired as to be incapable of supporting myself. My mind was enveloped in thick darkness, and I was particularly afflicted, because I had such a multitude of evil thoughts; and it even seemed to me that the sins of the whole world were on my shoulders. God knows what I suffered. I exclaimed, 'Where art Thou, my sweet Spouse? Return to me. Thou knowest that I can do nothing of myself; but that with Thee I can do all things. . . .' I could not even think of the suffering, although it touched me to the quick. And then came the additional trial of toothache, and pain in all my limbs, which lasted for the space of an hour. I offered it all to our Lord in union with His Passion. Nature began to lament, and to ask for a little repose; but I said to myself, 'There is no such thing as rest for thee; I shall take thee into the garden, and there thou shalt recreate thyself for a little.' My lower nature began to tremble before I got to the garden. When I got there, I found that it had frozen so hard that I was in danger of falling at every step. So I said to myself, 'How now, Veronica, are you satisfied? On, on!—round and round! cold and wind will do for you instead of rest. Take courage! All is little for the love of God.' Just then there came over me a great desire to call upon our Lord, and to seek Him. So I feared the ice no longer, but began to run, exclaiming, 'I long to invoke Thee, to seek Thee, and to find Thee, my sole and sovereign good. I invited the trees and plants to help me in calling upon our Lord. I kissed them, as well as the ground they grew upon. I embraced the trees, and said, 'You put me in mind of my dear Lord's cross.'"

She goes on to relate similar transports of her love, which resemble those of the Spouse in the sacred Canticles. She also mentions the insults which she had to encounter from two demons, who assumed the forms of negroes. But she was not at all dismayed. "All for Thy love, my God," she cried. "Oh, how cheerfully do I welcome pain! Come, oh come, my beloved Spouse. Satiate me with crosses and torments, provided it be Thy Will, for this is what I wish and desire. Delay no longer, but come, my Jesus." At last she returned to her cell, and spent the whole day in prayer and the severest penance, repeating from time to time the prayer of the great virgin and martyr St. Cecilia : "Fiat, Domine, cor meum et corpus meum immaculatum, ut non confundar"—"Grant, O Lord, that my heart and my body may be immaculate, that I may not be confounded."

Thus passed the days of that sacred novena, during which Veronica felt herself impelled on several occasions to write with her own blood a prayer to the divine Infant. She did so on the night of the Holy Nativity before matins; making with a penknife an incision in the form of a cross near her heart. This document she consigned to the care of her confessor. It ran thus:—

"Prostrate at Thy Feet, my Jesus, I solemnly protest that I desire to be evermore entirely Thine, and to have no other wish than Thy holy Will. Thou hast told me that lovers of the cross have to dwell in Thy Heart. I declare and subscribe myself with my own blood a lover of the cross. Take from me, my Lord, whatever may be a hindrance to my union with Thee.

Cause this heart of mine to be the abode of Thy holy love; let nothing remain in me but Thy holy Will. O my God, I pen with my blood this unalterable covenant, by which I bind myself to wish for nothing but the accomplishment of Thy Will. On Thee I rely for strength; to Thee I give my heart."

She had already drawn up something similar on the 14th of February, 1696, as follows:—

"J. M. J.

"My Lord, my God, my Spouse, Heart of my heart, I desire now to commune with Thy love. I implore on the part of my confessor a grace according to his intention; and I also entreat as a favour from Thy Sacred Heart, and Thy holy love, that my confessor may walk according to Thy good pleasure, and that he may labour and toil for the salvation of souls according to Thy Will. I pray that Thou, O Lord, wilt keep him in Thy Heart, as well as all others who have assisted, and who continue to assist, my soul, in order that they may all burn with Thy love, and live after Thine own Heart. O infinite Love, let the Wound of Thy love speak for me. Yes, indeed, my Spouse, I sacrifice myself as a perpetual holocaust, a victim of love; and I desire to unite this sacrifice with that which Thou didst make on the altar of the cross. I seal myself also with the sign of love, to signify that I wish to be always crucified with Thee, and that I crave nothing but Thy Will. O my Lord, I pray to Thee for the conversion of sinners, and I commend to Thee in particular those souls for whom my confessor would wish me to pray. O infinite Love, I address myself with love to Thee, Who art my Spouse, my God, and my All. I on my part am entirely Thine, and I protest unto Thee at this moment that I wish to be evermore entirely Thine. I intend to confirm at the present time all the protestations I have made to Thee with my blood: and I present myself anew in the quality of mediatrix between Thee and sinners. Behold, I am ready to give my life and my blood for their conversion, and for the advancement of Thy holy faith. O my God, in union with Thy Heart and Thy love, I invite them thus, 'O souls redeemed with the Blood of Jesus, I speak to you. O sinners, come all of you to the Heart of Jesus, to the fountain, to the immense ocean of His love; come, sinners, every one of you; abandon your sins, and come to Jesus.' Meanwhile, my beloved Spouse, let me love Thee with Thine own love, now and for ever. I ask the same for my confessor; give him Thy love, that he may forget himself, that he may divest himself of everything, and be united entirely to Thee. I implore the same grace on behalf of P.G., C., P., P.F., and P.F., as also for all those who are of help to my soul, and in fine for all my sisters.

"Sister VERONICA,
"Capuchiness."

Outside the paper is written in another hand, probably her confessor's:—"14th of February, 1696, with the blood of the wound which she received on Christmas day."

The above document is preserved with due veneration in the city of Castello, by Father Florido Pierleoni, postulator of her cause. There are two others which we have seen, also written with her blood, as follows:—

"J. M. J.

"My Lord, in the name of my confessor, I ask the following graces of Thee: purity of heart and intention, resignation to Thy divine Will, and desire for suffering; and on his behalf I consign to Thy Sacred Heart, and to Thy holy Wounds, his heart, together with all his powers, and his whole self.

"Sister VERONICA,
"Unworthy Servant."

The date is given outside in a different hand, 10th of May, 1697.

"J. M. J.

"My Jesus, I implore as a grace from Thee on behalf of Thy servant N., that Thou, O Lord, wouldst take off his thoughts from himself, and from all that may hinder the advancement and salvation of his soul, to the end that he may work advantageously both for his own soul and for all others confided to his care. Grant, O my God, that he may be entirely according to Thy Heart, and that in all he does, his aim may be solely the promotion of Thy glory, and the constant fulfilment of Thy holy Will. My Jesus, I consign him to Thy Sacred Side: grant that he may never withdraw himself from Thy Heart; but let him always live in Thy Wounds. Amen."

This sheet was folded in the shape of a letter, and superscribed "A. G. and M."

It would occupy too much space to relate minutely all the transports of love which she enjoyed that night. She frequently repeated as though in an ecstasy—"My Spouse, my Love, burn my heart with Thy holy love." And, thus inebriated as it were with love, she went to wake the religious at the hour of matins, exclaiming—"Sisters, do you not hear the matin-bell ringing? this is no time for sleep, make haste and rise." She did the same thing also at the hour of prime.

She was often permitted at the above season

of our Lord's nativity, to behold the divine Infant radiant with beauty, and covered with jewels. He addressed her as His Spouse, and she reciprocated that term of love. He offered to fulfil all her desires, and she replied: "I wish for Thee alone; through Thy merits, and those of Mary, Thy Mother, I crave the conversion of sinners; and I commend to Thy care our holy institute. Cause us to be entirely Thine. Take from us everything that is displeasing to Thee." But omitting an immense amount of similar matter, we will proceed to the details of the solemnity. The following is her own account:—

"In the hand of the divine Infant, I beheld as it were a golden rod, on the top of which was the appearance of a flame of fire, while the lower end was pointed with steel like a small lance. He placed the upper end against His heart, and directed the spear head to my own, so that I seemed to feel it pierce through and through. All at once I looked, and now there was nothing in the hand of the Babe; but all smiling He invited me to His love, and made me understand that I was now united to Him more closely than ever. Many things were communicated to me, but as I do not remember them all, I will write nothing about them. When I returned to myself, I was like one delirious, and knew not what I did. I thought I could feel the wound at my heart open, but I did not venture to look and see if it were so. I took a little cloth, and after applying it, found that it was stained with fresh blood; I also felt great pain. When your reverence commanded me to examine whether there was a real wound there, I did so, and found that there was one, open, but not bleeding. It was large enough to admit the blade of a knife, and the divided flesh was visible. On the first day of the year 1697 (eight days after this wound had been received) it bled again, and continued open for a good while. May it all be to the glory of God."

We must inform the reader that this wound, together with the blood which proceeded from it, was shown by order of her confessors to several nuns, as is mentioned in the processes. It was a very special favour, by which our Lord was pleased to recompense the heroic fidelity of His beloved Spouse.

CHAPTER VII.

JESUS PRODUCES IN HER A STILL GREATER RESEMBLANCE TO HIMSELF BY IMPRINTING UPON HER HIS SACRED STIGMATA.

It is a well-known proverb that the mutual affection of two lovers either finds or produces resemblance, as well in heart as in will and disposition. This is true in the case of human love, but much more in that love which is exchanged between God and man; so much so indeed that the souls which love God most are rendered most like to the divine Majesty by the surpassing nobility of their virtues, as we see in the lives of the saints. But although the resemblance which divine love produces in man, is more properly found in the soul, yet it has sometimes pleased God to indicate by outward signs what is passing within. Thus He has bestowed on a few of His holiest servants an exterior as well as an interior resemblance to the divine model of all sanctity, our Lord Jesus Christ, by imprinting on their persons His five principal

Wounds. It is universally known that this privilege was vouchsafed to the great saint and patriarch Francis of Assisi, as also to S. Catherine of Siena, though in the case of the latter the stigmata were invisible. Several others are mentioned by Theophilus Raynaud, an author worthy of confidence; for instance, the Blessed Lidwine, Blessed Ida of Louvain, Blessed Gertrude of Oost, Blessed Christina, who is mentioned by Dionysius the Carthusian—Blessed Helena of Hungary, Blessed Stephania Soncinate, Blessed Osanna of Mantua, Blessed Lucy of Narni, Blessed Joanna of the Cross, with others: he adds that as many as thirty-five persons of both sexes, who have received the stigmata, besides S. Francis, are named by Peter of Alva in his work entitled, "Prodigium Naturæ, portentum Gratiæ" —" A Prodigy of Nature, a miracle of Grace."

Our Veronica was permitted to share in this high privilege. She had attained to so lofty a degree of love and union with God that she had merited the favour of being in a sensible manner joined to Him in mystic nuptials, and she afterwards gave such extraordinary proofs of fidelity, as well as such wonderful conformity of soul with Him, that she deserved at length to bear His likeness in her body by the impression of the sacred stigmata. We have seen how her heart was visibly transfixed by a dart of love from Jesus Christ on the Feast of the Nativity in 1696. In the following year the wound was repeated, and she received similar ones on her hands and feet, reflected from the five most holy Wounds of her crucified Lord.

Before relating the details of this event, we must remark that although there is sufficient certainty in the cases mentioned above to satisfy every sensible person of their authenticity, particularly in the instances of S. Francis and S. Catherine, which are celebrated by the Church in her masses and offices, yet of neither have we proofs so convincing to human criticism as those which relate to Veronica; for besides the public declaration of all her companions, who, by order of the superiors, examined her one by one, five of them gave their personal testimony juridically in the process (though that was not terminated until after their death). Four also of her confessors were eye-witnesses of the fact, and deposed accordingly; moreover there was the attestation of the Bishop, Mgr. Lucantonio Eustachj, on whom the duty devolved of entering into repeated and most rigid investigations for the purpose of informing the sacred tribunal of the Inquisition at Rome. Still, although the case is as clear as noonday, there are critics sufficiently unreasonable to doubt the genuineness of this her gift. We consider, however, that her own description is the best proof of the authenticity of what she relates. When we meet with sentiments of such profound humility, of such deep contrition for her imperfections, of such tender love towards God, of such earnest desire for suffering, by all of which her narrative is accompanied, we cannot help recognizing the work of God. The following account is given in her own words.

She begins by recounting to her confessor the promises by which the exalted favour in question had been preceded. "The 29th of March, 1697. Praised be the Lord! To-night, after a great deal of suffering, I beheld in a state of recollection a vision of Jesus crucified. Suddenly He caused me to comprehend a little of my own nothingness and incapacity. I stood before the Lord like one speechless, unable to say or do anything. I was in pain, but it was the pain of love. The more helpless and incapable I felt myself, the more thoroughly did I learn that in myself I was nothing; and the increasing light which illuminated me on this point caused me to see more clearly Jesus crucified. All at once our Lord assisted and enriched me; for everything that is good in a soul is His. He made me understand this, and told me that it was His desire to renew my wound, and seemed to ask me, moreover, whether I would have it to be so. O infinite love of God! At the same moment He infused His love into my soul, and gave me intimate communications of His greatness and His power, making me at the same time conscious of my own nothingness, which enlightened me still more with respect to Himself. He caused my soul to penetrate ever more into the depths of His infinite love, and repeated the question, 'Art thou willing that I should wound thee? I am come to take away from thee everything that is a hindrance to my love.' I said nothing; I felt myself as nothing; I had not courage to say, 'Strike me, O Lord,' neither could I answer no. Then our Lord said, 'Tell Me, what dost thou wish for? I am come to renew thy wound; but what sayest thou? dost thou desire it?' I was hereupon raised into a state of rapture, and transported as on wings very near the Lord. Being completely resigned to His Will, I said to Him, though without speaking, 'Lord, Thou knowest that I wish for nothing but the accomplishment of Thy Will. Behold me prepared for whatever may please Thee.' All at once I beheld a great light leave the Feet of Jesus, and come towards me. When it had come close to me, it assumed the appearance of a small flame. In the middle of it was a large nail, which pierced my heart through and through. God knows what pain I felt. Then I returned to myself, crying aloud, 'My Jesus!' Immediately I was caught back into my state of ecstasy. The same vision was before me of Jesus crucified, but in His left Foot there was no nail. He said to me, 'Now thou art Mine; but I am not yet fully satisfied.' I replied as I had done before, 'O Lord, behold I am completely Thine: work Thy Will in me, for I can do nothing.' He informed me that on Good Friday He would wholly transform me into Himself, and that He would seal my hands and my feet with the marks of His holy Wounds, in order that I might be entirely His. He told me that for the present my wounds should be hidden, but that it was His Will to crucify me again and again, to the end that I might be totally dead to myself and to everything."

Veronica goes on to say that she prayed very fervently for her confessor, for her directors, and particularly for her own soul, as well as for those of her sisters, and all her order. With deep humility, which could not have been the fruit of diabolical illusion, she continues, "Hereupon our Lord in a special communication made me know and understand that hitherto I had been a religious only in name, and that it was now time to be one in reality. He told me also that in order to comprehend the full meaning of the word 'religious,' I must enter the school of His Wounds, and learn it all there. He communicated light to my soul, such as I am unable to describe. He made me understand that I had never yet abandoned the little world which is myself, and that, therefore, I had been a religious only in name and in habit. He then reminded me of our father S. Francis, and our mother

S. Clare, the founders of this holy institute; and told me that I must be denuded of self and of everything, and then be crucified with Jesus as they had been. After this our Lord said to me, 'Look on Me; dost thou see how much I have done for thy salvation? I desire thee to be solely intent on my service. Direct thy whole mind and all thy thoughts to Me. Commit all thy works into My hands, and be careful to co-operate with what I work in Thee.' Immediately after this He vanished from my sight. On returning to my natural state I felt anxious to be divested of self, and earnestly desirous of corresponding with our Lord's Will; I wished also to observe our holy rule in deed and in truth. I desired every sort of suffering, and exclaimed from my heart: 'My Lord, crucify me with Thyself, otherwise I shall not be satisfied. I desire to please Thee, and I know that it pleases Thee when Thy spouses suffer for Thy love. I long for pains and crosses, in order to give pleasure to Thee Who art my highest good. Praise be to God!

When our Lord had prepared her by means of these saintly affections, which were ever on the increase, for the crucifixion to which she aspired, He came to satisfy her desires according to His promise, on Good Friday, which fell that year on the 5th of April. As it is more than ever necessary to keep to her own words, the reader will permit us to give the passage entire, although it is rather long.

"The 5th of April, 1697. Laus Deo! I have passed the greater part of the night in recollection. From two to four o'clock I had a vision of Jesus Risen in company with the most Blessed Virgin and all the saints, as I had seen them on other occasions. Our Lord commanded me to begin my confession. I did so, but no sooner had I said, 'I have offended Thee, and I confess to Thee, O my God,' than I became overwhelmed with contrition, and could say no more. The Lord then directed my guardian angel to make my confession for me. He did so accordingly, placing his hand on my head, and began to accuse me thus: 'O eternal and immortal God, I, the guardian of this soul, in obedience to Thee, the supreme Judge, and for her salvation, begin now, in her name, to declare everything that she has ever done to displease Thee in thought, word, or deed.' Whilst he spoke, all my transgressions seemed to surround me. I beheld the countenance of our Lord no longer covered, but unveiled; it was full of mercy and compassion, and He made me understand that He was going to pardon me. He showed me His pierced Side, and His wounded Hands. When the angel accused me of my gravest sins, my pain and sorrow increased, but our Lord encouraged me by saying, 'I forgive thee, and annul by My Blood every fault of thy life. From this moment I accept thee for My beloved.' Again I was enraptured, and my soul was drawn, it seemed to me, to our Lord, Who by His words communicated to me a close union. I received more light as to my sins, and my heart was penetrated with sorrow on account of them; but as my angel recounted them one by one, they disappeared from before me, to my great relief, and my soul remained purified as God willed. He informed me that this was the effect and fruit of His sacred Wounds, which He had impressed on my heart; again He showed me His Side, His Hands, and His Feet, and said to me, 'I wish to mark also thy hands and thy feet.' O God, Thou knowest what I experienced amid these excesses of love—it was such that I can neither write nor speak of it. I can only mention its effects, which were, extreme grief for my sins, a fuller perception of their malice, together with such horror and detestation of them, that I would gladly have chosen to suffer all that has ever been or will be endured by all creatures until the day of judgment, and all that the holy martyrs have passed through, if I could thereby annul and undo the grievous evil which I have committed. 'O my God,' I cried, 'mercy and pardon!' He replied, 'Yes, I pardon thee; I remit the whole debt through My Wounds and My Blood.' Here my angel closed the confession by a general accusation of all I had done, and presented me to Jesus completely purified. The Lord then rose and said to me, 'Vade in pace, jam amplius noli peccare.'—' Go in peace, and sin no more.' O God! I experienced wonderful things, but cannot describe them. The Lord then gave me His blessing, and the whole disappeared."

Thus concluded the first vision of that blessed night. "As soon as I returned to myself," she continues, "I felt a profound sorrow for all my offences against God; I would have endured any suffering for His love. I therefore performed many of my usual penances. The more I inflicted on myself, the more did my anxiety to suffer increase, so I said from my heart, 'Lord, more pains, more crosses.' I took the crucifix in my hand, and went on making various acts of resignation, praise, and thanksgiving. I do not remember the words I used in these acts, but I recollect often repeating the following prayer: 'My divine Spouse, crucify me with Thee. Yes, indeed, my Well-beloved, I pray Thee to make me feel the pain and agony of Thy sacred Hands and Feet. Do not delay; now is the time; crucify me with Thyself, my beloved Spouse.' I went to those holy Wounds, and kissed them, and said, 'My crucified Spouse, I implore Thee to give me those nails of Thine.' Then I addressed myself to His sacred Side and said, 'Heart of my heart, when wilt Thou pierce this heart which is Thine? I am waiting for thee to do so. Come, come, my God; here is my heart, and my whole self.' I uncovered the wound, and said, 'This wound of love, my God, pleads with Thee for the conversion of sinners, particularly of certain individuals whom I named.' Then I replaced the crucifix on my little altar, meaning to remain quiet for a little while, but I could not. I took it in my hand again, and said many things which just now I cannot recall; but I know that I said again and again, 'My Spouse, my Love! Thou art fastened to this Cross for the love of us. I, too, wish to be crucified for Thy love. Do not delay longer; now is the time.' While pronouncing these words my heart beat so violently that it seemed ready to escape from my breast. O God! what pain did I then endure! I cannot tell how I uttered all this, for I was, as it were, out of myself. All at once a deathlike agony came over me, and lasted for about an hour, during which time I was totally incapable of moving or speaking."

As soon as she recovered from this agony, she set herself to pray, and during her prayer she received the impression of the sacred stigmata. "Whilst I was praying for sinners," she continues, "I became recollected, and beheld in a vision Jesus crucified, with the Blessed Virgin of dolours at the foot of the cross, as she was on Mount Calvary. The Lord told me that He had come to transform me entirely into Himself, and to seal me with His Wounds. I turned to the Most Holy Virgin, and said to her with the utmost confidence, 'Behold, I am ready for everything; do thou, Most Holy Virgin, offer thyself on my behalf, with all thy merits, together with all the pains and dolours which thou didst suffer beneath the Cross at the time of our Lord's sacred Passion: ask pardon and mercy for me from thy Son. I can do nothing; behold my incapacity, and who I am. Prepare me for this grace.' Our Blessed Lady then presented herself at the Feet of her divine Son, and did all I asked in a moment. While she prayed for me, I was enlightened as to my own nothingness, and made to perceive that all I was now passing through was the work of God. I was enabled to see the love with which God cherishes souls, especially ungrateful ones like mine. I was also led to a more intimate acquaintance with my own helplessness and ingratitude, and I felt my own nothingness. O God! I cannot explain this at all; I can only say that the result produced in my soul was firm hope in God, and detachment from myself. God alone! and my soul alone! Here it was communicated to me by the Lord that it was His Will to regulate for the future my mode of life and all my actions; and He repeated the words, 'I am come to make thee like to Myself: I am going to crucify thee.' I cannot express the manner in which this pierced my heart. While our Lord spoke thus, He drew this soul of mine into a loving union with Himself: and it seemed to me that He heightened my state of recollection into one of rapture. At the same moment there came to me so earnest a desire to be crucified with our Lord, that I turned to the most holy Virgin, and said, 'O Mother of mercy and compassion, obtain for me the grace to be crucified with my crucified Spouse.' Accordingly she turned to her divine Son, and said to Him, 'Come quickly, and crucify this soul.' Our Lord replied, 'She shall receive that grace.' Once more He asked me, 'What dost thou wish?' to which I replied, 'Thou knowest, my Lord, what it is I wish for.' 'But I would hear from thyself what thy desire is,' resumed the Lord. 'My God,' I replied, 'the accomplishment of Thy holy Will.' And then our Lord said, 'I have desired thee thus, and now I will confirm thee in My Will, by transforming thee entirely into Myself! tell me, what dost thou long for?' 'O God,' I answered, 'my highest good, do not delay, I beseech Thee, but crucify me with Thyself.' Meantime I was filled with contrition on account of all my offences, for which I heartily implored forgiveness. I offered for it His Precious Blood, His pains and sufferings, especially His most sacred Wounds; and I did indeed grieve most profoundly for every transgression of my whole life. Our Lord said to me, 'I forgive thee, but I would have thee be faithful for the future: I confer on thee grace for this through these my Wounds; which, as a pledge, I am about to imprint upon thee.' All at once I beheld five rays of glory issuing from His most holy Wounds, which approached me like little flames. In four of them were nails, and in the other a lance as it were of gold, but all on fire: it pierced my heart through and through, while the nails transfixed my hands and feet. I felt great sufferings, but at the same time I felt that I was being altogether transformed into God. As soon as I had been thus wounded, the flames resumed their former appearance as rays of glory, and lodged themselves in the Hands, Feet, and Side of Jesus Crucified. Our Lord again assured me that I was His

Spouse, commended and dedicated me to the perpetual care of his Blessed Mother, consigned me afresh to my guardian angel, and then spoke to me as follows, 'I am entirely thine: ask of Me what grace thou wilt, and I will satisfy thee.' I answered, 'Grant that I may never be separated from Thee.' Then suddenly the whole vanished from my sight; I returned to myself, and found that my arms were outstretched and stiffened; moreover I was conscious of extreme pain in my hands, feet, and heart. I felt that the latter wound was open and bleeding. I was anxious to inspect it, but was unable to do so in consequence of the pain in my hands. At length, however, I succeeded, and found it wide open, with both blood and water proceeding from it."

Such is the account of this marvellous favour which Veronica drew up for her confessor. It is impossible after perusing it to set it down as the production of a heated fancy, still less of diabolical illusion. The Spirit of God is apparent throughout the entire narrative, and in the very style in which it is written. As soon as her confessor had communicated the whole matter to Mgr. Eustachj, that venerable prelate took certain prudent precautions, as all superiors and spiritual directors are bound to do whenever such extraordinary cases come under their observation, in order to test their truth and spirit. Investigations of a far stricter nature were subsequently made, when the sacred tribunal of the Inquisition at Rome had been informed of the circumstances. The bishop was then directed to proceed to severer tests, of which we shall speak in the third book, which contains the account of her heroic virtues. It was on the 5th of April, as has been already stated, that Veronica received the sacred stigmata. On the 12th of the following July, we find from her own writings that our Lord gave her a special invitation to share in His cross, and warned her of the steps which would be taken concerning her by the venerable tribunal in question. The first letter which was written on the subject by his Eminence Cardinal Cybo, secretary of the congregation of the Holy Office, to Bishop Eustachj, is dated on the 20th of the same month; the second was written on the 10th of August, the third on the 14th of September, and the fourth and last on the 5th of October. By this time the sacred tribunal was satisfied with the replies of the bishop and the examinations he had made, and directed him in the last-mentioned letter, "to investigate the matter no further, and to say nothing more about it, but to keep silence on the subject." Such are the precise terms of the document, and they are the dictates of prudence; for it was not only desirable to prevent gossiping on the part of the public, but also to preclude the possibility of a vain thought arising in the mind of the servant of God. The bishop was furthermore directed "to ask no more questions of the nuns, and to forward no additional particulars to the Sacred Congregation, which had gained sufficient information from his previous letters." Hence it is clear that the sacred tribunal took the same view which the bishop had done in his various answers, which for brevity's sake are omitted here, of the supernatural fact above related, as also of the sanctity of the spirit of Veronica; although for good reasons it declined to announce it openly during her lifetime. However, a sufficiently clear declaration was made indirectly in the year 1716, when the nuns being desirous of electing her abbess, application was made to the sacred tribunal for permission to do so, which was immediately granted in a letter from the secretary, Cardinal Spada, dated the 7th of March. His Eminence expressed himself "persuaded that the proposed step would be conducive to the honour of God, and beneficial to the souls of the religious."

CHAPTER VIII.

THE STIGMATA ARE REPEATED ON VARIOUS OCCASIONS, AND ATTESTED BY NEW AND SATISFACTORY PROOFS.

WHEN Veronica had been sealed with the precious marks of our redemption, she derived gratification both from the pain she felt, and also from the great resemblance which now existed between herself and her Crucified Spouse; but her joy was damped on receiving an intimation from the bishop, desiring her to cut an opening in her dress so that the wound at her heart might be seen, for his lordship was anxious to test the reality of the sacred stigmata in presence of competent witnesses. For this purpose he made choice of four, who were all distinguished for their virtue, and sufficiently advanced in years, viz., Father M. Antonio Tassinari, of the Servites; Father Ubaldo Antonio Capelletti, of the Oratory; Father Vitale, of Bologna, of the Reformed Franciscans; and the Father Prior of the Dominicans of that city, and at the time we speak of extraordinary confessor to the monastery where Veronica lived. Our Saint was obliged to exhibit her wounds one by one to each of these individuals, holding meantime a lighted candle in her hand. Such martyrdom was thus imposed on her maidenly reserve and deep humility that, as she afterwards mentioned in confidence to Sister Florida Ceoli, if God had not deadened her senses for the time being, she would have expired with confusion. His lordship also required her to show her wounds to her companions, and this was a fresh torment to her humble spirit. At last, being able to endure it no longer, she began to implore our Lord to allow her to retain all the pain of her wounds, but to withdraw the external marks from the eyes of others, as He had done in the cases of His beloved Catherine of Siena and other souls who were dear to Him.

But the Lord, instead of hearing her prayer, was pleased to renew her wounds on the 28th of June in the same year. The following description of their appearance is taken from the account which the bishop despatched to the Holy Office, as also from the juridical depositions of Sister Florida Ceoli, and others who had frequent opportunities of examining them :—The wounds in her hands and feet were round, and about the size of a farthing above, slightly diminishing underneath the palms of the hands and the soles of the feet. The punctures were red, and pierced quite through when open, and when closed they were covered with a thin scar of the same size. The wound in her side was just above the left breast, occupying the length of four or five fingers, placed transversely, and as broad in the middle as a finger, but growing narrower towards the two ends, exactly as would be the case with the thrust of a spear. This last was never covered with a scar, but was always open and red as though it had been recently inflicted ; it bled frequently, and filled the air with a sweet perfume.

It was on the 12th of July that Jesus informed

her during a rapture of the investigations which would be ordered by the Holy Office at Rome; and then Veronica set herself to implore her divine Spouse with the utmost fervour that He would deign to avert such public proceedings by withdrawing the stigmata. But the Lord, Who desired to make known the gifts and merits of His beloved spouse, replied as follows: " The Holy Office shall apply its tests, and shall declare that it is all My work; and soon after that I will take from thee the marks in thy hands and feet, but be prepared to suffer much. This is My Will; relate all that has passed to thy confessor." Such was the perfect resignation of Veronica that she simply prepared herself for whatever God destined for her.

The Holy Office expressed itself satisfied on the 5th of the following October, as mentioned above; and Veronica, mindful of the promise she had received, began once more to supplicate her divine Spouse that He would remove the outward tokens of His Passion. But during a vision, which occurred on the night of the 3rd of January, 1699, our Lord renewed the pain of her five wounds, and informed her that she must bear the visible impression of them until three years from their first infliction should have been completed; for that was the meaning of the words, "soon after that" in the promise referred to. The stigmata were again renewed on the 20th of the following February, accompanied with another assurance that they should be withdrawn after the expiration of the three years, but not before, as it was the Will of our Lord that the reality of His work should be recognized. At length, on the 17th of March in the following year, 1700, the Lord presented Himself to her, all over wounds, covered with blood, and crowned with thorns. "At the same moment," Veronica writes, "my own crown of thorns seemed to press on my brow, and caused me great pain. Our Lord also seemed to touch the wounds in my hands and feet, and while He did so my suffering was extreme. He said to me, 'Calm thyself; thou shalt have the grace thou seekest; in a few days I will take away the marks of these wounds, and thou wilt have them no more.' But I asked, 'Why wilt Thou not take them from me now?' To which He replied, 'I wish the three years to be fulfilled, as I have made thee understand several times.'"

It was not until the completion of this term, viz., on the 5th of April, in the year 1700, that Veronica obtained the favour she so much desired. It is well to refer to her own account, in order that we may remark the caution which she observed in dealing with visions, although by this time long experience had made her quite used to them, and her soul was now so much at home with God, if we may be permitted such an expression, that she could hardly doubt the reality of such favours.

"On the 5th inst.," she writes, "I passed the night in great pain. From the first hour until it struck three, I experienced various kinds of bodily suffering, besides trials and desolation, and temptations of every description. Praise be to God. At the third hour I renewed my protestations. I felt desirous that our Lord would impart to me a spirit of true repentance for my sins, and I exclaimed from my heart, 'My God, bestow this grace on me that I may be no longer ungrateful to Thee, but may in all things faithfully correspond to and accomplish Thy holy Will. I am ready for everything.' It seemed to me that at that moment I was made intimately acquainted with my true state. I became absorbed in recollection, and beheld a vision of Jesus crucified. I was greatly afraid, fearing lest it might be an illusion of the devil. So I seemed to make certain acts indicative of contempt. I raised my whole heart to God, and said, 'Do not suffer the tempter, O Lord, to do these things to me, for I do not want visions; what I desire is sorrow for my sins, and knowledge of myself.' Again I expressed my contempt and abhorrence, as well as my anxiety to dispel the vision. . . . But the Crucified One said to me, 'I am not Satan, as thou conjecturest, but Jesus, thy crucified Spouse. I am come to strengthen thee to suffer.' To which I replied, 'I do not believe that thou art Jesus, but rather the enemy who wishes to deceive me; and therefore I regard thee not. I desire and long to have true contrition and a knowledge of myself, besides a true love of God.' He replied, 'All these thou shalt have, and the favour which has been promised thee shall be granted thee now.' Suddenly I was seized with such sorrow for my sins that I felt as though my heart would burst with anguish. At the same time I seemed to receive intimate communications regarding the immense love and charity of God. . . . Then from His Wounds there proceeded rays of splendour which advanced towards me. Meantime I felt my heart pierced as with a sharp lance, and my hands and feet with heavy nails. The rays of glory returned to the Crucified Lord, and I seemed to behold jets of blood issuing from His Wounds, and reaching to the parts in which I felt so much pain, viz., the heart, the hands, and the feet. The suffering I endured was so great that it appeared as though the flesh was being torn from my bones."

These were the preliminaries to the favour she so much desired, for she continues her narrative; "Meanwhile I understood that Jesus was granting me the desired boon by withdrawing the scars which the stigmata had produced. He confirmed me as mediatrix between Himself and sinners, and told me that for some days I should receive as many graces as I should have pains and sufferings. He informed me also that it was His Will that I should frequently ask to suffer for the salvation of many souls. He communicated to me likewise a variety of other things which I am unable to describe. . . . When I returned to myself I found that I possessed some knowledge of myself, besides contrition for my sins, and a desire for every kind of suffering. I was on my knees, with my arms extended; and so stiffened through the pain in my hands and feet that I could not stir. I felt great pain at the heart, and I thought that my wound there was bleeding; but I was unable to ascertain the fact, for the nerves of my hands and feet were drawn back in such pain that I thought I should die. I continued in this state for a long time. At length I began slowly to recover myself. I lighted the lamp, and found that the scars which had covered the wounds in my hands and feet were loose and separated. I was greatly pleased at this. The wound at my heart was still open, and bleeding more than on other occasions; it caused me such pain that I felt as if I should breathe my last every moment. All this occurred between the fourth and fifth hours of the night, which was just the time when I had received that grace (viz., the stigmata); and thus the three years were completed. To God be all the glory."

Though the external marks had been so far withdrawn, it must not be imagined that every outward symptom was removed. Several eye-witnesses attested in the process that where the wounds had been there still remained certain red spots of the same shape, sometimes of a deeper, sometimes of a fainter, colour. Her humility shrank from the idea of even these being seen; so she found some pretence for wearing little bandages, which concealed them, and she frequently entreated our Lord to cause them to disappear. But our Lord told her that this must not be until a short time previous to her death; and the same witnesses declare that during the last days of her life these red spots grew paler, assuming a purplish hue, and at length became white, like the rest of her skin, only somewhat more smooth and transparent. This was found to be the case during the examination to which her body was subjected after her death.

But although the outward marks of the stigmata were withdrawn, as we have seen, in April, 1700, suffering from them was not at an end, and they were even sometimes renewed. We find from Veronica's own writings, that such was the case on the 6th of April, 1703. It was also declared by various witnesses that the stigmata were several times renewed till within a few days of her death; and on these occasions blood used to flow from them. Moreover Sister Mary Magdalen Boscaini, when she gave her evidence in the apostolic process, maintained that they were renewed about three hours before the Ave Maria every Friday in the year, on all the greater feasts of the year, as also on the 17th of September, which is the day on which the church commemorates the stigmata of S. Francis, on the 4th of October, which is the feast of that saint, and whenever she was put under obedience to request the favour. As an instance of this, on Good Friday, which fell on the 19th of April, 1726, Veronica having mentioned to her confessor, Father Raniero Giuseppe Maria Guelfi, that our Lord Jesus had twice made choice of this day to renew her five wounds, he being anxious that the fact should be more fully certified, and also for the greater trial of her obedience, directed her to pray that our Lord would deign to renew them a third time. She received this order with joy and alacrity, and fell into an ecstasy at the feet of her confessor. On recovering her senses she declared that the boon had been granted. He therefore sent her to the window where holy Communion was given, in order that he might inspect her hands; and then to his amazement he beheld them wounded and bleeding. Wishing that this evidence should be corroborated by that of other witnesses, he pretended that he did not believe her, and said that she must be mortified on account of her disobedience; accordingly he desired her to show herself to the Mothers Sister Florida Ceoli, and Sister Mary Magdalen Boscaini. They both had a perfect view of her five wounds, which were open and dropping with blood, as they subsequently deposed in the process.

Although after all that has been said, both in this and the preceding chapter, it is impossible that any doubt should occur to the mind as to the reality and supernatural character of the rare gifts which we have recorded, the matter may be further illustrated by the following circumstances. In the first place, it is worthy of remark, that when the above-mentioned wounds were open, they emitted so delicious a fragrance throughout the whole of the convent that it alone was sufficient to inform the nuns whenever the stigmata had been renewed: and on several occasions the religious were convinced by ocular demonstration that they had not been deceived. When the bandages which had been applied to these mysterious wounds were put away, they communicated the same sweet perfume to everything near them. This fact is attested by Sister Florida Ceoli. The second remarkable circumstance is that when by order of the bishop the medical professors exerted their utmost skill to cure the wounds of Veronica, so far from being able to heal them, their remedies only caused inflammation. But a still more convincing proof than either was her being able to live and work in the midst of it all. After her death, when the physician and surgeon examined the wound, which penetrated from above the left breast to the heart, they both agreed that it was physically impossible for a person to live with such a wound, and that her existence must therefore have been the result of a miracle. This conviction was strengthened when the nuns declared that they had frequently seen breath proceeding from it: and yet Veronica lived in this condition for about thirty years; and when her hands and feet were thus pierced, she would walk with agility whenever her duty required it, and do whatever her offices or the community life required. At length, when the wounds became closed, it was more clear than ever that the whole was supernatural. Such was the opinion of Gentili, the surgeon, who examined the case; for in the course of nature a wound does not heal without becoming covered by a scar. This is a fact of which daily experience assures us, but Veronica's wounds, on the contrary, as soon as they closed, were covered with perfectly smooth skin, on which there was not the least rising or prominence to distinguish it from the rest.

Notwithstanding all this, which is sufficient to convince every competent judge, the subject of this extraordinary favour had her own doubts on the matter, until it pleased God to remove them by the following vision. Father Antonio Tommasini, of the Society of Jesus, who had earned the reputation of sanctity during fifty years which he had spent in the holy and apostolic ministry of a missioner, was appointed extraordinary confessor to the convent a short time before his death. One day Veronica entreated him to confer with her on the subject of her doubts, and to tell her if the stigmata were indeed the work of God. "My daughter," replied the good Father, "if God in His mercy permits me to reach heaven, and if He will then allow me to appear to you, I will visit you, and tell you all. But at present I can only desire you to remain in peace." Soon after this he died. We find in Veronica's journal, under date of the 29th of March, 1717, that during an ecstasy, in which she was holding converse with our Blessed Lady, Father Tommasini appeared to her, together with S. Francis Xavier, and other saints. The Mother of God then desired Father Tommasini to keep the promise which he had made to Veronica: in obedience to this direction from the Queen of heaven, he accordingly turned to our Saint, and told her that in the first place she was to indulge no fears on the score of the stigmata, because they had been imprinted by God: secondly, that she was to employ her life in the practice of humility and self-annihilation, and that in all her occupations she was to keep herself in the presence of God, and with Him:

and lastly, that she was to practise the most exact obedience, because "a soul that is perfect in this virtue is liable to no judgment at the hand of God, for whatever she does through holy obedience is sure to be the Will of God." "These three injunctions," continues the journal, "penetrated so deep that they seemed to be engraven on my inmost heart. The Blessed Virgin confirmed all that the Father had said." The humility which Veronica evinced when she received this assurance of the reality of her gifts after twenty years of doubt and apprehension, is truly remarkable. But we must not omit to mention the grateful testimony which she adds in praise of her benefactor. "Meanwhile," she writes, " our Blessed Lady showed me that the soul of Father Tommasini wore on his breast a most precious jewel, which shone as with the united splendour of a multitude of suns: indeed the sun which we see in the firmament is dark in comparison with that brilliant light. . . . I was given to understand the reason why he wore this gem. It was because during the whole of his life on earth he had always kept his heart fixed on God, in God, and for God alone; and therefore he wore the jewel at his heart, to symbolize the interior presence of that divine love which would fain have drawn the whole world to God if that had been possible, in order that every creature might love God Who is Supreme Love." Surely this is the eulogium of a real apostle; and we leave it to the reader to decide its value, coming as it does from such a source.

CHAPTER IX.

VERONICA PARTICIPATES IN ALL THE OTHER DOLOURS WHICH CONSTITUTED THE DIVINE PASSION.—WONDERFUL MARKS IMPRINTED ON HER HEART.

THE bitter chalice and the crown of thorns, together with His five principal Wounds, were not the only tokens by which Jesus was pleased to show the special love which He bore to His spouse Veronica. It was His Will that she should share in all the sufferings of His Passion. In proof of this we have, besides her own account, the depositions of many eye-witnesses, which were made in the processes, the deponents having had the most indisputable evidence as to the facts in question. One of the remarkable symptoms referred to was a very considerable curvature of the right shoulder, which bent the very bone just as the weight of a heavy cross might have done. When Gentili, the surgeon, examined the body after death, he declared that the above circumstance was prodigious and supernatural; for, as he subsequently stated in the process—"If it had occurred by natural means, it would have prevented her from moving her arms; whereas," he continued, "I have myself frequently seen the Venerable Sister Veronica using her arms as freely as other persons, and carrying about heavy articles of dress when she used to render charitable assistance to those sick religious who were my patients. In the same way, during her last illness, I saw her move her right arm without the least difficulty, and that too where the shoulder was particularly depressed; she was unable to use her left arm, for that had been incapacitated by an apoplectic stroke."

But, in order not to multiply references, we will confine ourselves to the testimony of Father Giovan Maria Crivelli, a celebrated Jesuit missionary, as being not only the most circumstantial, but also thoroughly authenticated, as the reader will presently see.

The bishop, Luc'Antonio Eustachj, having heard from the nuns of the extraordinary trials, contortions, and agonies to which Veronica was so frequently liable, and which her medical attendants were unable to obviate or explain, and having been also informed by her confessors that they were the results of her experiencing at certain times all the sufferings of the Passion of Jesus Christ, which were conferred on her by an especial privilege, his lordship became desirous of being further enlightened as to the facts, not being certain as to whether it was the work of God or an illusion of the devil. For this purpose he summoned the above-mentioned Jesuit Father from Florence in the year 1714, having heard that he was much skilled in the direction of souls. Father Crivelli accordingly came in November, and the bishop having thoroughly informed him as to the details of the case, in order that he might be the better enabled to carry out his plans, appointed him extraordinary confessor to the convent for the space of two months, during which time he withdrew their ordinary director. Father Crivelli caused Veronica to make a general confession, and disclose to him the entire state of her conscience, as well as all the gifts she had received. Comparing what he heard from her own lips with what the other nuns had observed concerning her, it occurred to him, or rather he was enlightened by God, to apply a test, which would at once discover whether the spirit which guided her were good or evil.

This was the employment of purely mental precepts, which it is impossible for the devil to divine, since they can be known to none but God. One morning he summoned Veronica to the confessional, and desired her to engage in prayer. He told her to ask God and our Blessed Lady to make known to her whatever he should enjoin her to do by simple internal acts of the will. Veronica expressed her ready acquiescence, and began to pray. Meantime, the good Father conceived in his mind, without either moving his lips or making the slightest gesture, the five following injunctions:—In the first place, that the wound in her side, which was then closed, as well as those in her hands and feet, should re-open and bleed; secondly, that, when open, it should continue so as long as he might wish it; thirdly, that it should close up again as soon as he willed that it should, in his presence, and in that of others whom he might appoint; fourthly, that in his presence, and at whatever time it might seem good to him, she should visibly undergo all the sufferings and torments which Jesus Christ endured in His Passion; and, lastly, that, when she had gone through the scene of crucifixion, stretched on her bed as usual, she should, in his presence, and before whomsoever else he might appoint, stand upright on her feet in the air, as he should command her to do.

Having willed these five orders, which, as we have already remarked, were merely internal, he left her a certain interval of time to continue her prayer. Then he called to her, and asked if the Lord and the Blessed Virgin had made them known to her. Veronica replied frankly that they had not. "Renew your prayer, then," he said. She did so; and when he called to her again, a short time after, she was able to repeat the five injunctions, word for word, in the order in which he had conceived them. The Father was amazed, and immediately recognized the Spirit of God. But, concealing his astonishment, he said: "Between speaking and doing there is a great difference. But I shall reserve myself for some other opportunity of ascertaining whether my orders can be literally accomplished." Veronica candidly replied that she was quite prepared to obey him, and, with the assistance of God and most holy Mary, to fulfil everything he had commanded, for, she continued, "I confide simply in the virtue of holy obedience, in the Will of God, and the aid of most holy Mary."

Some days after this he returned to the convent, and desired her to put in execution the first of the five orders which he had previously given her, viz., that the wound in her side should re-open and shed blood. He wished this to occur whilst he celebrated the holy sacrifice of the Mass, at which he bade her assist. As soon as he had offered the divine sacrifice, and made his thanksgiving, he summoned Veronica to the confessional, and inquired if her wound were open and bleeding. She humbly replied, "Yes." "That is not enough for me," rejoined the Father, who wished for more evidence. "Apply a white handkerchief to the place, and then give it me." Veronica obeyed, and the handkerchief, when she gave it him, was soaked through with warm blood, which emitted a most delicious perfume. He then went on to the second point, that her wound should remain unclosed until he should direct to the contrary. She promised submission, and so her trial was concluded for that day.

Father Crivelli went at once to the bishop, informed

his lordship of everything that had occurred, and showed him the handkerchief steeped in blood, and all fragrant, so that the prelate was filled with amazement. Just then the Father was obliged to go to Florence, to arrange some business with the Grand Duke Cosmo III. He remained absent for about three weeks. When he returned to the convent, he asked Veronica if her wound had continued open all this time. Being assured that it had, he repaired with this information to the bishop, and requested his lordship to accompany him after dinner to witness the fact with his own eyes, as also to observe the accomplishment of his third order, which was that the wound should close up again directly he signified his will to that effect. They arrived about four o'clock in the afternoon, and Veronica having been ordered to take her place at the window where holy Communion was given, the Father put a pair of scissors in her hand, and commanded her, in virtue of holy obedience, to cut a hole in her habit just where the wound was. She immediately obeyed. The bishop held a lighted candle, and both he and Father Crivelli saw the open wound, and the warm blood which issued from it. The latter, being encouraged at the sight, exclaimed, "It is well. This moment, I enjoin you, let the wound close." For a very short interval she remained absorbed in prayer. Then being asked whether she had obeyed, she answered, "Yes." The bishop and Father Crivelli looked through the opening which had been cut in her dress, and examined the wound with a lighted candle. It was completely healed, and covered with natural skin like the rest; the only thing which was left to mark the spot being a very slight discolouration. They were both amazed, and left her, scarce able to express their admiration for this wonderful work of God. It is worthy of observation that the diary of Father Ubaldo Antonio Cappelletti makes mention of a similar direction, which he had once given her, in obedience to which her wound had closed up on the 31st of July, in the year 1705.

Veronica's capacity for obeying the fourth order which the Father had imposed on her still remained to be tested. It had relation to the immediate subject of the present chapter, viz., her participation in all the sufferings of our Blessed Saviour. One morning, in the same month of November, our Saint presented herself at the confessional, and informed Father Crivelli that she had been instructed by the most holy Virgin to assure him that his fourth command should be obeyed on the evening of the 29th inst., being the Vigil of S. Andrew; that at the third hour of the night she would begin to experience the various sufferings of the divine Passion; that he was to be present; that the proper time for their continuance, including her participation in the seven Dolours of our Lady, would be twenty-four hours; but that, nevertheless, if he should command it, the whole would come to an end immediately. Father Crivelli replied to this with a doubtful air, and said that it remained to be seen what God would permit to take place. He went away to inform the bishop, and having obtained his sanction, returned to his college. Early on the following morning a messenger from the convent came to summon him in great haste, declaring that Veronica was dying. But he, knowing as he did beforehand what was about to occur, was in no hurry whatever, but began discoursing of the event with Father Giulio de'

Vecchj, the rector of the college. The summons being repeated, he set off for the convent, in company with the rector. Having entered Veronica's cell, he found her in her religious habit on her bed, with a coverlet underneath, and the usual woollen counterpane over her, in a state of extreme exhaustion and gasping for breath. He revived her by causing her to make acts of the theological virtues, and by sacramental confession. He then spoke to her about her state, and ascertained from her that from the third hour of the night until then she had been enduring our Lord's agony in the garden, His seizure, His bonds, besides all the blows and insults which He underwent in being led before the tribunals of Herod and Pilate. She had just got to that point in the divine Passion. Father Crivelli procured a light, and pointed out to his companion the deep marks which had been impressed on both her wrists, as though by cords; at which sight, we find it stated in the deposition, they both experienced those sensations of awe and compunction which are generally produced by supernatural and divine operations. The Father then asked her what mystery was to follow? She replied that the scourging was the next. He encouraged her to bear it generously; after which he repeated the sacramental absolution, and desired her under obedience to submit to the cruel torment which was before her, on the understanding that it should cease the moment he should signify his will to that effect.

This command having been given, it was put into immediate execution. We cannot do better than refer to the account which was given by the witnesses of the scene. They deposed as follows: "We saw her on her bed shaken and agitated to such a degree that it was both fearful and wonderful to behold. Most violent were the movements by which her body was impelled, first one way and then another; her head sometimes striking the wall with such force that the very planks of the bed were driven from their places, and the walls of the cell or infirmary were visibly shaken, as though by an earthquake. The noise was so great that the nuns who were about the house ran to the spot, in a fright lest the convent should be falling down. I was obliged to order them to withdraw, for fear they should become still more alarmed. Father de Vecchj himself was so excited, partly through the compassion he felt for Sister Veronica, who was enduring such unheard-of torments, and partly through the fear which he could not but feel at a scene which was at once so terrible and amazing, that he could bear it no longer; he was obliged to leave the cell, and return to our college, without saying a word. I permitted her to continue in this suffering for a good hour, if I remember right, and then I gave her an obedience that the torment should cease by pronouncing the words, 'Enough, let it stop;' and, wonderful to behold, she who had previously appeared rapt from all objects of sense, and absorbed in the contemplation of the mystery which she was passing through, and devoid of all strength, returned to herself in a moment, all traces of suffering were over, and she was left in a state of perfect tranquillity."

It appears from the same account that this occurred between the sixteenth and seventeenth hours (Italian time). Father Crivelli being anxious to say Mass, and, relying on the obedience of Veronica, directed her to rise from her bed, to repair to the choir without any assistance, and hear Mass on her knees. She executed this order with alacrity.

When the holy Sacrifice was over, he desired her to return to her bed, and then in presence of the Abbess, Sister Maria Tommasini, and some other religious, he put her under obedience to proceed with the mystery next in succession to that which he had already witnessed; and he declares that he saw on her head the visible impression of the crown of thorns. She next seemed to endure the weight of the cross in carrying it up to Calvary. Those present inferred this from the nature of the extreme suffering which she endured. "I plainly saw," continued Father Crivelli, "that the mystery of the crucifixion succeeded in all its agony. It was as clearly depicted as anything could be, short of a literal crucifixion on a material cross. As soon as I had given the word of command, her frame became extended, and her arms expanded in the form of a cross. The nerves of her hands were drawn, and her arms strained exactly as if nailed on a real cross. Her feet also were affected in a similar manner. Her head was bowed down, and her breast heaved, as though she were passing through her death-struggle. The extreme suffering which she endured was evinced by the cold perspiration which rose on her brow, by the tears which rolled down her cheeks, and by all the other external symptoms which attend the last agony of the dying. When she had remained in this condition for about half an hour, I saw that she was on the point of expiring, so taking courage from the success which had followed my previous injunctions, I commanded her by virtue of holy obedience to let all her torments cease. I was obeyed, and no trace remained of what she had undergone, save the debility of exhausted nature."

Father Crivelli goes on to state that he recruited her spirits by causing her to make acts of the theological virtues and by getting her to repeat the usual protestations against all the works of the devil. After this, he made her recite in his presence the divine office for the day, with Sister Florida Ceoli. Then calling to mind that the Blessed Virgin had intimated that Veronica was on the same day to experience her Dolours, he put her under obedience to endure them, telling her that he wished to observe the motions of her heart. "And in fact," he continues, "she experienced within her heart each one of the seven Dolours in so sensible a manner that I heard every palpitation as distinctly as the strokes of a clock. I knew it to be so, because I observed the spot from whence it proceeded, and perceived the agitation which it occasioned in her bosom."

A short time after he gave her an obedience that this also should stop. It did so in a moment, and she was herself again. About midnight, he caused her to take her supper in his presence, and having blessed it, he looked on while she ate it, without the least feeling of that nausea which almost always affected her at her meals. Filled with amazement at all the wonders which he had witnessed, Father Crivelli then returned to his college.

Thus passed S. Andrew's Feast. On the next day, the good Father went to acquaint the bishop with all that had happened, and to request that his lordship would do him the favour to accompany him some day to the convent, in order that he might be a spectator and witness of the execution of his fifth and last precept, viz., that she should go through the scene of crucifixion in an upright attitude. They agreed to fix on a certain day in December. When it came round, they repaired to the convent in the afternoon.

Having caused the doors of the church and of the choir to be closed, Father Crivelli commanded Veronica, who was at the communion window, by virtue of holy obedience to be crucified upright in a manner visible to the bishop and himself. For a brief interval she was rapt in prayer, contemplating the mystery in question. "All at once," says Father Crivelli, "she sprang to her feet with her arms extended with violence in the form of a cross. Her whole person was powerfully outstretched just as would be the case on a real cross; and her whole body was so moved that the choir and its benches were shaken, and the religious heard the noise. It sounded as if her bones were being put out of joint, and the convulsive movement of the nerves in her arms was so apparent that they produced in our minds both wonder and fear. As I was desirous of testing the case to the utmost, and perceived that in the midst of this fearful agitation, she occasionally gave rapid starts from the ground, I said to her from time to time, 'Rise higher—higher!' She did so, her whole frame being elevated into the air, so that her feet, for the moment, did not touch the ground. Soon after, she fell suddenly from her upright position flat upon the pavement of the choir; she remained there for a little while in the same attitude of crucifixion, and then resumed in an instant her previous upright position. When this torment had lasted for about half an hour, both his lordship and myself were of opinion that it had better come to an end, so I gave her an obedience that it should cease: it stopped immediately, and we saw her in a moment on her knees before the grate, in a recollected and humble posture."

The Father then asked her what was the meaning of

her unexpected fall on the floor in her crucified state, to which she replied, that it was owing to "the turning over of the cross; for that the Jews having nailed the hands and the feet of our Lord Jesus Christ, turned the cross over, in order that they might clinch the nails on the other side."

"After all this which I have deposed above," concludes Father Crivelli, "Sister Veronica was dismissed by the bishop; and we both left the church overwhelmed with amazement and admiration at the wonders we had seen." And certainly there is nothing more marvellous to be met with in the life of S. Mary Magdalen of Pazzi, or in those of S. Catherine of Ricci, S. Teresa, S. Catherine of Siena, or any other saint of the highest order.

But there was one peculiar feature in Veronica's case which we do not find in the biographies of other saints. We allude to the numerous and extraordinary signs which were engraven on her heart. We say numerous, because a few things of the kind were discovered in the heart of the Blessed Clare of Monte Falco and the Blessed Margaret of Città di Castello. In Veronica's there were no fewer than twenty-four, viz.—a Latin cross with a C marked at the top of the upright beam: in the centre of the transverse beam was an F: at the right-hand extremity of the same was a V, and at the left an O. Above the cross, on one side, was a crown of thorns; to the left of this was a banner on a staff lying transversely over the cross, and divided into two parts terminating in points—on the upper one was imprinted the letter I, and on the lower one the italic *m*. Near the top of the banner was a flame, and underneath, a hammer, a pair of pincers, a spear, and a reed with a sponge at the top. To the right of the cross, beginning from above, was a representation of the seamless vesture of our Lord Jesus Christ, another flame, a chalice, two wounds, a little pillar, three nails, a scourge, and seven swords, besides three letters in different places, namely, two P's and a V.

All these signs, excepting the chalice, are described in the process of information by Father Raniero Guelfi, which contains an account of the examination to which he was subjected on the 26th of September, 1727, about ten weeks after Veronica's death. On the Holy Saturday of the same year, our Saint had mentioned to him under obedience as her confessor, that during Passiontide the representation of two flames had been imprinted on her heart, as also a banner marked with the initials of the most holy names of Jesus and Mary. The father ascertained from her in the course of conversation that there were also other signs engraven on her heart. So he wisely conceived that it would be well to get from herself an authentic document, the accuracy of which he would be able to test after her death, and he commanded her to draw a picture of her heart, just as she had described it to him. Veronica obeyed, but as she did not know how to draw, she got Sisters Florida Ceoli and Mary Magdalen Boscaini to assist her. However, she did not tell them that she had any serious object in so doing, but treated the matter as though it were a mere joke or fancy. She designed it on a piece of red paper cut out in the shape of a heart; attaching to it the figures in question, which were cut out of white paper, with the exception of the two flames and the upper division of the banner; these she made of a deeper coloured red: she then traced the nine letters with a pen and ink, and drew lines which connected all the instruments together. She had completed her work by the Feast of Pentecost, and placed it in the hands of Father Guelfi, three days previously to her being seized by the apoplectic stroke of which we shall speak in the next chapter. During her illness he consigned it to the keeping of the bishop, having marked it with his own seal and signature, which he recognized in his examination during the informative as well as the apostolic process.

The same Father, moreover, adds, and his evidence is confirmed by that of various competent witnesses, that the mysterious instruments of which we have spoken were in the occasional habit of moving and emitting sounds, more or less audible, according as our Saint exercised the corresponding virtues, or was ordered under obedience. These facts were more thoroughly authenticated after her death. A formal examination was instituted according to directions received from the Bishop Codebò, by the medical professors, Giovan Francesco Gentili, surgeon, and Gian Francesco Bordiga, physician, in the presence of Monsignor Torrigiani, then Governor, afterwards Cardinal of holy Church, as also of the Chancellor Fabbri, the Priors Don Francesco Maria Pesucci and Don Giacomo Cellini, Don Giovanni Falconi, Don Cesare Giannini, Father Guelfi, the artist, Luc'Antonio Angelucci, and several nuns. They discovered, in the right-hand division of her heart, a well-defined cross, at the upper end of which was the letter C. Besides this, they found a little crown of thorns, two flames, seven marks, meeting at the points in the shape of a fan, to indicate the seven swords; the letters V and P, a lance and reed crossing each other, a banner attached to a spear, divided into two parts, on which were the letters I and *m,* and a nail with its head sharpened into a point, as we generally see the nails of the holy cross represented. The remainder of the signs already described were not discovered, because the bishop did not choose to have the investigation carried further, for fear of spoiling the heart; for our Saint had been now dead thirty-four hours, and his lordship was also unwilling to occasion inconvenience to the bystanders, particularly to the nuns, who were already too much affected by the sight before them, and by the grief which they felt at the loss of so holy a companion and superioress. They had all seen enough to convince them of the accuracy of the rest, and the function was accordingly closed. From what they had already seen and juridically tested, that print was engraved which got into general circulation.

Before we bring this chapter to a close it may not be unacceptable to the reader to be made acquainted with the signification of those mysterious signs and letters. We have the authority of Father Guelfi for what we are going to state; he heard it from the lips of Veronica, and brought it forward in his deposition. The two letters on the banner, viz., the I and the *m,* stand for Jesus and Mary, the C for charity, the F for faith and fidelity to God, the O for obedience, the two V's* for humility and the Will of God, the two P's for patience and suffering. The two flames represent the love of God and of our neighbour; the banner is the symbol of the victories which our Saint had gained during the course of her life, and the seven swords mark her participation in the Dolours of Mary. The remainder were the instruments of the most bitter Passion of our Lord Jesus Christ.

* In the original Italian these letters are the initials of the virtues for which they stand.

CHAPTER X.

THE EXTRAORDINARY GRACES AND FAVOURS WHICH ACCOMPANIED HER LAST ILLNESS AND HOLY DEATH.

THE crowning with thorns, the imprinting of the stigmata, and the painful impressions made on the heart of our Saint were several times renewed during the last thirty years of her life, as we have already mentioned. The frequent, one might almost say the perpetual, excesses of her love of God, besides the overwhelming sufferings which it pleased our Lord to bestow on her, together with the severe penances which she voluntarily imposed upon herself, had the inevitable effect of undermining her health, and eventually causing her death. Her companions relate in various parts of the process the frequent and severe maladies to which she was subject from time to time, and for which, generally speaking, no remedy could be discovered by her medical attendants, but of which she was invariably cured in some unexpected and miraculous way; so that it was commonly said in the convent that Veronica only lived by miracle. Father Ubaldo Antonio Cappelletti was the only person who took down in his diary an account of these illnesses and recoveries. He did so for his own instruction, from the year 1702 until 1707. His narrative was inserted in the process; it makes mention of no fewer than thirteen of these occasions on which she was reduced to extremity, and he had to assist her in his capacity of confessor to the establishment.

While these diseases lasted, Veronica would flatter herself that now at length she was about to be delivered from the burden of mortality, in order that she might take her flight and be united to her Immortal Good. She frequently received in her heart loving invitations from her divine Lord, and seemed to be on the point of possessing Him; but again, when she least expected it, the prospect would recede from her view. At last the time came when she was assured that the boon was granted, and her anticipation was both clear and unmistakable. As early as the year 1694 she had been informed from above, as she hinted to her confessor, that she had still thirty-three years to live. The event proved that this number signified the years which were to elapse until her death. Perhaps it was also an intimation of the thirty-three days which were to be the duration of her last illness. She was satisfied of this herself, and predicted that it would be so. She also declared that she would have to endure a threefold purgatory from creatures, from obedience, and from the devil, and so it came to pass. In the year before her death she appointed, by her authority as abbess, Sister Mary Magdalen Boscaini to be sacristan of the inner chapel of the most holy rosary. When Veronica committed this charge into her hands, she said to her expressly, "This is the last time that I shall dispense these offices." Upon which Sister Agnes inquired, "Are you going to die so soon, then, mother abbess?" She gave an approving smile, and it turned out as she had said. At several of the chapters which took place during the last year of her life, when Sister Gabriella Brozzi was kneeling before her to confess her faults according to custom, it was observed that the saintly abbess addressed to her alone the following words in addition to other good counsel:—"Sister Gabriella, let us prepare ourselves;

we have not much longer to live." In fact the following July, as we shall presently see, Veronica died, and Sister Gabriella followed her two or three months later. But Veronica spoke still more plainly to the above-named sister, Mary Magdalen Boscaini, on the eve of her fatal illness. That religious, having come to her by order of her confessor to mention some spiritual trial which afflicted her, remarked that she would await her abbess' leisure; but Veronica very soon after came to her cell and said, "We had better perform the obedience this evening, for who knows whether we shall ever have another opportunity?"

The following morning being the 6th of June, 1727, within the octave of Pentecost and a Communion day, the holy abbess, who well knew what was about to happen, manifested unusual anxiety that the sacred function should proceed with the least possible delay. She had left the confessional, her countenance glowing even with more than its wonted sanctity, and perceiving the sacristan, Sister Mary Joanna Maggio, who deposed to the fact in the process, she bade her make haste with the taper which she was in the habit of using to light the four candles which burned within the communion window. It was eleven o'clock, Italian time; and Veronica no sooner received the holy Eucharist than she was struck with apoplexy, which rendered her left side utterly powerless, but neither deprived her of consciousness nor of speech. The nuns ran promptly to assist her, and placed her on a stool made of walnut-wood, which is still preserved. She raised her eyes to heaven in rapture, and the sacristan tells us that her countenance was joyful as she said to those around, "I go, I go," thus informing them that the stroke would be a fatal one.

As they could not bring her to herself by any of the usual remedies, they put her in a chair and conveyed her to the infirmary. Not to prolong her suffering, they lodged her in the first room, although it was dark and resembled a prison. She had already spent much time there, as we shall see in the next book. Notice was immediately sent to her confessor, Father Raniero Guelfi, at that time an Oratorian, and afterwards archpriest of the illustrious college of S. Eustachio at Rome, also to the bishop, Mgr. Alexander Codebò, the physician Bordiga, and the surgeon Gentili. As soon as our Saint beheld her confessor, the first thing she asked him was to give her the holy Viaticum, although she had so lately communicated, but this he thought it necessary to refuse. Presently the bishop arrived, and the moment she saw him she began to declare with the greatest humility that she was the most unworthy inmate of the monastery, that during the fifty years of her religious career she had failed to correspond with the grace of God, and had not succeeded in acquiring a single virtue; she requested his pardon and that of all the religious who were present, for the scandals she had given them, and implored them not to imitate her, for she had been a great sinner. She then requested his lordship to give her the blessing *in articulo mortis*, and to grant her permission to receive holy Communion daily during the remaining portion of her life. The bishop granted the second favour she had asked; the first he postponed for a more suitable occasion.

Her malady increased, and was aggravated by the addition of a violent fever, acute pains in her head and teeth, calculus, nervous and spasmodic affections in all her joints, and such nausea, that she was unable to retain any description either of food or medicine; so that throughout this terrible illness she could only swallow a few drops, and that with the utmost difficulty. On the third day the physician had her conveyed with care into the third cell of the infirmary, where she lingered for thirty days more, and then expired. It may be conceived that everything was done which human care or skill could suggest to save so precious a life. The nuns, the bishop, and the whole city, did all they could, particularly the medical men, so high was the estimation in which they held her. The latter tried bleeding, applied hot irons to the nape of her neck, and administered their most costly drugs. All this constituted the first description of purgatory which she had to encounter, viz., that which was to come from the hands of her fellow-creatures. The remedies which were resorted to served only to increase her sufferings. The same may be said of the attentions which were paid her by the religious. Although she never complained, it was clear from her convulsive movements that every posture was painful to her. They sought to relieve her by changing her position, but although they did this with the utmost caution, it only made her worse. Once she declared that her sufferings were like those of hell. She particularly felt the absence of her former spiritual director, the Servite Father Tassinari. It was the Will of God that during the whole time of her illness he too should be incapacitated by sickness. It was the only thing for which Veronica showed any regret, but she resigned herself to the providence of God.

The second purgatory, that of obedience, tried her still more. She ardently desired to unite herself to her Beloved without delay, but she would not do so without the permission of her confessor; she therefore repeatedly asked him to give her leave to die. He always refused until the very last, as we shall hereafter see. She was so much afflicted at these denials that on one occasion she turned to the bystanders and exclaimed, "How strange to feel oneself dying, and yet to be unable to die!" Her maladies had weakened her to such a degree that although she did not hesitate to take whatever was offered her, she was unable to swallow either food or medicine. This cost her several reproofs, both from the nuns and her confessor, on the score of disobedience; which was peculiarly mortifying to her, since there was no virtue of which she had shown herself more jealous, both in theory and practice, throughout the course of her life, than that of holy obedience. Father Vincent Segapeli, an Oratorian, was invited by Father Guelfi to assist him in the care of Veronica. One night, when the bell rang for matins, he turned to our Saint, reduced as she was, and deprived of the use of one side, and said to her, "Sister Veronica, do you not hear the bell ringing for matins? will you not go?" This was enough to cause her to make a strenuous effort to rise; but the father was struck with admiration at her heroic obedience, and commanded her not to stir. A still greater proof of humility and obedience came under his observation. Perceiving that her hands were covered with certain little bandages, which her superiors had permitted her to wear for the purpose of hiding the stigmata, he inquired contemptuously, "What is the meaning of these bandages? This is sheer hypocrisy." In a moment she presented him her right hand, for she could not move the other, and cheerfully replied: "I am ready to do as you please; obedience gave me them, and obedience shall take them away." But it cost her humility a severe pang to be obliged to display those marks of honour. This was all deposed in the process by Sister Mary Joanna Maggio, who was highly edified, as was every one else who happened to be in the cell.

The third kind of purgatory was to come from the demons. Several times they attempted to terrify her, by appearing under the form of brutal negroes; or they would assume the shapes of asses, and bray in her ear, in order to increase the pain in her head; or one of them would take the appearance of her physician, and predict the most revolting kind of diseases, for the purpose of subduing her indomitable patience. But the worst of all was their transformation on one of her last days. She was quite alone, and beheld the bishop entering her cell; he declared to her in a threatening manner that she was at last discovered, and that her whole life had been one tissue of malicious hypocrisy, and diabolical illusions; he added that in the afternoon he would return with the officers of his court, in order that in their presence, and in that of all the nuns, she might acknowledge and abjure her treachery. This was taken down from her own lips by Sister Mary Magdalen Boscaini, Sister Mary Celestine Tosi, and Sister Mary Celestine Meazzoli, who deposed accordingly in the process. They had been lingering about the infirmary for some reason, when their holy abbess called to them and said, "My daughters, recommend me from your hearts to God, pray for me." They asked her what had happened. She replied, "The bishop has been to me, and has told me that he knows my whole life to have been spent in hypocrisy, and in deceiving either myself or others; he says that he will come again in the course of the day, in company with others, in order that I may abjure my hypocrisy in their presence, and before the whole community. If they say so, they must have been enlightened as to the true state of the case, and I am ready to obey." Such was her humble distrust of herself, united with heroic obedience. The three nuns were astonished at what they heard, and assured her that the bishop had not been to the convent that morning. "What do you mean?" asked Veronica. "I believe his lordship is just going downstairs, and what you say is only to spare me pain." The fact was that the bishop had really not been seen that morning; and thus they discovered that it was merely an illusion of the devil, invented for the purpose of driving our suffering Saint to despair. Probably the lapse of memory which occurred to her often at this period in her frequent confessions, was another device of Satan, unless we look upon it as a trial permitted by God. During her self-examination she would prepare what she meant to say to her confessor, but when she was on the point of accusing herself, she had forgotten it all. For this reason she was often reproved by her confessor, who charged her with negligence in order to try her. This got to be known in the monastery; and Sister Florida Ceoli, her assistant, asked her why she did not confess, to which she replied with the utmost humility, "Our Lord knows what pains I have taken in order to make my confessions, and how much I desire to do so. But when I attempt to accuse myself of my faults, I find that I have utterly forgotten everything." With still greater humility, she on more than one occasion asked her novices if they could remember anything that she ought to mention to her confessor. Out of compassion for her they suggested one or two things, just as one would do to a child when preparing it for its first confession. "God reward you," replied Veronica, "I will accuse myself as you advise."

These three kinds of purgatory, besides the other sufferings which we have described, constituted the first class of special graces conferred by God on His servant. We call them graces, although to a superficial observer they may not appear such. But let the reader bear in mind that the portion which our Lord Jesus Christ chose for Himself on earth, was an uninterrupted course of sufferings from the first to the last moment of His life. There was no favour which Veronica more desired, or more ardently implored of her Crucified Spouse on the day of her solemn nuptials, than *suffering, pure suffering*. However, this was not the only boon, precious though it might be, which God in His bounty bestowed upon her during her last illness. She derived the highest gratification from the repeated visits of the bishop. She always requested him to let her hold his pectoral cross in her hands, caressing and kissing it with the utmost affection; and, when she had been blessed with it, she would say that she felt quite comforted. But far greater was the consolation she derived from holy Communion, which she was permitted to receive every day, according to the promise which had been made her. On these occasions her whole heart beamed and glowed with love. The mere sight of a crucifix, which she was in the habit of calling the door-keeper of the heart, and which she always kept near her, had power to relieve her in the midst of the most excruciating pain. She gave a proof of this one day by calling some of the younger sisters to her, and saying, "Come here; love lets itself be found here. It is the cause of my suffering. Tell every one so." Then she asked them to sing a hymn on the Incarnation of the Divine Word, which touched her so much that she wept freely. Being asked the reason of her tears, she replied with all the energy of love, "Who would not weep at the thought of such love?" She was constantly making fervent acts of the theological virtues, of resignation to the divine Will, and of profound humility, which are the true refreshment of the soul. Her physician, who visited her several times a day, was extremely edified, as he expressed in the process. He was particularly struck by an answer she once gave him, when, seeing her more than usually tried, he encouraged her to make an act of conformity with the sufferings of Jesus. To this she replied with the greatest humility, "In order to obtain merit by suffering, it must be accompanied by virtues, of which I am utterly destitute. Still, I am quite willing to bear it all; I would fain suffer even more, if such were the Will of my Lord."

Thus passed thirty days of her illness, during which her danger had been several times so great that she had thrice received the holy Viaticum, and had been fortified on one occasion by the Sacrament of Extreme Unction, at her own earnest request. During the last three days of her life, she appeared to live in almost perpetual ecstasy; her eyes being for the most part closed and immovable. She did not say as much, but it was the general impression that during her ecstasy she frequently beheld Jesus, her divine Spouse, Mary, her powerful Advocate, and those saints to whom she had a particular devotion, especially S. Francis and S. Clare. At last it became evident that her departure was at hand, and for the fourth time she received the holy Viaticum. Before it was administered, although her voice was so feeble that she feared it would be impossible to make herself heard, she requested her father confessor to ask in her name the forgiveness of the religious who surrounded her, for the bad example she had given them, as well as for all the faults she had committed during the term of her superiorship. Sister Christina Eleosari was not present, for she was confined to her bed by illness; so Veronica asked that a message might be conveyed to her. After our Saint had occupied herself for a considerable time in holy affections to Jesus in the blessed Sacrament, she took great pains to impress upon her spiritual daughters the importance of exact fulfilment both of the laws of God and of the Church, as also of the rules and constitutions of the convent, and of the maintenance of peace and mutual charity among themselves. She gave them all her crucifix to kiss, and said, "Never lose sight of the infinite love which He has shown us."

On the morning of the 8th of July, which was her last day on earth, she received her fourth visit from the bishop, and obtained leave from his lordship to have the Sacrament of Extreme Unction repeated. She accompanied it with intense acts of faith, hope, and the most perfect charity. She then asked for his pastoral blessing, and for the papal benediction *in articulo mortis*, both of which he bestowed on her amid the tears of the bystanders. Her confessor then proceeded to give her the blessing of the order, that of the most holy rosary, and of the seven Dolours. She then remained perfectly tranquil, her right hand never relaxing its hold on the image of her crucified Lord, towards Whom she poured forth in silence her tenderest affections. About the middle of the night she entirely lost the power of speech, and her agony commenced. The confessor went through the usual recommendation of a departing soul, accompanied by the prayers of all the nuns, who never left Veronica during the whole of the night. Dying as she was, it was evident that she joined them as well as she could with her internal petitions, although she could not use her voice. Throughout her agony, which lasted for three hours, like that of our divine Redeemer, she did not give the least sign of agitation or alarm. As morning broke, her confessor, being informed that she had but a very short time to live, said to her, "Take courage, Sister Veronica, you are very near that which you have so ardently desired." At these words her joy was inexpressible, and she began to look fixedly at her confessor. He continued to recite the prayers which the Church has appointed for the dying, and suggested the usual pious acts, without thinking why it was that the dying Saint kept her eyes fixed upon him. At length God gave him light to remember that Veronica had often told him that she would not even wish to leave this world, until dismissed by holy obedience, which she now asked by her earnest gaze. Animated by a lively faith in God, he approached her and said: "Sister Veronica, since it is the Will of our Lord that you should now go to enjoy Him, and since it is the pleasure of His divine Majesty that you should not pass away from us without the order of His minister, I give it you." Veronica immediately dropped her eyes in token of submission; then she looked round on her daughters to take a last leave and blessing, after which she bowed her head like her crucified Spouse, gave her last sigh, and her blessed soul winged its flight to the bosom of her Beloved. This took place about seven o'clock in the morning on Friday, always to her a day replete with heavenly favours, the 9th of July, 1727. She was in the sixty-seventh year of her age, and had spent fifty years in religion, and eleven in the office of abbess.

We shall not attempt to describe here the commotion which ensued, not only in the convent, but in the city at large; nor the honours of her funeral, for we shall reserve such details for the following book. We must not, however, omit some description of her person, as it will be acceptable to those devout to her. Her external appearance gave indications of the heavenly gifts which enriched her soul. Veronica was of middle height and fair complexion; her face oval and beautiful, though she had a slight mark to the right of her under lip; her eyes were bright, and their expression habitually cheerful. Although she practised such severe mortifications as those we are about to describe in the next book, she was not emaciated, a grace which she perhaps obtained from our Lord, in order that her fasts and penances might be concealed. Her manners were courteous and obliging, and qualified with great modesty and religious reserve; so that we may apply to her the eulogium which S. Ennodius gives in his life of S. Epiphanius, Bishop of Ticino: "Modesty, which is the mother of good works, shone conspicuous in him. The grace of his person was an index to his soul. The sweetness of his beaming smile harmonized with the melody of his discourse. The calm splendour of his eye reflected the peace of his soul. His marble brow might have borrowed its whiteness from the very source of light. His countenance was a beautiful mirror of his life." In like manner, there bloomed in Veronica, as the spring in the fields, that modesty which is the mother of good works. Her outward loveliness was an image of her inward beauty. Her radiant smiles added charms to her words; while the lustre of her eye indicated the serenity of her spirit. Her forehead was fair as ivory, and her appearance was altogether an emblem of her life.

BOOK III.

OF HER HEROIC VIRTUES, AND OF THE GIFTS WHICH SHE POSSESSED IN COMMON WITH OTHER SAINTS.

CHAPTER I.

JESUS CHRIST HIMSELF BECOMES HER VISIBLE INSTRUCTOR IN CHRISTIAN AND PERFECT LIFE. HER CONSTANT DESIRE OF GREATER PERFECTION.

WE have already witnessed such numerous instances of the heroic virtue of Veronica, that to some persons it may appear superfluous to devote a separate treatise to the same subject. But so many of her actions are illustrious on account of their exceeding sanctity, that we should fail in one of the principal duties of a biographer, if we were to omit to recommend them to the imitation of our readers. We are obliged, as it is, to make a selection, for if we were to mention all, we should swell this volume to an unreasonable size. We shall, therefore, confine ourselves to the most remarkable facts.

But before entering on this narrative, it is well to remember the source from whence she derived such supernatural grace. Jesus Christ, Who is Incarnate Wisdom, was pleased to constitute Himself her Master and Guide; and thus from her earliest years she had been instructed in this heavenly science by Him Who is at once the Author and Model of all that is most holy. Veronica was not more than three years old when she was permitted to behold our Lord, as we have already seen in the second chapter of the first book. She was then taught that she must belong entirely to

Jesus, that her heart must be changed, that she must practise certain rules of life, and aim at retirement, mortification of the senses, silence, obedience, and the avoidance of all curiosity. Then again in her sixth year she saw the Divine Infant, and was reproached by Him because she had sometimes diverted herself with juvenile sports, in company with other children. When she had attained the age of nine years, He excited within her an ardent longing for holy Communion, and infused into her soul special lights, in order that she might make a good preparation, and an exact confession of her past life. He also kindled within her heart a holy fervour the first time that she was permitted to receive the holy Eucharist, which was on the 2nd of February, 1670. These three circumstances are found in the diary of Father Cappelletti, which we have often had occasion to quote. Veronica herself confided them to him on the 19th of December, 1702, when she related to him the vision she had had on the 2nd, in which our Lord had shown her her heart under the figure of iron, and had reproved her for want of correspondence to His grace, and reminded her of the rare favours which had been vouchsafed her as a child. The reader will recollect this vision in the third chapter of the first book.

But still more distinct and elaborate were the instructions she received from our Saviour during the night which followed Easter day in 1697, after the solemnity at which her mystic nuptials had been renewed, and when He gave her a precious ring with three gems. During that night He appeared to her, and said, "Wilt thou do whatever I shall command thee?" To which she replied, "Yes, my God, I will do all with Thy grace." At the same time she received an intimate knowledge of her own nothingness, and deep sorrow for her sins (sure signs of the truth of her heavenly vision), and our Lord, after bestowing His blessing, continued as follows : " I am about to give thee rules for thy conduct. 1. I wish thee to be faithful, to be diligent, and to co-operate with all that I, thy Spouse, work in thee. During this life thou must be like a corpse, unconscious of self, and leaving the care of all to Me. 2. I wish from thee a strict obedience to thy confessor and superiors, and that thou regard thyself as a novice who has only just come into religion. Such is My Will, and I confirm thee now as My spouse. Let thy obedience be blind, particularly as regards thy confessor, conferring with him clearly and definitely. 3. Make it a rule in all thy works to have an upright and pure intention of promoting only My glory. In everything let thy object be the accomplishment of My Will, which thou shalt ascertain from the lips of My representative. 4. I command thee to observe a rigorous silence : never speaking save on religious subjects, when charity requires it, or when it is expedient for thine own good or that of others. 5. By means of mortification and contempt thou mayest advance along the path of humility. Let all these things guide thee in thy works, that thou mayest never lose sight of thine own nothingness. 6. I wish thee to go barefoot, and to ask leave for this of thy confessor in My Name. 7. I enjoin thee to write a full account of all this for thy confessor, and to describe all the operations which I work in thee, simply, sincerely, and accurately, in order that My great love for thee may be seen and known. Maintain thyself in peace, for it shall all conduce to the benefit of thy soul, and to My honour and glory.* 8. Never give an opinion or counsel to any one, until thou hast first asked My direction in prayer. 9. Be sure, O My spouse! to have always firm confidence in Me, and distrust of thyself. I wish thee to walk between fear and love, so that fear may preserve thee in knowledge of self, and love draw thee to close union with Me. 10. I have chosen thee to act as mediatrix between sinners and Myself: I confirm thee now in that office, not merely by inspiration, but by word of mouth. Let it be thy business to save souls; for their salvation and My glory thou must be ready to sacrifice thy life and thy blood. 11. For the future thou shall keep thyself in the exercise of My divine presence; and in whatsoever condition thou mayest be, fasten thyself to the simple and naked cross, and bind thyself to it by My Will. 12. I wish thee to be entirely transformed into Myself. I make over to thee My Passion, My merits, and all the sufferings of the thirty-three years of My Life, that thou mayest work with Me and suffer with Me. In all things conform thyself to My Will; divest thyself of all besides, so that thou mayest truly say—'I AM CRUCIFIED WITH CHRIST.'"

These divine rules for attaining to sublime perfection, are transcribed word for word from Veronica's written documents of the year 1697. They would have sufficed for ever, but so great was the care with which our Lord regarded the spiritual profit of His well-beloved disciple and spouse, that He did not fail to renew the remembrance of His instructions, in whole or in part, by means of almost daily visions, as may be seen by any one who chooses to consult her volu-

* This was said because she was always afraid of pride and vainglory, when writing about her own gifts.

minous writings. A very remarkable instance of such a repetition occurred in the year 1700, on the 5th of April, when our Lord appeared to her for the purpose of removing the scars of the stigmata. She writes as follows concerning that occasion: "Our Lord wishes that I should lay myself out for the good of my neighbours, and that I should have neither human respect nor self-love; and that I should go, either by night or day, to give counsel to whosoever may need it at my hands; for He assures me that He intends to speak through me for the advantage of others. Our Lord has also convinced me how negligent I have hitherto been in this respect; and how, through this, other souls have lost the fervour of divine love. At the same time He made me aware that He desires me to be entirely denuded of self, without reflection upon myself. It is His Will that I should be prepared for everything, and that I should mention whatever occurs to my confessor. Again He said to me, 'Be faithful; be faithful.' To which I seemed to reply, 'Grant me some particular direction as to this.' 'Be faithful in everything,' He said. 'But be specially careful,' He added, 'to cherish zeal for My honour, to accomplish My Will, to sever thy soul from self, to practise prompt obedience, to be contented in the midst of pains and labours, to delight in being treated contemptuously, to be charitably vigilant on behalf of others, to attract all to My holy service, to be exact in religious observance, and to live like one dead, never allowing thyself the smallest gratification. Thou must also exercise thyself strenuously in humility and obedience.'"

Again, on the 4th of December, 1707, Father Cappelletti tells us in his diary, that he heard from her own lips, that after she had received holy Communion, our Lord appeared to her, and gave her a fresh rule of life, which contained an abstract of the former, with the addition that in the morning of the day she was to meditate on His most sacred Passion, beginning with the prayer in the garden, and continuing until evening with all the other sorrowful mysteries; and then beginning again as at first. Her attention was thus to be fixed hour by hour, or rather moment by moment; and she was to relate to her confessor all the details of God's work in her soul—an indubitable sign, like all the rest, of the reality of these heavenly graces.

The devil took occasion, from these frequent lessons given by our Lord Jesus under a visible form, to deceive Veronica by assuming a similar one, but she was too great an adept in the science of her divine Master to be seduced by his artifices. She mentions several of these occurrences under the date of the year 1700. Once he took upon him the appearance of our Lord, and presented himself before her with his countenance all resplendent, showing her a large book, and informing her that it contained a summary of perfection. But she perceived his artifice in a moment, and nobly replied, "Infernal monster, I have no need of thy books; I want no other book but the crucifix, and the Will of God. Of myself I can do nothing; I am full of imperfections." Such unfeigned humility put Satan to instant flight, leaving behind him an offensive odour in her cell. Another time he assumed the same glorified aspect, and said to her, "Stand firm, and doubt not; I am come to console thee, and to teach thee how thou must conduct thyself." Whereupon the faithful disciple of Jesus smiled, and then, in a tone of grave contempt, inquired, "Deceiver, who art thou ? Thou art the devil, art thou not ?" So the traitor departed; but, as he did not despair of ultimate success, he presented himself again under the same form, and with a cheerful countenance said, "I am for thee; do not doubt." To which she replied, "Mind your own business. I do not care for you; I hope in the mercy of God. I desire Him, and trust in Him;" saying which she spat in his face. The proud demon was immediately put to flight, but presently returned, and said, "I do not wish thee to practise such severities as thou dost. Human nature should be kept in subjection just so far as that it may serve the spirit" (an excellent aphorism, but misapplied). "I give thee, as regards conferences, a rule not to trouble thyself about any more. What thou hast done already is enough for me." But the prudent virgin ridiculed these suggestions, and replied accordingly; "I do not need thy lessons. Mind thyself. I desire to do the Will of God, and His representative must know all. I shall continue to do this in spite of you." This was enough to banish at once the father of disobedience.

It is, however, time to quit this not unprofitable digression. The celebrated adage of S. Ambrose, in his book concerning virgins, strikes us as appropriate here—"The first desire of learning springs from the nobility of the master." It is not, therefore, surprising that Veronica, who had been favoured with the personal instruction of our Lord Jesus Christ, should exhibit so much ardour in aspiring to the sublimer degrees of that perfection of which He is the Master. And, in fact, if we could only look through all her precious writings, which are so voluminous as to fill a large box, we should find that in all the visions which she describes, in the midst of the most signal favours which she received from God, she never manifested the least desire for these extraordinary privileges; and on the innumerable occasions on which she spoke familiarly with God, she never asked for anything but contrition for her sins, knowledge of her own nothingness, conformity to the divine Will, the conversion of sinners, crosses and pure suffering, and the grace of divine love. It appears that these desires were, in a certain sense, by special privilege, innate in her, as is clear from considering the history of her earliest years; and that, like the passions of other children, they grew with her growth, and strengthened with her strength. We have already seen that they were not mere empty hankerings and desires; and this will be still more manifested by what follows.

CHAPTER II.

VERONICA'S HEROIC PERFECTION IN THE THEOLOGICAL VIRTUES.

LET not the reader be surprised at our devoting only one chapter to a subject which comprehends the basis, not only of the Christian life, but also of the most sublime holiness, viz., faith, hope, and love of God. We have not taken this course from any lack of heroic actions on the part of Veronica, but because it would be superfluous to go over again minutely the ground we have already trodden in our first and second books, especially since we have seen the sacred familiarity which existed between her saintly soul and God during more than sixty years, her almost daily visions, and the wondrous mystery of those espousals to which she was so graciously raised by our Lord Jesus Christ. It is obvious that the most lively faith, the firmest hope, and the most ardent charity must have reigned in such a soul. Nevertheless, in order to accommodate ourselves in some degree to the ordinary style of biographers, we will not omit some distinct mention of these; but a selection must be made, both for the sake of brevity, and the reasons given above.

To begin with faith: as God was constantly before the eyes of Veronica, she regulated all her actions by the maxim, *God sees me*. This is attested in the process by her former director, Father Segapeli. So habitual with her was this exercise of the presence of God, that her days passed without her perceiving it. She admits as much in her journal, under date of the 3rd of April, 1697; adding, "On several occasions the Lord was at my side, in the literal sense of the words. I was aware of it, and was thus enabled to perform in a short space of time, what, under ordinary circumstances, would have required whole days." Thus we see how, in her case, a life of extreme activity could be combined with an almost perpetual contemplation. She was in the constant habit, when abbess, of conversing with her novices and the whole community upon the mysteries of the Faith, though never in a controversial manner, for she could not bear people to ask the why and the how of every mystery. If any one attempted to do so, she would reprove them, and tell them that our province is to believe and not to investigate. This is an excellent rule, particularly for the unlearned. Veronica, although a person of moderate natural endowments, and very little education, as Father Guelfi and others testify, could yet speak so learnedly on the subject of divine mysteries and perfections, that the most profound theologian could not have excelled her. Hence it was a common opinion among the nuns that on several occasions when she held chapters as their abbess, it was the Mother of God herself who addressed them through the mouth of Veronica; which opinion was confirmed by her own declaration that not she herself, but the Blessed Virgin, was the abbess of the convent.

She burned with the most intense desire to see the holy faith propagated throughout the world; and if she had been permitted, she would fain have compassed the globe, in order to evangelize idolatrous lands, and seal her testimony with her own blood. The following is a striking instance of the spirit which animated her. When Father Crivelli was confessor extraordinary to the community, Veronica one day requested him to preach them a sermon, in which he was to invite all idolaters, Turks, heretics, and schismatics, to come and embrace the truth. The good father smilingly inquired, "Of what use can the invitation be, when those to whom it is addressed are unable to hear it?" But she pressed him so earnestly, that at last he complied, and delivered a sermon at the grate, such as he would have preached to the most barbarous tribes of India. Veronica literally danced for joy, and could not sufficiently express her gratitude to the father. It seemed to her as if she were herself preaching in the midst of the savages, and reaping a rich harvest in the conversion of many souls.

In order to satisfy in some degree her desire for martyrdom, on the night of S. Laurence's feast, and frequently at other times, she would impose on herself various fearful sufferings, for the purpose of imitating that saint and martyr. She made for herself a species of hurdle of thorns, on which she lay without any protection for the space of three Misereres recited slowly. After this she would squeeze herself under a basket, and remain thus painfully imprisoned until the day was far advanced. Then she would give herself six hundred and sixty-six blows with a scourge made of thorns, and end by holding her tongue for a great length of time under a heavy stone, praying the holy martyr to obtain from God the conversion of the whole world. Even when she was a novice, she had such earnest longings after martyrdom, that while she was conversing one day with the mistress of the novices upon the subject, she was seized with such a violent palpitation of the heart, that it seemed as though it were breaking. The novice-mistress heard three loud cracks, so that she feared our Saint was about to die on the spot, and wished to take her to the infirmary; but Veronica, who knew the real state of the case, assured her that nothing serious was the matter. It was on this occasion, perhaps, that the letter F, signifying Faith, was imprinted for the first time on her heart. We pass over such particulars as are common to other saints; for instance, the supreme veneration which she entertained for all sacred persons and things, her pious attention to every act of religion, her special devotion to the Blessed Virgin, to her guardian angel and patron saints, and the peculiar interest which she felt in celebrating the greater solemnities of the Church; and proceed to the consideration of the next theological virtue.

Let it not be thought that the exercise of hope necessarily precludes all fear as to one's eternal salvation, for the Philippians are exhorted by the apostle to work out their salvation with fear and trembling. In fact, the theological virtue of hope, whose object is God, takes its rise in the fear of our own weakness and natural corruption. Such was the case with Veronica. In a letter of hers, written to Bishop Codebò on the 18th of January, 1725, she thus expresses herself: "May the most holy Virgin obtain for me the salvation of my soul; I always fear and tremble." From this diffidence of herself she rose to firm confidence in the mercy of God. She would therefore frequently sing the 135th Psalm, which begins, "Praise the Lord, for He is good," and which terminates every verse with, "for His mercy endureth for ever." Accordingly she had no fear of death, but was, on the contrary, anxious to die. Sister Florida Ceoli, who lived twenty-four years with her, bears witness to this fact. If our Saint refrained from praying for death as a boon, it was only in order that she might suffer more; and this was an evidence of her hope for that reward which God has promised to those who suffer.

But this virtue was chiefly conspicuous in the trials through which she had to struggle. Among the temptations by which the devil strove to effect her ruin, those of distrust and despair were not the lightest, or the least frequent. "Thou art ours, thou art ours," said the evil one. Upon which Veronica retorted—"If I am yours, why do you tempt me?" But it may conduce to the instruction of many to hear her own account of her conduct during these attacks.

"It is under obedience," she says, "that I write the details of some of those assaults which are so frequently made upon me by the devil. They are of various descriptions. To displease him, I shall sum them up in general, and then descend to particulars. Satan seems to mock me; but he has good reason to do so, for I am a vile worm of earth: I am nothing, I can do nothing, I can will nothing. The Will of God is my stay. Though I can do nothing, I rely with a firm faith on the power of God. I trust myself to His power. He fights for me. I glory in His infinity, I hope in His mercy, I fold myself in the arms of His immense love and unlimited power. The farther I enter into the greatness of God, the more strengthened I feel; and I derive from this a generous readiness to wrestle with all the powers of hell. Again I repeat that of myself I can do nothing, I am good for nothing; I take my stand on the consideration of my own nothingness; and the more deeply I bury myself in this abyss, the more do I find myself drawn to the contemplation of the divine attributes. I fix my gaze upon the mercy of my God, and behold as in a mirror the love with which He has blessed, and continues to bless my soul. . . . It is in this divine charity that I place my trust, when I see my nothingness and incapacity without the grace of God." Her writings are full of these sentiments.

Since she was herself so good a combatant, it is not surprising that she should have excelled in assisting others when engaged in similar conflicts. We could give many illustrations of this; but, for brevity's sake, we will content ourselves with one, which is related in the process by Sister Florida Ceoli, whom we have so often had occasion to name. She was the next in authority to Veronica, and died in the odour of sanctity; her evidence, therefore, has great weight. When she was a novice under Veronica, she was a good deal troubled on the subject of her own predestination, and the devil did his best to foment her fears. One day in Holy Week, in either 1703 or the following year, while she was taking the discipline with her novice-mistress, in memory of the Passion of Jesus, the arch-fiend tried to interrupt her in this mortification, saying, "Wilt thou see if thou art going to be condemned eternally? Behold hell open before thee!" And at the same moment the terrified novice saw before her eyes a great whirlpool of fire, and began to weep violently. Her saintly mistress perceived the cause, and said to her, "Do not be afraid: have faith. The devil is a liar; what he shows you is merely an illusion." So saying, she embraced her affectionately. These few words, with their accompanying embrace, brought such consolation to the poor novice, that her agitation was calmed in a moment. Subsequently the same Sister Florida attributed to the heroic hope of Veronica the abundant assistance in the way of alms which during her government flowed into the monastery, for when she had at first assumed the superiorship the establishment was in a wretched condition, overwhelmed with embarrassments, and destitute of necessaries. When our Saint became abbess, she paid off the debts, enlarged the building, and supplied it with all that was requisite.

Lastly, in order to give some idea of her intense love of God, of which we have already seen many instances, we must briefly remark that her exterior would often present signs of that ineffable charity with which she was possessed, and, as it were, inebriated. On several occasions she ran, as though out of herself, along the open galleries of the convent and in the garden walks, springing on the trees, and inviting all creatures, whether reasoning or not, to join her in loving and blessing her God. When she addressed the community as abbess, the most tender expressions would burst from her lips in speaking of God, whom she termed "Father," "Friend," and "Spouse of Souls." Thus would she excite her daughters to a grateful correspondence of feeling with her. On the Vigil of Pentecost she spoke with such impressive energy on divine love, that the whole community was melted into tears, and the religious declared that it seemed to them as though on that day they had witnessed a renewal of S. Peter's preaching after the descent of the Holy Ghost in the Cenacle at Jerusalem, so-powerfully were they moved. Sister Florida adds that one evening when our Saint was speaking on a similar topic, she beheld her countenance suddenly assume an appearance of angelic beauty. She declared that her hand was then seized by Veronica, who continued in an ecstasy for the space of an hour and a half, and that she found it impossible, with all her efforts, to rescue her hand from that grasp. She also mentions a still more remarkable fact. Father Antonio Cappelletti had given directions to two of the religious that whenever they saw her in these raptures of love they should deluge her hands and feet with cold water: this was done, and several times the water, when applied, was seen to boil, as though it had been brought into contact with a strong flame.

Hitherto we have dwelt on the tender character of her love. A few words must be said on the strength which distinguished it. The supreme affection which she entertained for God induced her to destroy everything in herself which might displease Him. Hence arose the intense contrition which she displayed in manifesting the slightest imperfections to her confessor. This is attested by the last confessor she ever had, Father Guelfi, who mentions that she was in the habit of prefacing her self-accusations with the words, "I have offended God," while this declaration cost her such pain, that her heart seemed ready to break, and it frequently happened that it stopped her breathing. She appeared to be in a certain manner jealous of inanimate things—for instance, she would embrace the trees and the stones, kissing them, and blessing them, because they never disobey God or transgress His commandments. Suffering, unmixed suffering on behalf of her Beloved, was the object of her most earnest desires. This burning charity was symbolized by the flames impressed on her heart, and was illustrated by the following vision:—She writes that on Easter Day, in the year 1698, Jesus appeared to her, and holding in His Hand a heart, which He drew from His Breast, pronounced the following words, "Tell me, whose is this heart?"—"Lord, it is Thine," replied Veronica.—"Tell me, whose is this heart?" repeated our Lord; and she gave the same answer as before. But Jesus, as He had done to St. Peter, turned to her again with the same inquiry, "Tell me, whose is this heart?" and for the third time Veronica replied, "It is Thine."—"If it is Mine, then," resumed our Lord, "I shall put it back in its proper place." Then, showing her His own divine Heart within His opened Side, He placed Veronica's above it. At this sight she became all on fire with love. She had innumerable favours like the above, particularly on occasions of sacramental Communion. The blessed Eucharist was often administered to her in a visible manner by angels, by the most Holy Virgin, and by Jesus Christ Himself. Father Cappelletti alone mentions no fewer than five of these instances within the years 1702, 1703, and 1704. He obtained his information from her own lips at the time he was her confessor, and he gives very conclusive evidence of this, for he states that on several mornings when he was saying Mass at the convent, he gave her a purely mental command to be communicated at the hands of angels, and that after the termination of the holy Sacrifice, she herself mentioned to him the command she had received, and its accomplishment. His diary mentions the 21st of November, 1702, as being the date of one of these occurrences. Such rare privileges, like those of which our second book is full, belong to the class termed gratuitous (*gratis data*), because they have no foundation in the merits of the recipient: although, as we may learn from the lives of other saints, God in His ordinary providence does not grant them excepting to such souls as are most enamoured of His divine Majesty. Hence we may infer the greatness of Veronica's love for her Supreme Good.

CHAPTER III.

HER REMARKABLE ZEAL AND CHARITY TOWARDS HER NEIGHBOUR.

LOVE for our neighbour is the twin sister of love of God, and is concerned with both the temporal and spiritual advantage of others. In the former it may be termed charity, and in the latter, zeal. Veronica shone conspicuous in both. With regard to the first, from her very infancy she seemed inclined, by preventing grace, to relieve others. As she grew in years, she advanced in charity. When it fell to her as a religious to have the charge of the turn, and still more afterwards, when she became abbess, she did her utmost to assist the poor who applied to the monastery for alms; and although she could not personally attend the prisons and hospitals, she visited them in spirit by desires and prayers, as she one day admitted to Sister Mary Boscaini, who was asking her how to employ herself during a season of dryness of spirit.

It was impossible to surpass the charity which she evinced towards the sick members of the community, particularly when she was abbess, for then she enjoyed more liberty as to the disposal of her time; night and day she was to be met with at their bedside; she would visit them at any sacrifice of her own convenience, in case they should be in want of assistance. In order that they might be better attended, she added two to the usual number of infirmarians, and whenever she could, she nursed them with her own hands. Her heroism was specially manifested in coming down every day to the gate of the monastery, to dress the wounds of Sister Antony, an external sister, who was suffering from a dreadful cancer in the breast. When any sister was dying, Veronica, unmindful of her own convenience, hardly left her side, even for meals, but did all in her power to administer to her bodily as well as spiritual relief. She acted in the same way towards Sister Margaret Marconi della Penna di Billi, who, besides being in consumption, was much wasted away.

She never left the patient's bed for several days, neither would she have thought of taking any nourishment, if the sisters, moved with compassion, had not brought her some little refreshment. Hence all the nuns were anxious in their last illness to have her at their side.

There was a religious of a disagreeable temper, who, when attacked by a slowly-consuming cancer in the breast, became almost unbearable to those who waited on her. Veronica was constantly in and out of her cell to see if she wanted anything; but the nun frequently drove her away, although her abbess, by her unbecoming deportment, and told her to take care not to come into her presence when she was dying. When that time came, she repented of her previous impatience, and asked pardon; after which she could not bear any one but Veronica at her bedside. The latter, who was always on the watch, no sooner heard herself summoned by night or day, than she replied, "Here I am, sister; what do you want?" And she persevered in this assiduity to the last. When any of the sisters died, she would lay them out with her own hands, place them on the bier, convey them to the choir, keep watch over them to the end, and at length bury them, doing her best to pray and to procure prayers for them.

Her zeal for their spiritual welfare was not less striking. We have already seen that our Lord Jesus Christ appointed her to act as mediatrix between sinners and His divine justice. The more effectually to incite her to this mediation, He caused her to see, and even experience, the bitterness of those pains to which transgressors are destined. She mentions several instances of this in her writings.

In December, 1696, after she had been running about the garden in a state of ecstasy, during pouring rain, exclaiming that she wanted to find her God, she at length paused, and said, in the midst of her sighs, "My God, my Infinite Love! I would fain have this boon, that Thou shouldst be no more offended. There is nothing I would not do to prevent the loss of so many souls. O God! O God! I feel that my heart is opening." "At this moment," she continues, "God gave me some idea of the ingratitude of creatures, and how much this sin displeases Him. I beheld our Lord in the sufferings of His Passion, scourged, crowned with thorns, and with a heavy cross on His shoulders. He said to me, 'Behold, and mark well this place; it shall never have an end: My justice and My rigorous indignation constitute its agony.' I seemed to hear a tremendous noise; a multitude of devils appeared, holding fast bound in chains a variety of animals. The latter suddenly assumed human forms, but they were so ugly and hideous, that they frightened me more than the demons themselves. . . All at once they resumed the appearance of beasts, and were precipitated into an abode of utter darkness, where they cursed God and His saints. Here I was enraptured, and our Lord communicated to me that this place was hell, and that its inhabitants were departed souls, who, in consequence of their sins, had been condemned to those bestial forms, and that some of them had been religious when on earth. O my God! what is there I can do to prevent these crimes? I was made to understand that the sin of ingratitude is one so displeasing to our Lord, that whoever is guilty of it crucifies Him, as it were, afresh. Religious commit many sins of this kind, and are lost in consequence. Jesus showed me His cross, His precious Wounds, and His Blood, which streamed down on the earth, and said to me, 'The value of this is infinite; I gave it all for the salvation of souls, but I find few to avail themselves of it.'" In another of these visions—for she had very many such—she relates the various kinds of torments which she beheld, and adds that unless she had been supported by her angels, and the most Blessed Virgin, she must have died of simple fear. She concludes; "I say no more, because I cannot say enough. All that I have said is nothing. All I ever heard on the subject from preachers, and all I ever met with in books, is nothing. Hell never can be understood, nor the anguish of its pains and torments."

Visions like these had the effect of exciting, to an almost incredible degree, her zeal for the conversion of sinners. Incessant were the prayers and penances which she offered up in order to bring them back to God. This is attested by Father Crivelli, her extraordinary confessor, who was better acquainted with her than any one else. In order to render her efforts more efficacious, she requested that in the course of his missions he would cause whatever pious souls he might meet with to make a spiritual alliance with her, for the purpose of obtaining from God, by their joint exertions, the repentance of those who had strayed from the right path. "And it is my firm belief," adds Father Crivelli, "that many of the most important conversions which took place during my missions, were the result of her prayers and penances; particularly as I was in the habit, when pressed by great difficulties, of invoking mentally the assistance of those very prayers and penances. And I was animated in my work by the conviction which

God frequently impressed on me, that Veronica was present with me in spirit, when I preached missions."

Still more striking was an idea current among many, and founded on various expressions dropped by our Saint: namely, that it had been granted her, for the promotion of this, her great object, to experience during her mortal life the torments of hell, save only the pain of loss and the privation of God. With respect to the supplications which she offered up for sinners, she is declared by eye-witnesses to have shed tears of blood. Sister Mary Magdalen Boscaini deposed as follows, after mentioning the terrible mortifications which she added to her petitions on behalf of sinners and unbelievers: "Veronica," she says, "frequently shed tears of blood, when, in her deep recollection, God made known to her the state of sinners, the grievousness of the offences offered to Him, and their miserable condition. I say this happened frequently, because several of the nuns have told me that on various occasions they were witnesses to this fact, viz., our present abbess, Sister Clare, who was the companion of our Saint, and the two lay sisters, Giacinta and Frances. I myself have more than once seen these tears of blood in her eyes. I have also seen a black veil of hers spotted in several places with the blood which she shed on these occasions. This last circumstance is attested in writing by Father Raniero Guelfi, her confessor, who gave the veil in question to my uncle, Don Domenico Boscaini, prior of S. Sisto, at Pisa. This document I have read. Father Guelfi had the veil either from Father Girolamo Bastianelli, or from Father Bald' Antonio Cappelletti, I do not exactly remember which."

Whilst our Saint was abbess, she frequently gave orders for processions and special devotions, and would request that each one of the community would pray for the conversion of one sinner, and implore Almighty God to send all the sufferings and chastisements on herself, their abbess, in order that the boon might be granted. Such fervent prayers were the fruits of that charity which our Lord teaches us is the highest of all; for Veronica offered herself as a victim of expiation, and consequently her petitions could not return unanswered from the throne of mercy. Sister Florida Ceoli says, "I saw her literally shedding tears of blood. I dried them with my own hand. She was in the act of praying for the conversion of a sinner, whose name I withhold out of respect; and being in a state of ecstasy, she said in my presence: 'Courage! I hope we shall gain this soul.' I afterwards learned from her confessor that she had told him that the soul in question would be converted to God, and the event proved the truth of her prediction. His subsequent life and death were holy; his conversion was a notorious and public fact, as was also his happy decease."

One of the religious had a brother who lived a life of dissipation. His sister commended him to the prayers of Veronica, and, to the amazement of all, he abandoned his evil courses and became a good Christian. A religious in another convent was at the point of death, and exhibited the worst symptoms of impenitence; and our Saint received orders from Father Tassinari, her confessor, to assist the dying nun in spirit. This direction was promptly and zealously obeyed by Veronica, who, during several days, was perceived by her companions to be in a state of profound abstraction; and it was evident that she suffered much interiorly. But they were all extremely consoled when the fruit of her labours appeared in the sincere contrition with which the dying religious ended her life. A lady, who was devoted to worldly amusements, and particularly fond of dancing, was attacked by a dreadful cancer in the foot. Her conscience was disturbed by remorse; and the agonies consequent on her disorder drove her to the brink of despair. Her daughter and the Jesuit Father Ticciati, who was at that time extraordinary confessor to the monastery, got our Saint to pray for her. Her pleadings were successful, for the unfortunate lady expired, after giving satisfactory tokens of eternal salvation. At her death she was assisted by the above-named father, and still more by the powerful intercession of her saintly mediatrix.

Another lady of Castello, who had led a most scandalous life, was dying of a lingering disease, and endeavoured to procure the prayers of Veronica on behalf of her soul. The answer returned by our Saint was that she must publicly ask pardon of the whole city, if she wished to be saved. Everybody thought that she could never be brought to do this, but through the earnest prayers of Veronica an immediate change was effected in her heart; she sent for all the parish priests of the city, and requested them to ask from the altar, in her name, the forgiveness of the people for all the scandal she had given. She died a true penitent. Hence we see that the prayers of the saints do not of themselves suffice to effect a conversion; there must also be the co-operation of the sinner. In fact, whenever any one was commended to her intercession, she directed what was to be done, and her conditions were no sooner complied with, than the happy result followed. The reverse was the case if her suggestions were not attended to. A zealous priest, having requested her to plead for a certain person, she replied, "Yes, Father, I will pray, but the pitchers are not ready at the well." By which she meant that her petitions would not be supported by the good-will of their subject. We find from her writings, that on one occasion when she was engaged in prayer to our Lord, Who was then visibly before her, to the intent that she might be assured of the conversion of certain individuals, which she had very much at heart, He answered her with a smile full of majesty, "Tell them that it is not enough to call upon Me, they must come themselves and seek Me."

The zeal of Veronica knew no limits. It extended itself to the whole Church militant and suffering. She was frequently invited, by celestial visions, to offer up her sufferings for the prosperity of the holy Catholic Church. Once the Blessed Virgin said to her expressly, "My daughter, pray for the necessities of Holy Church; they are great." On the 12th of December, 1707, Jesus Christ Himself appeared to her under the semblance of His Passion, and asked her to accept three days of special suffering before the Feast of the Nativity, to be applied to the wants of our holy Mother the Church, and of the convent in which she lived. The days were to be fixed by her confessor, Father Cappelletti. He appointed the 16th, 21st, and 23rd of the month; and describes in his diary the nature of the sufferings which befell her on those days. They chiefly consisted in a participation in the heaviest sufferings of the divine Passion, added to various ill-usage from the devil, and the most bitter spiritual desolation. She endured also terrible palpitations and tremblings, the details of which are taken from the above-mentioned diary: "Her head was all swollen and pierced, as though a nail had been driven into the middle of it. There was another great nail which went through from ear to ear. Her eyes were full of thorns, which made her alternately burning hot and icily cold. Her nose, too, was swollen, and full of pain. Her mouth, palate, and tongue were in a state of burning inflammation. Her throat, also, had swollen to such a degree as to threaten suffocation. Her arms and legs had the appearance of being bound to the very bones. She felt as though her whole body was at one moment being squeezed under a press, and at another crushed beneath a mill-stone. Sometimes she felt heavy as lead, and cold as ice; at other times she had the sensation of being scorched and utterly consumed in a furnace. Her own breath seemed to her such that she wondered any one could bear to be near her; she even asked the sisters how they could endure such a stench. She said the same thing to me, but really what she referred to was neither perceived by me, nor by any one else. Everything that she took seemed to her to possess the same quality. It was all dreadfully bitter, moreover, and occasioned her great inward distress and vomiting." On the third of these days, which fell on a Friday (as did the first) our Lord appeared to her beneath the weight of His sufferings, and again asked her to apply all she endured to the necessities of holy Church, informing her that the wants of our spiritual Mother at that time were nothing when compared with what they would one day be. And truly the late unfortunate times have already verified the prediction.

Ten years later, viz., in 1717, when Christendom was in terror from the Turks, Veronica multiplied her prayers and penances more than ever; for which reason she was maltreated by the demons, who are the principal causes of the disasters which befall the Church. There is a notice of these conflicts in her journal for that year. "The devils inflicted blows on me," she says, "exclaiming, 'Accursed one, accursed one! dost thou think thou canst keep us bound? Thou art a fool, thou art an idiot, thou art our captive.' I laughed at their boasts, and said, 'I am bound to the Will of God; here I take my stand; may the divine Will live in me; I wish for nothing else. Even so, infernal monsters! strike me, scourge me, do whatever God allows you. Lying traitors that you are! I belong to God. With Him I wish to remain, to accomplish ever His holy Will.' In the innermost recesses of my soul I blessed God. I had recourse to *Mamma mia*, most holy Mary. I said to her from my heart, 'Most Holy Mary, defend me, assist me; thou knowest that I am nothing, and that I can do nothing.' I endeavoured to bury myself in my own nothingness, at the same time that I made acts of faith and confidence in God and Most Holy Mary." Her hopes and prayers were not in vain, for in the August of the same year, the Christians gained a great victory over the Turks, as our Lord had revealed to her in the preceding March would be the case, in accordance with which revelation she had ever since predicted the event.

We must not forget her cares on behalf of the Church suffering. Father Tassinari, who was her special confessor for forty years, declares "that the same charity which influenced her dealings with the living, characterized her zeal on behalf of the dead.

She prayed night and day for the souls in purgatory. She performed very severe penances for them; and entreated Almighty God to impose on her all kinds of sufferings, however dreadful, in order that they might be liberated from those flames; and if she could have suffered enough to set them all free, she would fain have emptied purgatory." We can form some idea of the species of penalties to which she subjected herself on their behalf, from an account written by herself on the 1st of January, 1717. "I write under obedience," she says; "I have spent this last night in the midst of pains of every description. Blessed be God! I have endured all kinds of bodily torment, in the way of freezing cold, burning heat, nervous convulsions and shocks, pains in all my bones; I have been pierced with steel weapons, and stretched from wall to wall. I have also experienced the sensation of being buried, so that I was unable to breathe. I was carried down into a deep place, where I found nothing but serpents and fierce animals. It seemed to me that I was gnawed by all these creatures; and the agony which this caused me every moment was such that I was on the point of death. With regard to the pains of purgatory, I can only say that if the souls who are there could return to us, they would be unable to describe them, for whatever they might say would fall short of the reality. . . . . The pains of the body are nothing compared with those of the soul. O God, thou knowest how fearful they are! To be banished from God! To be deprived of God! In such a state every moment seems an eternity. An hour passed in such a condition is more consuming than every other suffering or cross."

Veronica was not left without a reward for all that

she endured. "From the conversations which I had with her," says Father Tassinari, "as well as from her own writings, I have ascertained that by the merits of her holy obedience in offering up suffrages for the dead, she obtained from our Lord the liberation of an innumerable multitude. During her ecstasies, Almighty God and the Blessed Virgin vouchsafed to reveal these favours to her. She was frequently permitted to see the objects of her care set at liberty, while she herself was left to suffer the most severe trials for a long time. Among the souls set free by her intercession was one of a priest, and one of a religious of her own convent, named Sister Constance Dini of Mercatello, who died in October, 1703; as also that of a certain Sister Catherine. The last-mentioned soul appeared to our Saint in the form of a globe of light, deriving its lustre from a magnificent sun, which signified God. Three times, however, a small cloud came between these two objects, and obstructed the passage of the sun's rays. Then the globe assumed the appearance of Sister Catherine, and the ever glorious Virgin, who was present at the vision, said to Veronica, "Ask this soul whether the applause which was given her in the world is any pleasure to her now?" Veronica put the question, and was answered, "Although it pleased God to grant me a special grace of detachment, yet transitory things were impediments to me; that little cloud which came between me and the sun was a sign of this. As God is most pure, the soul which is anxious to be united to Him must keep clear of the smallest obstacles, inasmuch as the least impediment or spot will prevent it from enjoying His pure love." Our Blessed Lady then desired Veronica to ask her what kind of life was most pleasing to God. She replied, "A life of sufferings, a life of humiliations and ignominies endured for God." These answers are sufficient proof of the genuineness of the heavenly vision.

Sister Florida Ceoli bears witness to the liberation of the soul of the Count Monte Marto, husband of the Countess Gentilina. Father Guelfi attests the deliverance of his father, Louis Ferdinand Guelfi, on the Feast of the Assumption, 1725, after three days of purgatory. He also mentions the deliverance of his sister, called in religion Sister Mary Gaetana, who died in the convent of S. Clare, in her native place, Borgo S. Sepolcro. That of Signor Giulio Spanaciari rests upon the evidence of his daughter, Sister Mary Constance. Those of Mgr. Eustachj, of the auditor, Monsignor Magi of Florence, of Father Cappelletti, and of Pope Clement XI. of holy memory, stand upon the testimony of Sister Mary Victoria Fucci. Sister Mary Magdalen Boscaini brings forward the deliverance of the father, mother, and uncle of Father Crivelli, all of whom died at Milan. These were all the fruits of Veronica's prayers and mortifications, and were all revealed by apparitions, or in some other unmistakable way. We see now with what good reason the letter C, signifying *charity*, was stamped upon her heart; as also the two flames, which typified her sublime love of God, and her heroic charity towards her neighbour.

CHAPTER IV.

HER SPIRIT OF POVERTY AND MORTIFICATION, AND HER ANGELIC PURITY.

It is customary to pass from the theological to the cardinal virtues, which are the foundation of all morality. Enough has been said in the tenth chapter of the first book on the subject of her prudence and justice towards men. What our Saint did towards God, with regard to the choice of her last end, the means of attaining it, and the rendering to God what was due to Him, we have already seen; and it will be proved to us more strikingly by what is to come. In this chapter we will consider her perfect observance of her vow of evangelical poverty, and her admirable, rather than imitable, mortification. These, combined with her angelic purity, constituted the virtue of temperance in an heroic degree.

She appeared to have an instinctive fondness for evangelical poverty; or rather, we should say, she was endowed with that grace so early, that even in childhood she was resolutely opposed to all those pomps and vanities which are apt to charm the female eye. It was her love for rigid poverty which induced her to make choice of the Capuchin order, and in this she excelled others in an extraordinary degree. She was accustomed to wear the very oldest habit she could get. Sister Florida Ceoli declares that when Veronica was abbess, she wore a habit which had as many as ninety-eight patches in it, and the only wonder was how she could keep it from falling off. At last the assistant earnestly requested her to substitute another for it, but our Saint would not consent, except on condition that she should ask for one not quite so bad in chapter as an alms. The furniture of her cell consisted of a poor little bedstead, made of two planks, with a worn-out coverlet laid on it, and a canvas pillow stuffed with straw, a small stool, a table with a devout print on it, and an earthen vessel for holy water.

As she gave so bright an example herself, she was able to urge the observance of this virtue on others. At an early stage of her career, when she occupied no position of authority, she obtained so much influence by means of her truly religious deportment, that she persuaded the nuns to give up their silk cushions for lace and embroidery, as well as pious pictures on parchment, silver pins, medals, and little crosses, because in her opinion such things were inconsistent with the poverty which ought to be practised by Capuchin nuns. When she became mistress of novices, one of her spiritual daughters attests that she was always exhorting them to love the very simplest poverty; "and so impressive was her mode of speaking," continues Sister Boscaini, " that neither the other novices nor myself could help eagerly petitioning for the very commonest things in the way of pillow-cases and coverlets, exchanging those fine linen ones we had brought with us from the world for others of coarse cloth or canvas.

She used to make us pick up every little thread that lay on the ground, and examine the sweepings of the noviciate, in case they might contain anything that could be turned to account. She did this in order to accustom us to the practice of that holy poverty of which her own conduct afforded so illustrious an example; for she observed herself the same carefulness which she required from us." She took away from the noviceship all musical instruments, birdcages, and such things, for they were not conformable with the virtue which she so tenderly loved. It may be easily conceived that no consideration whatever could induce her to accept anything that was either costly or superfluous. Donna Julia Albani Olivieri, the aunt of Clement XI. of holy memory, presented her with a silver reliquary, containing a fragment of the true cross, but Veronica lost no time in placing it in the hands of the bishop, and she acted in the same way when a Roman prelate sent her a medal and twelve silver crosses. When she was abbess, she would never keep the pecuniary contributions which were sent to the convent, but handed them over to the bishop, in order that they might be reserved for some pressing emergency. When any such occurred, she sent to ask for as much as was absolutely necessary, declaring that the bounty was thus doubled in her eyes, as it came first from her benefactors, and then from the charity of her ecclesiastical superior. She also put a stop to the giving of presents unsuitable to the institute, allowing only such as were of trifling value.

Notwithstanding her zeal for this virtue, it pleased God to increase it by means of various visions. Among the souls which were released from purgatory by the prayers and penances of Veronica, we have already mentioned the name of Sister Constance. Soon after her death in the monastery, Veronica beheld her tormented with flames, because she had kept certain little papers on her altarino. Our Saint immediately ran, as though beside herself, to the oratory of her departed sister in religion, and began stripping off its little ornaments, exclaiming, "Ah! if Sister Constance could but return to us, how carefully would she set this place in order." Jesus once appeared to her and pointed out to her a certain spot where she beheld a multitude of demons throwing dirt into certain grottos, which were like sanctuaries. Our Lord informed her that these were the cells of religious, furnished at the instigation of the devil with curiosities and unnecessary articles. Lastly, S. Francis appeared to her, and reproved her because she had not used her authority as abbess with sufficient severity in removing all abuses against poverty. In order to encourage her to do this, our Lord appeared to her, holding a banner in His Hand, and said to her, "I am thy Victory." She was recommended to co-operate strictly with her confessor, for the purpose of promoting the most rigid poverty in the monastery.

We are told by Sister Boscaini "that all these things animated her to bring the whole community to a state of thorough detachment. She would never permit a single religious to have anything she could call her own, or even to have the disposal of anything, however slight might be its value. She had many difficulties to encounter in achieving her end, but she manifested throughout an invincible fortitude, combined with alacrity and cheerfulness. . . . When she visited the offices, she was careful to banish everything that seemed opposed to the most rigorous poverty. Once in my time, some of the infirmarians had brought more fagots than were absolutely necessary from the wood-house into the infirmary, so Veronica ordered them back, considering that such an abundance was incompatible with the exactness required from those who profess poverty. Another time, having discovered that certain officials had provided such a number of brushes for the use of the convent that there would be enough for their successors after them, she reproved them sharply, and, as a penance, obliged them to carry the articles round their necks in the public refectory, accusing themselves of their fault. She would permit only a very small number to be retained. She administered a similar reproof to the two lay sisters who worked in the garden, because they had blackened with soot and pomegranate bark a certain bench in the chapel of our Father S. Francis in the garden, for she considered such a thing superfluous, and contrary to poverty. She also directed that the black colour should be washed off the bench." The same deponent goes on to state that Veronica gave up herself a representation of the Infant Saviour in plaster, though she had been permitted to keep it.

She was very particular that whatever presents were made to the nuns by their friends and relations should be delivered into the hands of the superior, to be distributed for general use. In a certain annual chapter of detachment which she introduced, she required an account from each individual of the smallest things they might have, such as chaplets, pictures, &c., and if any one ventured to conceal anything, though ever so carefully, she was sure to know it by light from above, and to question them accordingly. One of the choir religious had hidden a piece of a black veil, and having sprinkled it with lavender-water, wore it on her head. She was severely taxed with her offence by her zealous abbess, and punished by going without her black veil for several days, like a lay sister.

Such rigid poverty was of itself a considerable mortification, but it was nothing when compared with the rest. To form some idea of this, it will be as well to refer to the style of living practised by the community at that time. We have the official statement of Sister Mary Teresa Vallemanni, which was sworn to in the deposition made to the judges of the process and the sub-promoter of the faith; when examined by them, she replied as follows:—" The Capuchin nuns of our convent observe perpetual abstinence from flesh meat, and every day is a fast with us, Sundays excepted. In the forenoon we take for dinner some soup made of herbs, or such things, and an egg; occasionally we have a little fruit. On those days when we do not eat eggs (viz., during the forty days' fast of Advent, beginning immediately after All Saints, and lasting till Christmas—besides the ordinary Lent of the Church, that of the Holy Ghost, from the Ascension to Pentecost, and the Wednesday, Friday, and Saturday of every week), in addition to our herb soup we are allowed a small portion of salt or fresh fish, not more than five pounds being allotted for each day, we being at present thirty-three nuns and one servant. . . For our evening collation a small vessel of boiled bread is prepared for such as require it; the others take instead a little salad, with a morsel of bread, or else a small quantity of fruit, for instance, a few grapes, or a couple of chestnuts or walnuts, or an apple, or a radish." Veronica attended to these rules with the utmost precision, as the witnesses declared unanimously; but these general mortifications were nothing in comparison with those peculiar to herself.

In order to mortify her natural delicacy of appetite, she would frequently collect the leavings of the soup of the more aged nuns, and make her own meal upon them. Her ordinary portion of food was so very small, that Fabbri, the physician, weighed it, and said it was impossible that she could have subsisted upon it naturally. This wretched pittance, however, became a source of real torment to her, in consequence of the disgusting things which the devil, in his anger, was accustomed to mix up with it, namely, bunches of hair, dead mice, insects, leeches, &c. All these things Veronica ate, although the violence thereby done to nature was so great, that more than once Sister Florida Ceoli, who was looking on, and had been authorized to do so, snatched away her plate from her. Our Lord was pleased that she should share the bitterness of His chalice, and on several occasions infused into her food a certain liquor, which communicated to it an almost insufferable taste, as the lay sister, Giacinta, who had tasted it, affirms.

The reader may recall that peculiar fast which she observed for five years, and judge if it were possible to surpass such mortification. Father Crivelli states that her "repose during the night was so brief and interrupted, that it might almost have been termed a time of waking as well as of sleeping. Even during the short space her slumbers lasted, which, perhaps, did not exceed an hour, she was constantly waking and exercising herself in most intense acts of love of God; and then she would drop off again with her mind full of these holy affections; so that it was a season more of prayer than of rest. . . . Meanwhile the devil did not relax, but gave her enough to do in combating his attacks, and conquering him; for it was particularly during the hours of night that God permitted the powers of darkness to assail her."

This was but a small portion of the trials of Veronica. We must request our readers to call to mind the overwhelming sufferings which were connected with her participation in the chalice of our Redeemer, her crown of thorns and the wound inflicted on her heart, besides all the torments of the divine Passion, the sacred stigmata, and various kinds of agony which she so frequently endured throughout the course of her long life. "Her penances," deposed Father Crivelli, "were of so terrible a nature, that one is at a loss to conceive how she could have lived through them without miracle. She used the discipline to a fearful extent, macerated her body with sharp instruments, and wore an under vest woven with thorns, which she called her embroidered robe. . . . On my asking her whether, when she put it on, she kept it on also by night as well as by day, she replied in the affirmative. I had half a mind to forbid her to do so; but reflecting on her great zeal and spirit of penance, I permitted her to continue it, only limiting the times and seasons at which she might wear it." Father Casoni, S. J., one of her directors, states that she was in the habit of taking the discipline for whole hours together, to imitate the scourging of our Lord Jesus Christ. This was a function which occupied her for two hours and a half, when she went through the whole at once. Sometimes he desired her to distribute it over the days of a whole week. On such occasions her instruments were bundles of thorns, nettles, and iron chains. She would also tear her flesh with pins and iron combs, and imprint on herself the holy Name of Jesus, by means of heated slates.

The processes of her canonization furnish us with various other instances of her penance. She frequently slept on the bare floor; sometimes under her bed, which, being very near the ground, acted as a kind of press, and prevented her from turning. When she slept on her bed, which has been already described, she was not satisfied unless she could strew it with thorns, bones, and broken crockery; and then she called it the "repose of thorns." Sometimes she got the lay sister, Giacinta, who was in her confidence, to cover her with a large basket made of rushes, and then to put on it heavy weights, so that she could not rise. This she called "the prison;" and frequently remained thus confined during nearly a whole night, in consequence of the lay sister having fallen asleep at the appointed hour for releasing her. The same thing happened when our Saint caused herself to be buried under a pile of wood in the wood-house. When praying at night before the blessed Sacrament, she bore on her shoulders an enormous log weighing upwards of seventy pounds: she alleged as a reason that she wished to feel the weight of her sins. She loaded herself in a similar way with the kneeler belonging to S. Francis' chapel; and with this on her back she traversed the garden walks when they were covered with ice. Sister Giacinta also says that she would often spread hot wax on her flesh, and squeeze it with pincers, which were not seldom heated. She generally wore sandals that had no soles, in order to conceal from others that she was barefoot. If she happened to have on a pair with soles, she put into them beans and small stones. Often at night she ascended the long staircase leading to the infirmary on her bare knees, marking every step with a cross, which she made on it with her tongue, so that traces of blood were left behind. Besides this, she would put her tongue on the window sill, and press it with a heavy stone: this she did even when she was in the world.

But Father Battistelli, another of her confessors, mentions something still more painful. There were in her cell two large hooks fixed into the wall, as far apart as the ends of the cross-beam of a cross, and to these were attached two running knots of cord, in which, mounted on a stool, she inserted her wrists. She then got Sister Giacinta to take away the stool, and remained suspended in the air for several hours in unspeakable agony. One night the lay sister forgot to come and take her down, and Veronica was brought to the very verge of death. The nuns heard of this, and told her confessor, who forbade her ever to do the like again. So also during the last years of her life Father Tassinari prohibited all the extraordinary penances which she had been in the habit of imposing upon herself, and permitted her only to continue the more usual methods of mortification, fasting, disciplines, and haircloth. Although she regretted this, she yielded a ready obedience, for she had never done anything without the cognizance and approval of her directors.

Yet all this was not sufficient to satisfy her ardent desires. She was continually praying that God would send her *pure, simple suffering*. It was out of the abundance of her heart that she gave utterance to the following beautiful expression. She heard a sweeper passing under the windows of the monastery, and inquiring if there was any one who would buy his goods. " Why is there no one," exclaimed Veronica, " who is ready to buy sufferings? If there were but any one to sell them, I would purchase all he had." Father Crivelli relates a still more striking instance of her passion for unmixed suffering. " The genuine desire of our mother, Sister Veronica," he declares, " was that she might suffer more : her thirst after sufferings was absolutely insatiable. I recollect that one day when I was anxious to moderate the force of her longing, she told me that she could not live without suffering, for it was the sole benefit of existence. I remarked—' I suppose you would wish to imitate S. Teresa, who said, " To suffer, or die !" or S. Mary Magdalen of Pazzi, who used to say— " To suffer, not to die !" ' She replied that in order to suffer still more, she would choose neither to suffer nor to die. On my bidding her explain herself, she answered that suffering consists in being deprived of what we desire ; since if we have the object of our wishes, our state is one of enjoyment and not the reverse—therefore as she desired to suffer and to die that she might see and enjoy God, it was a far greater pain to her not to die and not to suffer." This is both admirable and true, but it only applies to such souls as, like Veronica, are enamoured of the cross. Was anything more remarkable ever met with in the lives of the greatest penitents? Truly she might be called a martyr of penance.

When surrounded by this thick hedge of thorns, it is not surprising that the fair lily of angelic purity should have flourished. We saw in the first book with what care heaven watched over our Saint from infancy. Well may her chastity have risen to an heroic degree after she was honoured with the mystic espousals of the Immaculate Lamb. A symbol of her soul's fragrance was the delicious perfume of Paradise which her body diffused around her. Even during the most frightful assaults which she had to encounter from the demons, and when she shared in the mystery of our Lord's scourging, not the smallest part of her was seen uncovered, through the watchful care of her Beloved. We will content ourselves with summing up all that might be said on this point, in the words of Father Crivelli, in the process—"She possessed this virtue in so eminent a degree that she might be termed the very picture of purity. She seemed like a spirit, scarcely conscious of the burden of humanity. Her example was such as to inspire similar sentiments in the minds of all the other religious." We will now proceed to glance at another bright example given by our illustrious model.

CHAPTER V.

HER PATIENCE AND IMPERTURBABLE GENTLENESS.

VOLUNTARY sufferings, however appalling in their nature, have something in them which is gratifying to our own will. Those which come immediately from God, or with His permission from the devils, can be endured, because we are soothed by the reflection that we receive them from the Hand of God, and we know that they are the earthly inheritance of His beloved ones. But those afflictions which are brought upon us by our fellow-creatures, either through their malice, their errors, or any other reason, are those against which our human nature more especially revolts: consequently when such are calmly endured without any resentment, it proves the existence of a very high degree of patience and forbearance, both of which proceed from fortitude, the fourth and last of the cardinal virtues. We shall omit here any particular description of the frequent and very painful maladies from which Veronica suffered during the course of her religious life, and which only caused her regret on account of the trouble which they occasioned to her companions. She felt their sympathy so acutely that she was accustomed to say, " Suffering is not suffering to me; my suffering consists in being pitied." Neither shall we enter in this place on any details of the horrible assaults made on her by the demons, but confine ourselves to those trials which came from her fellow-creatures in one shape or another. Let us first remark that no one ought to be surprised, much less scandalized, that among a community of religious, many of whom were saintly persons, there should be found some who deviated from the path of duty. Still less ought we to be astonished that God should sometimes permit the most holy men to fall into certain mistakes of judgment, out of which a good deal of suffering accrues to others. Furthermore, many actions are lawful on the part of superiors and spiritual directors, for the purpose of testing the virtue of their subjects, which would be utterly unlawful in private individuals.

The community of the Capuchin nuns was distinguished for its spirit of religion and sanctity when Veronica entered it (indeed, it was for that reason she selected it, as we have seen, from among many others), and its character subsequently rose under her direction and blessed example. Nevertheless there were certain nuns who deserved the name neither of saint nor religious, just as among the apostles there was a Judas Iscariot. From these the sanctity of Veronica had much to bear. Even when she was a novice, she had a companion who set herself to persecute our Saint, carrying slanderous tales about her to the abbess and novice mistress, and treating her in the most rude and contemptuous way, even before others. But Veronica was not in the least irritated by her conduct; and so far was she from rendering evil for evil, that she did not even seek to justify herself. On the contrary, she only resorted to the evangelical vengeance peculiar to the saints, and repaid evil with good, subduing it by means of benefits. She would humble herself so far as to kiss the feet of this companion; she assisted her in every possible way, and even thanked her for the treatment she had received at her hands. She only requested her to forbear in public for fear of giving scandal to others: she did not mind what was done to her in private. The reader must not suspect that either of her three fellow-novices, whose names are mentioned in the eighth chapter of the first book, had any share in this disgraceful persecution. Sister Clare Felicia entered and passed the year of noviciate with her. The latter has been unjustly blamed on this score by a certain writer; but so far from there being any ground for such an accusation, she was one of those who most admired and assisted Veronica in her extraordinary penances and virtues. This we have ascertained from the indubitable testimony of those religious who were her companions and contemporaries. Veronica's persecutor was clothed two years before herself, but was in the noviciate at the same time, according to the custom of the monastery, which requires the newly professed to spend two years under the direction of the novice-mistress. We heard her name in the monastery, but refrain from giving it. Besides the kindness she received in return from our Saint during life, she owed her after death a still greater favour, for she was one of those souls who were speedily delivered from purgatory by the intercession of Veronica.

The following facts, which are recorded in the processes, will serve to give us a better idea of her heroic patience. In the course of the long period during which she filled the office of novice-mistress, she had under her a couple of very intractable novices. One of them could so ill brook her gentle admonitions, that she was transported with rage against her, and, proving incorrigible, was dismissed from the convent, as Veronica had predicted before she even entered it. Nevertheless, the Saint obtained from the Blessed Virgin that this person should receive the holy habit of religion in another order, and be brought to repentance. She acknowledged her faults, and, in detestation of her ill-treatment of Veronica, she began to publish abroad her sanctity. She also, during an illness, implored with great profit the aid of her powerful prayers. The conduct of the other was so violent, that she one day struck her saintly mistress and wounded her lip. Veronica, who was only grieved on account of the scandal thus given, and the excommunication which the novice hereby incurred, set herself to petition our Lord so earnestly for her repentance that she shed tears of blood, as many eye-witnesses deposed. The transgressor did repent for the time being; but as she did not strike at the root of her natural ill-temper, she on another occasion grievously insulted Veronica, who was abbess, while she was cook. An old labourer came to the monastery, and it was the duty of the cook to give him his food. The holy abbess, not seeing this done as usual, and being moved with compassion for the poor countryman, went into the kitchen to administer a mild reprimand for her forgetfulness or dilatoriness, whichever it might be. But as the sister contradicted her, Veronica, being anxious to cut short the conference, said, "Now, make haste, and give him this," taking up the bread and a knife, with which she was to help the poor man. But the cook grew excessively angry, and gave her abbess such a vehement push, that if she had not been caught by the bystanders she must have fallen flat on the ground. They wished the offender to be immediately punished, as she deserved, but the superior wisely and prudently would say nothing then, because she was aware that correction is useless and even injurious while the person on whom it is inflicted is in the heat of passion. So when the religious pressed her to impose due penance on the culprit, she calmly replied, "We must have patience. I am only displeased on account of the sin against God." She conducted herself with the same tranquillity in the first chapter which she held; and the reward of her moderation was the contrition of the guilty person, who was filled with shame, and made due satisfaction to the community, after which she watched better over herself, and lived and died a very good religious.

Similar to the above are the following cases, which we shall relate in the words of Sister Mary Joanna

Maggio, who was an eye-witness, and deposed to them in the process. "I have not only heard of," she says, "but I have also seen, the venerable Sister Veronica enduring insults and contradictions without cause, particularly from a certain religious who is now dead, but who filled the office of sacristan conjointly with myself, during the superiorship of the venerable Sister Veronica, who bore all with courage and tranquillity, specially showing her charity towards the person who injured her. The religious in question wanted to make an altar in the choir for various sacred relics, which were to be placed there on the feast of All Saints, but she built it up too high in proportion to the strength of the foundation, so that it nearly fell down with the holy relics and myself; for she had desired me, as second sacristan, to get upon it. As soon as our abbess, the venerable Sister Veronica, perceived this, she directed me to come down, which I accordingly did; and she reproved the sacristan for having made her platform so weak that there was danger of the cases of the holy relics falling to the ground and being broken. This reproof was appropriate and necessary, prudent and moderate. However, the person to whom it was addressed did not take it in good part, but remarked with anger that the abbess might attend to herself, for that she did nothing but trouble her. To which our venerable superior replied without the least irritation, but with an air of suitable modesty and tranquillity, that her duty was to obey, and nothing else. Upon this the nun began to grumble, but our mother restrained her feelings, not choosing to administer correction to a person under the influence of excitement. However, when the chapter of faults came round she did not fail to do so, but in the most charitable way."

"Another time the same individual was rebuked by the Saint for her carelessness in arranging the usual crib of the Nativity in our choir. She handled the figures so carelessly that she knocked off a finger from the statuette of S. Joseph, and broke a candle which weighed seven or eight pounds. The admonition which she received was gently and prudently worded, but she gave a proud and impatient answer. Our Saint bore it with patience, and merely gave her a charitable correction at the ensuing chapter, in which she had to put up with insulting conduct, not only from her, but from another of the three ill-disposed sisters which the community contained in my time. Our saintly abbess, in quality of her office, corrected them with the utmost kindness, firmness, and love, which seemed to increase in proportion to their perverseness. She prayed and got others to pray for them, and imposed on herself various penances, as I have heard from those nuns who were her confidants. The delinquents were brought to their senses, and acknowledged the great virtue of the servant of God, by whom those who died before her desired to be specially assisted in their illness and death. As soon as it became known in the monastery that the Saint had received the stigmata, some of the nuns who did not like her stirred up a persecution against her, slanderously affirming that they were only appearances, and that she had artfully contrived to imprint them on herself. They said this even in her presence, and one of them declared that she would be lost for ever if she continued to maintain these appearances, and persist in her hypocrisy, for such she deemed her life to be. When Bishop Eustachj came to be informed of this event, he presented himself at the grate, and calling the saintly servant of God with our mother abbess (who must have been either Guerrini or Salari), he blamed her severely, and showed every mark of contempt."

The present is a good opportunity for adducing some instances of her invincible and exemplary patience and tranquillity during the trials which she had to encounter from her superiors for the purpose of testing her spirit. We may be allowed to remark that as in the case of those patients who have strong constitutions a physician is allowed to adopt very strong remedies, so the severe trials resorted to by her superiors cannot be called extravagant or indiscreet, seeing that they had proofs of the strength of her virtue. When Veronica received, on the 5th of April, 1697, the rare and precious gift of the sacred stigmata, Bishop Eustachj considered it his duty to apply to the sacred tribunal of the Inquisition at Rome, for directions as to the course he should pursue. At the same time he informed their eminences the cardinals, of the moral qualities of Veronica. In conformity with the instructions which came from Rome, to ascertain any illusion or hypocrisy there might be, he did his best to try her patience, humility, and obedience, as these are the undoubted characteristics of a right spirit. His first step was to depose her from her office as mistress of novices; he also deprived her of her active and passive vote, and called her excommunicated, and a sorceress, in a voice so loud that it resounded from the grate to the corridors of the nuns; he threatened also to have her burnt in the middle of the cloister. Then he caused her to be confined in a room of the infirmary, forbidding her to write to any one excepting to her sisters, who were religious at Mercatello, and those letters she was first to show to the abbess. He also prohibited her from ever entering the parlour. Then he forbade her to come to the choir either for Mass or the divine Office, excepting on feast days, and then no farther than the threshold, apart from the rest as though she were under excommunication, attended by the lay sister Frances, who was to re-conduct her to her prison. She was not allowed to speak to any of the other nuns, who were directed to treat her with the utmost rigour as a hypocrite and a deceiver. She was deprived for this period of holy Communion, and the time she might spend at the confessional was to be restricted by the abbess. Besides all this, the bishop caused her mysterious wounds to be medically treated; and, as if he suspected imposture, he had the gloves which were used sealed every time with the episcopal seal. Instead of getting better, swellings arose round them, so that it became necessary to bathe them with rose water, as we find from the letter of the bishop to the secretary of the Holy Office at Rome, dated the 29th of August.

These appointments of Providence must have been not only distressing to her nature, but great trials of her virtue, deprived as she was of the sacraments, and the other privileges of religion; and yet the following testimony of Sister Maggio is fully borne out by other witnesses. "While the venerable Sister Veronica was in this condition, abandoned as it were by all, both without and within the convent, and treated with utter contempt, she retained all her humility, calmness, and resignation. She reposed in the arms of her crucified Love : her sole desire was to glorify and imitate Him ; she thought nothing of herself, and was not disturbed by the contumelies heaped upon her, but, on the contrary, took the greatest delight in them." But there is no occasion to refer to other sources, when we have the authentic letter of the bishop to the Holy Office, which is above all suspicion of impartiality. Under date of the 29th of August, 1697, he states,—"She punctually fulfils everything she is ordered to do, and manifests great satisfaction at being exercised in obedience, as also at not being permitted to approach the grate. Neither by me, nor by her confessor, nor by the abbess, is she favoured with the slightest mark of distinction ; on the contrary, she is treated with less consideration than any one else." On the 26th of the following September, after relating what had been done, the bishop continues : " Sister Veronica never fails in the practice of the most strict obedience, humility, and abstinence, without evincing the least degree of sadness, but always ineffable serenity and peace. The nuns cannot help expressing their admiration of her to seculars. I try hard to prevent them from doing so, but I cannot succeed, though I am always threatening to impose some mortification on the most talkative of them, for I do not wish the curiosity and gossip of the people to be encouraged." On the strength of this letter, the Congregation of the Holy Office laid aside all doubt as to the virtue of Veronica, although it prescribed certain precautions against the dangerous curiosity and gossip of the city.

We have not mentioned the harsh measures which were adopted towards her by a certain abbess, at the instigation, probably, of Bishop Eustachj, in the year 1695. Not being satisfied as to the order which Veronica had received from God to keep that rigorous fast, of which the particulars are given in the fifth chapter of the second book, he attributed to affectation the violent repugnance which caused her to reject every kind of food. In fact, he rather suspected that, as some malevolent person declared, she was in the habit of eating when she pleased in secret. The devil contrived, by false appearances, to support this idea. So the bishop wrote to the abbess, directing her to shut up Veronica in a cell belonging to the infirmary, and to put some one to watch her constantly; also to give her nothing to eat but meat and broth. The superior received these orders while she was saying office in the choir with the other nuns, and Veronica, too, was in her stall. No sooner had the abbess glanced at the bishop's note than she stopped the office, and, turning to Veronica, with an indignant and commanding tone, exclaimed, "To the infirmary! To the infirmary!" She then drove our Saint from the choir as one unworthy to remain there, and confined her in the appointed cell, causing one of the lay sisters to bear her company. The religious who were present declare that Veronica went off immediately, without any sign of being troubled, and remained in her prison for fifty days with the greatest cheerfulness.

In our opinion, however, the trials which she had to encounter from the Jesuit Father Crivelli in 1714, must have been still more painful, not only because her spirit had been thoroughly tested in many ways during the previous year, but because she suffered from one of whose merit she had been assured by our Blessed Lady on the occasion of her first seeing him. That celebrated missionary arrived at Città di Castello in the above-named year, and was employed by Bishop Eustachj to try the spirit of our Saint still further, although that prelate had been already enlightened as to her great virtue in the matter of the fast, as well as in that of the stigmata. Yet as the extraordinary features of her life went on multiplying, he appointed the Jesuit her extraordinary confessor, and conferred full powers upon him. Father Crivelli availed himself of this authority, and having duly got up the case, began by putting her to the severest possible tests. At their very first interview he treated her as a sorceress and a hypocrite, and called her so repeatedly at the grate. One day, when she was in her stall with the rest, listening to the sermon, he obliged her to come out into the middle of the choir and sit on the floor, as being unworthy of taking her seat with them. In order to put her to shame before them all, he called to her in a loud voice, "Where is she? Let her come and sit on the floor." She did so directly, without being disquieted, and afterwards she thanked him gratefully for what he had done. At this time she was as much as fifty-four years of age, thirty-seven of which she had spent in religion, and twenty as mistress of novices. Father Crivelli deposes that one day he assumed a confidential air, and told her that she was likely to be scourged and burnt alive as a witch and a hypocrite, and says, "I found her so humble and resigned to be taken for such, that, to tell the truth, I wondered exceedingly. The more I endeavoured to mortify her by means of harsh words, taunts, and threats, the more did she humble herself. The following were the precise words she used : 'I would not willingly be a sorceress; but if your reverence knows that I am in the hands of the devil, be pleased to deliver me from them for the love of Jesus Christ.'"

From words he proceeded to actions. He forbade her to speak or write to any one out of the establishment, and appointed the lay sister Frances to be her superior, whom she was to obey in everything. He obliged the said Sister Frances to treat her in a manner which was at once rude and imperious; giving her now one kind of occupation and now another. Veronica yielded the most prompt submission to every beck and call, and maintained the same equanimity and sweetness of temper during the two months which this trial lasted. Then he gave her another of a different kind. He knew that there was a small closet in the infirmary which was dark and unused, the habitation of spiders and other insects. He ordered Veronica to occupy it instead of her cell, which was too good for her; and instead of having it swept out first, she was to kneel down and clean the floor with her tongue, and then stand up and do the same to the walls. She fulfilled this injunction with the utmost calmness; and, furthermore contrived, with the assistance of a footstool, to apply a similar process to the ceiling, swallowing both spiders and cobwebs as though they had been the most dainty viands. The nuns reported this to Father Crivelli, who sent for her, and, concealing the high estimation which he had formed of her virtue, scolded her, and called her stupid for having misunderstood his orders. She quietly replied that such food did her good. He left her in this place for two months, during which, whenever she had occasion to name her abode, which was generally called "the dark cell," she, on the contrary, termed it "the bright cell," because she had learnt more there than in any other place. Satan was so displeased at the light she received in that dark cell, that he did all in his power to force her to disobey, and to leave it. Every night he appeared to her under some horrible form, hoping thus to frighten her out of it. Often he came with a troop of his hideous companions, attacked her furiously, and struck her head against the walls; but she was firm and contented to the last, and even sorry to go away when removed by obedience.

We have taken these particulars, not only from the depositions of the nuns, but from those of Crivelli himself, in the process of information, wherein the reasons which he assigns for the opinion which he had conceived of her, not only in that year, but in the three which followed, during which he was the extraordinary confessor of the monastery, are given in these words: "The principal pleasure of Veronica consisted in suffering for the love of God; and the more afflictions she had, the more she wished for them. She had preserved her baptismal innocence, as I knew from having heard during those years both her general and particular confessions; for frequently I could not find in these last sufficient matter for absolution, and, therefore, I made her repeat her general confessions, though even in them I could scarcely find enough." He often recommended himself to her prayers, in which he had great confidence, for he had experienced their efficacy on several occasions. He it was, who, on his arrival at Rome in February, 1716, after the death of Bishop Eustachj, was appointed a missioner of the city by the father general, and was admitted to an audience by the illustrious Pope Clement XI. By the encomiums which he then delivered on the sanctity of Veronica, he obtained from the Holy Office permission for her election as abbess. She was, therefore, unanimously chosen to fill that office, which she retained till her death, with the sanction of the Sacred Congregation of bishops and regulars, who permitted her re-election for three successive terms of as many years.

CHAPTER VI.

HER WONDERFUL HUMILITY.

" OBEDIENCE and humility were the two predominant virtues of our mother, Sister Veronica, and constituted the basis of her exalted sanctity." Such is the declaration of Father Giovanni Maria Crivelli. Amongst all the witnesses who deposed to the heroic virtues of our Saint, the authority of this illustrious missioner is peculiarly important; not only on account of the zeal for souls which he evinced in devoting his whole life to missionary labours, and his skill in the discernment of spirits, but still more on account of his being appointed by the bishop for the purpose of examining Veronica, and putting her to many severe and satisfactory tests during four consecutive years, which no one else had the opportunity of doing. Throughout the whole of the process of information, we can find no deposition more minute and circumstantial than that which contains his examination from the 14th of July to the 16th of August, 1728, in the presence of Bishop Codebò, of the fiscal promoter, Lorenzo Smirli Mori, and the episcopal chancellor, Domenico Fabbri, on about two hundred and fifty points. Father Crivelli had been shown to Veronica under his natural form, several years previously, by Jesus Christ, who told her that he would one day make trial of her spirit. In the year 1714, when he first came to Città di Castello and entered the church of the Capuchin nuns to pray, she saw him again. She was at that time in the confessional of Father Tassinari, so that she could not have seen him by natural means; but the most holy Mary rendered him visible to her, so that she was able to describe him, to the amazement of her confessor and the nuns, who knew nothing about it. She declared moreover the object of his coming, and the good that would result to her soul. To him also she predicted many things, and disclosed her knowledge of his interior secrets, as he himself tells us. At his request, she obtained the deliverance of the souls of his father, mother, and uncle, from purgatory.

Veronica having expressed a desire that he should assist her at her death, he promised to do so, if possible. At the time of her last illness he was extraordinary confessor to the Capuchin nuns of Monte Castelli, having been sent there by Monsignor Gualtieri, Bishop of Todi; but it seems that notice was sent him in the following way. He occupied the apartments of the ordinary director, in which hangs a bell, communicating, by means of a rope, with the monastery, so that the nuns can ring it in case of necessity. On the evening of the

30th June, about 4 o'clock at night, he heard this bell ring. He and his companion listened to hear if it would sound again, but as it did not, he did not answer it. The next morning he asked the abbess why the bell had rung, and what had happened. She replied that nothing had happened, and that it was impossible that any one could have rung it, because the room where the cord was had been locked, and she always kept the keys herself. Another evening, at the same hour, he heard it again, as also on the 9th of July; but on inquiring the reason the same answer was invariably returned by the abbess. At length the news came that Veronica was dead, and he understood that these had been her summons—the first corresponding with her increased danger, ten days before she died, the second to give warning of her approaching decease, and the third to inform him of her death, which took place about 7 o'clock in the evening on the 9th of July.

We heard the following incident from one who had it from his own lips. Father Crivelli had taken from Veronica's cell a large wooden cross, which he always carried about with him, and conveyed to the Jesuits' College at Tivoli, where, at an advanced age, he died in the odour of sanctity. He used to say that when this cross should break, it would be an intimation that his departure was at hand, for that the venerable Sister Veronica had told him so. It was securely attached to the wall of his room at the college, when one day, without any apparent cause, it fell down and broke. Then the good old man said that he had but few days to live, and his words were verified. We trust the reader will forgive us for this brief, but not irrelevant, digression. It may serve to enlighten us as to the value of his testimony, and is a tribute of gratitude to so eminent a director, as well as to the rare holiness of our Saint. It will also, we hope, be agreeable to her, for during her life she had the highest esteem for him, and the deepest sense of her obligations to him.

But to come to the subject of the present chapter, her rare humility in thought, word, and deed. She had the lowest opinion of herself; her own nothingness was the habitual subject of her reflections. We have seen from her writings, that she prayed for nothing more than that the Lord would make her understand this well. But this was not all; she regarded herself as a grievous sinner; "and such she would have been considered," says Father Tassinari, who was her confessor for several years, "by any one who did not know her, and who merely formed his opinion from the way in which she spoke of herself in the confessional and in conversation. These confessions," adds Father Crivelli, "she would have wished to make, if possible, before the whole world, in order that she might be looked upon as the being who was most ungrateful to God, and the greatest sinner in the world." She did all she could to ensure this reputation. She spoke of herself in this way before all her companions; and to the novices, when she was their mistress, she would frequently make a kind of general confession, putting herself to the blush in their presence by relating the little faults of her childhood, as though they had been enormous offences, and dwelling on them with such energy and contrition as to draw tears from all who heard her. She would say over and over again, " In hell there is room for all; my place is there if I do not change my life." The lay sister Giacinta, her special confidant, attests "that she was constantly begging every one to pray to our Lord for her conversion, and for the salvation of her soul. She did this with such fervour and earnestness that you would have thought her heart was bursting. I recollect that one day our confessor, Father Ubaldo Antonio Cappelletti, told me that she had so bad an opinion of herself, that she was afraid of associating with the other religious for fear of contaminating them. It was evident that she considered herself as a being so very vile and abject among us all, that she seemed ashamed to show her face, as I have frequently observed." Father Cappelletti, in his diary, expresses himself in the following clear and energetic words : " She felt ready to die of grief every time that God gave her that intimate knowledge of ingratitude and sin. If she could have hidden herself in the very depths of hell, she would have readily done so. This filled her with such an intimate knowledge of herself, that she would fain have concealed herself in the innermost centre of the globe, so as never again to behold creatures, and to preserve them from beholding her, and being polluted and poisoned by coming into contact with her. She wished that all would drive her from them, and despise her as she deserved."

The fruits of this low self-estimation did not consist merely in saying disparaging things of herself, but, what was of more consequence, in a total absence of resentment under contumelious treatment. On the contrary, as Father Crivelli and others affirm, whoever despised her fell in with her wishes. An instance of this may be found in the tenth chapter of the first book, when it was related that she used to oblige her novices to tread on her lips. When she became abbess, she did not cease from the most menial employments, or from waiting on the lay sisters.

It will not be out of place to point out here the humility which she showed in declining the dignity of abbess. Father Crivelli, being thoroughly convinced of the sanctity of Veronica after the trials which have been already related, believed that it would be of the highest advantage to the convent if the suspension of the Holy Office could be withdrawn, and she were to be elected abbess. He consulted the Abate Giacomo Lomellini, the companion of his missions, and Bishop Eustachj, both of whom agreed with him. One morning, in the same year, 1714, after celebrating Mass in the church of the convent, he went into the confessional, where he found Veronica plunged in the deepest affliction. She implored and conjured him for the love of God to spare her the cross which he had in his mind for her. Father Crivelli, who really did not know what she meant, not having the least idea that she had had a vision, hastily replied that he could not tell whether she was dreaming, or what cross she was talking about. She then told him that while she had been assisting at Mass, S. Francis Xavier had appeared to her with a heavy cross on his shoulder, and had informed her that Father Crivelli was about to lay that cross on her in the office of abbess, which he destined for her. This vision was repeated on the two following mornings. The good Father was in reality amazed; but prudently concealing his astonishment, for the purpose of testing her spirit, he began to scold her and call her mad for supposing that he had any thoughts of making her abbess, whereas he did "not consider her capable of governing a set of hens." Veronica smiled and modestly replied that there was no occasion to deny it, for that she knew and saw how it was. On the morning of the third day she furthermore stated that she had seen the same cross making the circle of the choir until it came to the stall of the abbess, where it stopped. The fact was, that not only did Father Crivelli think of getting her appointed to that office, but he put his thought in execution, for in 1716, as we have already seen, he obtained from the Pope that the suspension should be withdrawn by the Holy Office, and that she should be elevated to the rank of abbess. But the lustre of so exalted a post alarmed Veronica so much, that she fell on her knees and implored the bishop, as well as the entire chapter, to save the convent from the ruin that must ensue from the choice of a superior so wicked, and incapable of promoting either its spiritual or temporal welfare. Her humility, instead of answering her purpose, had quite the opposite effect, since it only showed her worth and fitness; and in the event the monastery was her debtor for increased advantages in the way of enlarged buildings and additional supplies of water, as well as for the regularity of religious observance which it now enjoys. Her mode of government was so able, owing rather to the illumination she received from above, than to her natural talents, that Mgr. Eustachj said that she was fit to govern a world, and that every one should have recourse to her in the most difficult matters; yet she would never undertake anything without the advice of others. It is true that, whatever she proposed, every one acknowledged to be the wisest course. Her profound humility prevented her from using words of command, even to the lay sisters, or to the artisans and countrymen who worked for the monastery. She employed, instead, humble expressions of request, excepting in cases where it was her duty, as superior, to reprove any rebellious persons for their faults.

Her disposition was equally averse to human praise. In order to conceal her extraordinary penances and prayers, she chose the dead of night wherein to perform them, when all around her were sleeping. If she had occasion for the assistance of others, as when she suspended herself from the wall, or imprisoned herself in the basket, she selected the two most simple of the lay sisters, namely, Frances and Giacinta, on whose secrecy she believed that she could implicitly rely. In order to conceal the fact that she was barefoot, she wore sandals without any soles. She strove also to hide the mortification which she observed throughout the whole of a novena before Christmas, of never warming herself, by carrying about the usual pan of charcoal, with nothing but cold ashes in it.

Still more careful was she to conceal the heavenly gifts and graces which our Lord lavished upon her. It was nothing but obedience which induced her to make them known to her directors, and when she did so, she expressed herself in the most humble way. She would always say, "It appears to me that I saw," or, "It appears to me that I understood;" and she would always conclude by exaggerating her own iniquity and ingratitude to God. From her sense of her own unworthiness, she took her visions for dreams and impressions of the imagination. "I mention this," she writes in the year 1695, "out of obedience, and to conquer myself, but it really seems to me that I am talking nonsense. I do not know how to write a line properly. All these things seem to me to be dreams, and my own imaginings." She uses similar language in 1697, and in the following year. In 1703 she goes still further: "I am never confident," she says, "but always in fear and trembling lest these things should be devices of the devil; and I treat them with contempt every time that they occur to me, particularly visions. I relate them minutely, not because I believe them, but in order that the minister of God may know everything, and ascertain if there be any demoniacal illusion." She only liked narrating those visions in which God had reproved her for some imperfection. But inasmuch as she could not conceal the gift of the stigmata from general observation, but was, on the contrary, obliged to give all the evidence she could in proof of it, she took care to remark that it sometimes pleased God to bestow certain graces on sinners in order to effect their conversion, adding that that blessed result had not followed in her own case. She prayed incessantly that those marks of honour might be withdrawn, or at least the external and visible scars. It was three years before she obtained this boon, and it was not until just before her death that all traces of them were removed. Her humility, in short, was such as we do not find to have been surpassed in the life of any saint.

CHAPTER VII.

HER MIRACULOUS OBEDIENCE.

WE now come to the virtue which is the parent and fruitful origin of all others; for as the illustrious Pope and Doctor S. Gregory has remarked, it is obedience alone which engrafts the whole circle of virtues in the soul, preserves them, and trains them to perfection. Obedience is the offspring of humility, for none but the truly humble can subject their will and understanding to God and man. The obedience of Veronica was indeed the submission of both intellect and will, not only to God, but to all His representatives, whether her superiors or spiritual directors. It is not our intention at present to speak of that obedience which is paid immediately to God and His divine commandments (though of this we have abundant evidence), nor of her exact observance of the precepts of the Church and of her rule, nor of her perfect conformity to the divine Will. All this comes under the virtue of charity, on which we have spoken enough already, for no one can be said to love God, who does not observe His law and acquiesce in His Will. Yet we cannot omit one example of obedience which comes more properly under this head, and which is taken from one of her writings of the year 1696. "My Lord," she says, "I desire to please Thee, and to accomplish Thy holy Will. If Thou seest, O my God, that there is anything of my own choice in these desires, take it away, rid me of it. . . . . Lord, let thy Will be done; I am satisfied to be in the dark, and to be treated as Thou wilt. But I protest that whether Thou shalt manifest or conceal Thyself from me, I always intend to remain with Thee." Not content with this declaration, she signed a contract to that effect with her own blood.

But the kind of obedience with which we have now to deal is that which she rendered to her fellow-creatures as the ministers of God. This is the greatest trial to human pride, and it was practised by Veronica to a miraculous extent. We do not mean to speak merely of the act of obedience, but of the consent of the understanding and will. In order to do this with the greatest possible perfection, she had imprinted on her mind, as her confessor, Father Guelfi, assures us, the following maxim, which she would often repeat to herself, as it would be well that all other persons should do who have bound themselves by the vow of obedience : " If God in person were commanding me to do anything, should I not run to obey Him ? Now the obligation is the same, whether God makes known His Will directly, or through my superiors, His representatives." Knowing such to be her conviction, we have no difficulty in believing what Father Tassinari tells us in the process. "If it had been possible," he says, " she would never have moved a step or drawn a breath without the merit of holy obedience, as I know well, from the long, severe trial I made of her." Nor are we astonished at the following deposition of Father Guelfi : "During an ecstasy on the 1st of January, 1727, the Blessed Virgin having invited her to the banquet of eternity, she excused herself by stating that she had not leave for that. When she returned to herself she related this fact at my feet. She then asked me to give her leave to go to eternal glory ; but on my refusing to do so, she promptly resigned herself to obedience."

Her great affection for this virtue was never more conspicuous than during the severe trials by which she was proved. We have already seen what pains the devil took to withdraw her from the submission which she owed to her confessors and superiors. However, the only result of the traitor's machinations was an increase of that virtue in her. From that time forward she used to subscribe herself, "In spite of the adversary, daughter of obedience." We have seen the trials to which our Lord Jesus Christ submitted her, in the case of her remarkable fast, reproaching her frequently for not putting it in execution: to which she always replied by imploring Him, if such was His Will, to make her superiors consent to it. We are already aware of the severe tests to which her directors and superiors subjected her. She was always prompt in her acquiescence, and calmly prepared to obey the least intimation of their will. She requested them never to spare her, but to use words of command, such as, "I will that you should do so and so; I order you, I command you." Therefore she was never more pleased than during the two months which Father Crivelli made her spend under the lay sister Frances, who, although an excellent person, was extremely rough in her ways, and particularly so in her treatment of Veronica, according to the orders of Father Crivelli. She either kept our Saint working in her room, and watched her as one would an inexperienced and naughty child, or she set her to sweep the kitchen and poultry yard, or similar places. She was always scolding her for her stupidity. She put her in penance for several days, depriving her of her black veil, and making her wear a white one like a lay sister, to all of which Veronica submitted without a word of complaint.

There was one point, however, on which she found it difficult to obey, namely, when her confessors commanded her to give them minute details of her gifts and virtues, not merely by word of mouth, but in writing, for here humility and obedience clashed. It was a hard contest, but obedience proved victorious, as the reader will be pleased to see. When she began to write in the year 1693, she said: " I pen these lines simply under obedience, and with great repugnance. . . . . Believe me, every time I have even to mention these things, my repugnance increases; and having to write about them costs me much. But being commanded to do so overcomes it all, otherwise I should not write a line. . . . . I say all these things under obedience, but I assure you that the struggle is so violent that I scarcely know how to say a word." This aversion never wore off; in the year 1699, she repeats, " I find still the same repugnance to writing that I always did. In 1702 she says, " When I set myself to write the contents of this book, I had to do myself such violence, that I could scarcely finish a line." In 1704, " Whatever I have written has been done under obedience, and my aversion has been sometimes so vehement that I have been hardly able to write a word." In 1716 she says, " I have written under obedience, but it is like death to me." Again, in 1722, " I write by obedience, otherwise I should say nothing." Her writings are full of such expressions, and yet this aversion is coupled with the fact of her having penned so many manuscripts, that they fill a large box, without counting those which she tore up because they had been spoilt by the devil, and those which he afterwards burned in his fury. In order not to absent herself from any conventual office or employment, she was obliged to write all her papers at night when the community was asleep, so that she was not only obliged to take the time from repose, but also from her beloved prayers and penances, which she was in the habit of reserving for that time. We must not forget the frequent and most painful maladies to which she was subject; and it cannot be denied that her obedience was in this respect miraculous.

We will now give those real and tangible miracles which have passed through the ordeal of the processes. We pass over one which Father Tassinari relates, in which she died and rose to life again at his command, because, although we are inclined to think there is sufficient warrant for believing it, it is a matter most difficult of proof, and we mean to confine ourselves to such as are proved beyond all doubt. The fact of her understanding purely mental precepts was certainly supernatural, and occurred several times. Under the same head we may place her going down into the confessional, which she did frequently out of obedience, while she had fevers and other disorders upon her, and her returning thence in perfect health and strength at the command of her confessors. These occurrences were witnessed by the whole community.

One day, when the devils had been beating her, they threw her to the ground from the ceiling, to which they had lifted her, so that she broke her leg. Some days after, Father Cappelletti, for the purpose of testing her obedience, having had her brought to the confessional, said to her, " Have you faith? We shall see if you have. Ask our Lord to cure your broken leg directly." Thus enjoined, she began to pray confidently for this favour, and obtained it on the spot. Before the eyes of all the nuns she went out of the confessional and walked upstairs to her cell. From that time forth she always spoke of it as "the limb of obedience and of faith." On another occasion Satan held her hand over the fire so long that her nails were shrivelled, and the skin scorched up. Two hours afterwards Father Crivelli arrived, and, having heard from the abbess and Sister Ceoli what had happened, he summoned Veronica, and asked her whether she had faith in obedience. She replied in the affirmative. "Very well," said the Father, "in the Name of God Almighty, Father, Son, and Holy Ghost, Three Persons and One God, Living and True, I command you by the sign of the holy cross, which I make over your hand, that it be entirely healed." Then he asked her if she was cured, and she replied, "Yes." Just then Monsignor Eustachj arrived, and when he had been informed of what had taken place, Veronica was summoned to the grate. On seeing the wonderful cure which had been effected, he sent for the abbess and Sister Ceoli, and first of all asked them if they would know the scorched hand again. "Certainly," they replied. "Very well, look at it now," was the answer. Accordingly they both examined it; but not being able to discover the least trace of burning, they were amazed, and exclaimed, "It is a miracle!"

While Veronica was abbess, the three dispensers inadvertently poured into a vessel of putrid oil about three hundred pounds weight of good oil, which had been provided for the table. One of them, Sister Mary Tommassini, being in great distress, hereupon implored Father Guelfi to command their saintly abbess to bless the vessel. The confessor having issued the desired injunction, and his obedient penitent having faithfully executed it, the oil was found to be of so good a quality, that it was used in the refectory with general satisfaction. The lay sister Frances, who had charge of the garden, having lost all hope of getting rid of a sort of worm called in that part of the country *cicerbola*, which is very destructive to the roots of plants, had recourse to Father Tassinari, who was at that time their confessor, and requested that he would desire Veronica to bless the garden for that particular intention. She did so immediately, and all the worms came up out of the ground, and collected together in one spot. Then Veronica said, " Let us leave them to be food for our chickens." The fowls were accordingly turned in, and the garden was completely cleared of the nuisance.

Such extraordinary incidents sufficiently sanction our calling Veronica's obedience miraculous; and they might be added to those given by that great master of obedience, S. Ignatius Loyola, in his celebrated letter to his religious in Portugal, in which he commends the more perfect degrees of this virtue. But besides the mute language of these wonderful events, it pleased heaven to express an open approval of the blind and most perfect obedience of Veronica. To preserve her from all risks of illusion, her directors had commanded her to pay no regard, but, on the contrary, to exhibit marks of contempt, even if our Blessed Lady, or our Lord Jesus Christ were to appear to her in person, for such treatment is intolerable to the evil spirits, whereas those who come from heaven rejoice at it when it is done for a good object, and out of obedience. Among the innumerable visions of the most holy Mary which were vouchsafed to Veronica, she had one after the gospel of the first Mass on Christmas Day. The Queen of heaven held her divine Son in her arms, and was attended by a multitude of saints, among whom were distinguished the seven founders of the order of Servites. Having related this event in her journal, she adds, "As usual, I forced myself not to desire these kind of things, and I even despised the vision as an illusion of the devil. But the most holy Mary, with a gracious expression of countenance, and a smile full of majesty, said to me, 'Daughter, I am no evil spirit, nor are these my children such. Nevertheless, continue to act as thou hast done, for thou hast been often bidden to do so by obedience, and by myself.' She immediately caused me to adore the Most Holy Trinity; and at the same moment there came to me three rays of light, and I was confirmed as daughter, spouse, and disciple of the Three Divine Persons, as I have frequently described elsewhere. Then all those saints and blessed souls offered up an act of thanksgiving for me to God and the most Holy Mary. . . . . The Blessed Virgin then caused me to renew my profession, and when I came to that part of the formula in which eternal life is promised, all the saints answered, Amen, and all the instruments in my heart were moved." The last fact to which she alludes was one of not unfrequent occurrence; it was discussed and approved by the tribunal of the Sacred Congregation of Rites, who acknowledged it to be a real prodigy.

CHAPTER VIII.

HER TENDER DEVOTION TO THE BLESSED VIRGIN, TO HER GUARDIAN ANGEL, AND THE OTHER SAINTS.

WE have doubted whether we ought to devote a special -chapter to this subject, for what has been already said in the course of our narrative, is amply sufficient to mark out Veronica as one of the most devoted of the clients of Mary. But on the other hand, considering that this peculiar grace being, as the Fathers tell us, most efficacious in promoting our salvation, as well as one of the most beautiful of the prerogatives of the saints, we have resolved to dwell on it particularly, as there are many things concerning it which have not yet been drawn out.

Although we have read the lives of many other saints, we have never met, excepting in Veronica's case, with examples of familiar intercourse between our Blessed Lady and a child of three years old. It is, indeed, a peculiar privilege, and one never granted to any but chosen souls. Nor can it be supposed that the Queen of heaven would condescend to such holy intimacy with a soul that did not burn with love for her. Such communications must have marvellously increased the affection of Veronica for her who is of simple creatures the most worthy of love. We have seen that our Lord Jesus Christ deigned to be her visible instructor in virtue, and in this the Blessed Virgin also took part. Our Saint has left us many of the lessons which she received from her glorious Patroness; for Jesus Himself had been pleased expressly to commission His holy Mother to teach her, when He appeared in her company to

Veronica, and pronounced those sweet words, "My most beloved Mother, I wish this our beloved to be always guided by thee."

But we must not linger on what is plain. It is time for us to proceed to certain indisputable facts which will give us an idea of the caresses which took place between our Lady and her devoted daughter. It is well known that it is the cherished office of love to share in the sorrows of the beloved object. Therefore it was that Veronica was so fond of testifying her homage by participating in the martyrdom of the Queen of Dolours. On this theme she would often meditate and speak. When she did so, it was with such a feeling of compassion, that Father Tassinari declares himself to have been frequently moved to tears; and at such times she seemed to him a living portrait of her whose woes she depicted. And indeed these Dolours had made so powerful an impression on her heart, as to leave there the symbolic representation of the seven swords. She was so anxious that her religious should be incited to practise the same devotion, that she placed in the choir a statue of the Mother of Dolours, in whose honour she appointed a solemn procession on the third Sunday of every month, which is still kept up by the community. When she was elected abbess, and had accepted, according to custom, the keys, the rules, and the seal of the convent, she placed them all before the most holy Sacrament, and then, falling on her knees at the foot of the superior's stall, she directed Sister Florida Ceoli, her assistant, to place thereon their statue of the Mother of Dolours. This done, Veronica presented the insignia of her office to the sacred image, imploring the Blessed Virgin to be abbess instead of herself. Every evening before retiring to rest, she renewed the devout ceremony of surrendering the keys to her as to her superior.

There is no doubt that our Blessed Lady graciously accepted the offering of her client, with all the benignity of her maternal heart. We learn from Veronica herself that her heavenly Advocate appeared to her, and told her lovingly that she must not shrink from that undertaking, for that she would herself fulfil the functions of abbess. If any reader should be disinclined to believe this vision and statement of Veronica, he may be convinced by various facts, which were vouched for by nearly all the witnesses in the process, who deposed that during the abbess-ship of our Saint, they had sensibly and tangibly felt that the most Holy Virgin was their abbess, and spoke through the lips of Veronica. This was clear from the wonderful effect produced by her discourses at chapter, as also by the marvellous order and peace which characterized the community during the happy period of her rule, and the copious alms, both of money and provisions, which flowed in from all quarters so abundantly as to enable the building and other advantageous arrangements to be forwarded. In order that they might all recognize the maternal hand whence all this providential bounty flowed, these benefits invariably coincided with the approach or celebration of the more solemn feasts of our Blessed Lady ; so that it was a common saying among the nuns, " Our divine abbess has paid for the feast." Hence Veronica called her, not only the superior, but the procuratrix of the establishment. It is pleasant to read the following note which she sent on the 14th of April, 1723, to her bishop, into whose hands she committed all the money she received:—" Your lordship must forgive me, if I again trouble you with a letter. *Our Superior*, the most Holy Virgin, who provides us with money and other alms, is the cause of my doing so. It is she who now sends you thirty-three pauls. I ask permission to write to the manufacturer, to tell him to make some cloth for the religious. I know he cannot make it immediately, for he requires three or four months' notice. It will cost a good deal, but I am not afraid; I rely implicitly on the *Superior*, and on your lordship."

As specimens of her affection for our Blessed Lady, we shall select two of the letters which she wrote to Father Tassinari, and which were examined by the Sacred Congregation of Rites. On the 2nd of February, 1713, she writes:—" Father, do not be discouraged at the coldness of your daughter. Give her your charitable assistance, by commands, penances, and sufferings. I speak from my heart when I tell you that I can no longer endure myself. I am satisfied with the Will of God, but I am in fear and trembling lest I should be banished from God on account of my ingratitude. I go to the feet of most holy Mary, and there I make my protestations, renew my vows, and offer up my hearty prayers. But only think! she does not wish for my prayers. I go on, and throw the blame on your reverence, saying: '*Mamma mia*, I can do nothing else. Holy obedience sends me to thee; thou art bound to hear me. After all, I am thy child, and the child of thy servant. Thou art the Mother of Dolours—behold me who am full of sorrow. I repent of my sins, I grieve for my ingratitude; I know that I dare not lift my eyes to heaven. Full of confidence in thy mercy, I resign myself to thy will like one dead.' Then I experience a sensation at my heart which I cannot express, but so secretly, that I can hardly feel it. To God be all the glory."

Again, on the 12th of March, 1721, she writes:— "I live contented in the midst of troubles. Oh, how sweet and precious it is to live for the love of God! Although my Mamma is hidden, I know she assists me; and I bless her for such great charity. If it were not for her, woe to me! I receive every blessing from her, and your reverence knows that it has always been so. It is very surprising. If you only knew, my father, the way in which the most holy Mary treats my soul, you would be beside yourself with delight. I ask her for graces, and she immediately enfolds me in the Will of God. I am sure to receive some grace, not that which I ask for, but that which God pleases to send me. So I have good reason for praying, and I feel that the Blessed Virgin stirs me up to do so. She does all for me in God's way, and I agree with her."

In the last of these letters, the powerful protection vouchsafed to Veronica by Mary is specially apparent. But perhaps another anecdote may be useful to excite others to a similar devotion. Besides showering such abundant supplies from every side on the convent, while our Saint was abbess, the Queen of heaven not seldom condescended to assist her in those laborious occupations which she still continued. One day when she was employed with others of the community in washing their clothes, it was observed that she accomplished her work in an incredibly short time, and with wonderful perfection; and they several times heard her exclaim : " Most holy Virgin, art thou going to do everything thyself and leave nothing for me?" Then they were no longer surprised at her amazing progress, but were struck with admiration at the condescension of Mary, and at the merit which Veronica must have acquired to receive so high an honour.

Many years after she had received the stigmata, Mgr. Codebò, the new bishop, directed her to draw out in writing full and precise details of the event. Veronica was a good deal perplexed, for she did not thoroughly recollect all the circumstances, and she was afraid either of failing in obedience, or of deceiving her superior by any incorrectness in the narrative. But in the midst of her difficulties our Blessed Lady appeared, and related the whole distinctly to her.

In connection with the present subject, and with her writings, is the following beautiful incident, which Sister Florida Ceoli witnessed with her own eyes. About seven years before her death, Veronica was ordered by her confessor to write down in a fresh book an account of the state of her soul. She obeyed, but as the things which she had to relate were for the most part such as were likely to do her honour, she expressed herself as laconically as possible. In the evening Sister Florida saw that she had nearly finished her task, and the next morning, on entering the chamber of her holy abbess, she found her in tears and deeply afflicted. She inquired the reason, and, as Veronica had great confidence in her, arising from their similarity of spirit, she replied that during the night she had had a vision of her guardian angel and most holy Mary, who, having received from the angel the book she had been writing, looked it over, and reproached Veronica with disobedience in not giving a much fuller account. Our

Blessed Lady then desired the angel to cancel all that she had written, and told Veronica that she must write the whole of it again better. As soon as our Saint returned to herself, she took up her book, and found it perfectly white, as though no one had ever written on it; in which state she showed it to Sister Florida, who had seen it on the previous evening almost covered with writing. Nor was this the only rebuke which Veronica received from the Mother of God, who, wishing to raise her to a still higher degree of perfection, frequently reprimanded her for her faults, informing her how she might obtain the full approval of her divine Son. These reproofs were the best tokens which our Lady could give of the great love which she bore Veronica, as well as of her special protection and care for her.

A still more striking instance of this maternal affection was related in the process by Father Tassinari, who was acquainted with all the secrets of our Saint. According to his testimony, which is above all suspicion, the Blessed Virgin would frequently place her divine Infant in the hands of Veronica, particularly during the feasts of Christmas. On several occasions she communicated our Saint with her own hand, taking the Sacred Host from the altar, or from the tabernacle. Frequently in her visions our Blessed Lady seemed to play with the heart of Veronica, drawing it from her bosom, showing it to her with those mysterious marks which have been already described, and then replacing it near her own or that of her divine Son, exclaiming, "Heart of my heart!" Then, again, she would make an exchange, putting into the bosom of Veronica her own and that of Jesus. Such exchanges are well known to be no more than sensible symbols of the invisible operations of grace in the heart of Veronica, but as such clearly they demonstrate the resemblance of her heart to those of Jesus and Mary, as well as that conformity of will and affection which existed between the three, and which is the most sure sign and fruit of that solid and tender devotion which Veronica cherished towards the Queen of heaven and her divine Son.

Before closing this chapter, the reader must permit us to say something of her devotion to her guardian angel and her patron saints. There is no room for details of the novenas and other works of piety which she daily offered up in honour of these inhabitants of heaven. Her visions proved how acceptable they were. She frequently beheld her guardian angel presenting her at the Throne of the august Trinity, or making intercession on her behalf at the tribunal of the divine Judge, or before the bright throne of the Queen of heaven. Many times she saw S. Joseph, the great spouse of Mary, S. John the precursor of our Lord, the great apostle S. Paul, her own patriarch S. Francis of Assisi, and her mother S. Clare, SS. Catherine of Siena, Teresa of Jesus, Rose of Lima, Dominic, Francis Xavier, Pellegrino Laziosi, Aloysius Gonzaga, and others; a certain sign that she had merited these rare favours by her devotion to them. We cannot conclude without remarking how much those persons err, who seek to gain a vulgar reputation for wit among the irreligious by ridiculing the devout practices which the Church sanctions in honour of the saints. In the lives of all the heroes of our holy religion from the very earliest ages, we find examples of similar homage to those immortal warriors, who, having completed their earthly career, have attained crowns of eternal glory. Such examples should make us smile at our modern reformers, while we follow the footsteps of those who have preceded us in the faith, and are now enjoying the rich harvest of glory in heaven, and on earth the honour of being raised on the altars of the Church.

CHAPTER IX.

HER GIFTS OF PROPHECY AND MIRACLES DURING LIFE.

It is natural that a soul enriched with such heroic virtue and such extraordinary privileges, should be likewise adorned with every other ornament with which God is pleased to decorate His saints before the eyes of the world. To begin with prophecy, which is a gift that has been vouchsafed to nearly all the saints. Veronica possessed it to such an extent that it was commonly said in the monastery that nearly all her words were so many prophecies, for they invariably came to pass. The reader may recollect how she predicted her own death. Sister Mary Magdalen Boscaini relates of herself, that having applied for admission into the convent of S. Clare in the time of Mgr. Codebò, the bishop was just then unwilling to admit any one. Her parents and an uncle, who was a priest, were opposed to her wish, and called her mad for wanting to be a Capuchin nun, particularly as her constitution had been injured by a serious illness. She was extremely distressed at this opposition, and despaired of attaining the desired boon; but Veronica told her that in time she would overcome it all, and so it proved. The same thing happened to Sister Florida Ceoli. She had come, like the former, from Pisa, to apply for admission, but the nuns had no sooner seen her than they discouraged her advances, thinking her unsuited to their community. But Veronica plainly told the bishop that a chapter had better be held, and that the votes would be unanimous in her favour. The event verified her prediction; and both these individuals became of great use to the monastery by their exemplary virtue. An opposite case was that of Margaret Ranucci, who was received by Mgr. Eustachj. Veronica, who was then novice-mistress, distinctly told him that the young lady was not meant for them. However, she was clothed, but two months afterwards she left them and went to Perugia, where she entered a convent of "the Poor," as they were called. She uttered a similar prediction on the admission of Signora Clarice de' Marchesi del Monte, who was not even clothed, but went away and entered the enclosed convent of the same city.

Upon the death of Mgr. Eustachj, the Capuchin nuns prayed for the election of another good pastor. Veronica did so particularly, by order of Father Crivelli, who, as her director, enjoined her to mention every light that she might receive from heaven. This fact is related by the good father in the process. After she had prayed for some time, she said that she had seen a bishop's mitre, bearing in front the two capital letters A.C. Father Crivelli inferred that these would be the initials of the future bishop, so he glanced his eye over the directory of *Cracas* to see if any of the prelates had a name and surname corresponding with these letters. The only one he could find was Mgr. Antonio Cansacchi. He thought this must be the one, and the rumour got abroad through the whole city; but news came from Rome that quite another person had been fixed upon. So Father Crivelli said to Veronica, " Your prediction has ended in smoke." But she replied that she had no such doubts herself, because she had since seen the mitre with the same letters, and six additional ones at the sides. Presently intelligence arrived that the individual who had been elected was a most worthy ecclesiastic of Bologne, named Alessandro Codebò, not yet a prelate. Every one was astonished. Father Crivelli does not tell us what these other six letters were; but we learn from the evidence of others that before the election took place they saw a sketch made by Veronica of the mitre as she had seen it, and afterwards heard the interpretation from herself. In the middle were the letters A.C., signifying Alexander Codebò; on one side were the letters M. V. D., Mariæ Virginis Devotus—devout to the Virgin Mary. On the other side were the letters P.E.O., for Pastor Ecclesiæ Optimus—an excellent pastor of the Church. These epithets were merited by the new bishop during the whole course of his life. Sister Boscaini attests that during his lifetime Veronica informed her confessor that he would be succeeded by Monsignor Gasparini. This came to pass six years after the death of our Saint. The same religious adds that when the see of Cortona became vacant, she foretold that it would be occupied by Mgr. Gherardi.

When Father Raniero Guelfi was a young man, she told him that he would one day be an Oratorian, notwithstanding the opposition of his father. When he was in the Oratory, she told him to go to Borgo S. Sepolcro, for that his father was at the point of death. Finally, she predicted that he would assist her in her passage from this world; and all these things came to pass. When Father Vincent Segapeli, an Oratorian, was dangerously ill, she assured him of his recovery, though all had given him up: the same happened to Father Tassinari, another of her confessors, who had been given over by his physicians on account of gangrene. When Father Crivelli was summoned to Rome by the General, Father Michael Angelo Tamburini, in order that he might take the place of Father Merlini, she told him plainly that he would not remain there, but would shortly return to Città di Castello, and so he did. She predicted the birth of a son to the Emperor Charles VI., and her words were verified, though the child's life was short. She also foretold the destruction that would be caused by the plague at Marseilles, when it was reported in Città di Castello that its ravages were over in that city.

We should weary the reader if we were to recount the innumerable prophecies with which the processes are filled, so we will conclude with one relating to Signor Don Giacomo Lomellini, who was the companion of Father Crivelli in his missions, as he had been of the celebrated Father Segneri the younger; for he deserves honourable mention. Veronica was indebted to this holy and zealous ecclesiastic, for he had been her director during the period when Father Crivelli was obliged to absent himself, in order to proceed to Florence. When Father Lomellini was dangerously ill at Città di Castello in December, 1714,

Father Crivelli ordered Veronica to recommend him to God. She did so, and afterwards said that most holy Mary had appeared to her with a cross adorned with five jewels, which she informed her were intended to represent the virtues of Lomellini; adding that he would not die until she should see the same cross again, decorated with a larger number of gems, to indicate the greater virtue which the good priest would have by that time attained. She repeated this intimation to Father Lomellini himself. At the beginning of the following year, Father Crivelli set out with his companion to give the spiritual exercises at Perugia; and there Father Lomellini fell sick again. Thence they proceeded to Foligno, where, perceiving that his companion was suffering from fever, Father Crivelli sent him to Sarzana for change of air, while he returned in March to Città di Castello. He had no sooner arrived there than he asked Veronica what she thought of his beloved companion. She said that she believed him to be near his end, for that she had had a vision in which Father Segneri the younger had appeared to her, holding in his hand the same cross which she had previously seen, all covered with jewels, which circumstance coincided with the notice she had then received from most holy Mary. Hereupon Father Crivelli wrote to Sarzana to congratulate Father Lomellini on the approaching termination of his sufferings, and on the rich reward which was prepared for him in heaven; but before the letter could reach him, Father Lomellini breathed his last.

To the spirit of prophecy may also be referred the power of penetrating secrets buried in the heart; although this may more properly be termed the faculty of searching hearts. We have had instances of this in the tenth chapter of the first book, and therefore we will only give one example here. Bishop Codebò was consulting with Father Guelfi, her confessor, as to what should be done with her after her death. The next time Veronica saw that prelate she said to him, as if she had heard the whole discussion : "My lord, I beg that you will do with my body exactly as you please, without troubling yourself in the least." We have seen how she was able to divine the mental precepts of her confessors, and also her discovery of Father Crivelli's design of causing her to be appointed abbess. We will conclude with Father Crivelli's own words: "I must acknowledge that, from the opinion which I entertained of her gift of reading hearts, I used to treat her with reverential fear and deference; being convinced that she knew everything that was passing in my heart."

The evidence of such a witness renders all further remark superfluous. We shall not attempt to speak here of her gifts of supernatural science and discernment of spirit; nor even of her ecstasies, which were still more wonderful, for the reader has read much of these in the course of the narrative, but will pass on to the miraculous cures which she effected.

The following cases are selected from the processes. A Capuchin nun of her own convent was afflicted with a festering wound in one of her limbs, which she could never bring herself to show to a surgeon. At last the torment she suffered was such that she told Veronica, who visited her with the utmost charity, and bathed the part affected with a little rose-water. The next morning it was found that she was completely cured. Another, who was suffering from a violent headache and other bad symptoms, applied to our Saint, who had no sooner touched her head than every trace of indisposition vanished. Sister Catherine Cappelletti, who was cook in the year 1719, was troubled with an inflammation in her eye, in consequence of a piece of egg-shell having flown up into it. Her companions and Gentili, the surgeon, did all they could, but were unable to extract it. The swelling and pain became so great, that the surgeon resolved to use his lancet the next morning, though he protested that it would be running a great risk. During the night his patient was in convulsions, and Veronica was informed of this at matins by Sister Mary Constance, the infirmarian. Therefore, as soon as the office was over, she went to the sufferer, and recommended her to try to rest a little; to which the sister replied that it was impossible, in consequence of the spasms she felt. Then the saintly abbess embraced her, pressed her head to her own bosom, blessed her, and departed. She had hardly left the cell when the invalid fell into a quiet slumber, which lasted till morning. She woke up when the infirmarians came, and being asked how she was, replied that she had slept all night. They went up to her and examined her eye, which they found perfectly free from the splinter of egg-shell, and without the least swelling or inflammation. When the surgeon arrived, he was astonished to find that there was no need of the operation he had proposed, for the eye was perfectly well, and remained so ever after. The same Sister Catherine suffered for several years from a severe and incurable headache, and when Veronica was confined to her bed in her last illness, she fell on her knees before her, and implored her to bless her, lest the excess of pain she felt should deprive her of her senses. Our Saint laid her hand on Sister Catherine's head and said, "You will not lose your senses; on the contrary, you will be cured." From that time forward she never had the slightest return of her headache.

Sister Mary Fucci (sister, we believe, of Canon Vincent Fucci, a priest of high character, who died at Rome, at an advanced age, and was a great friend of ours), had a great number of warts on her hands, of the size of a farthing. They often opened, and no remedy could be found for them. According to the usual routine of the convent, her turn came round to serve in the kitchen, but Veronica, who was then superior, would not allow her to do this, thinking that the community would object to have their food touched by her. Sister Mary, however, was extremely grieved at this prohibition, and resorted to the unwise expedient of cutting her warts, although it caused her extreme pain. The bleeding which ensued was so copious that she ran into the kitchen to stanch it with cold water, but unsuccessfully. While she was so employed, the holy abbess came up, and, ascertaining how matters stood, reproved her gravely, and added, in order to frighten her a little, "Are you not aware that such a foolish step as that which you have taken may cause your hands to fester?" Then she ordered her to get herself attended to, and not to rise for matins that night. Sister Mary Fucci happened to have at hand a piece of Veronica's scapular, which was commonly called "patience." In this she wrapped her wounded hands, having removed the bandages which the infirmarians had put on; after which, she passed the night in refreshing sleep. When she awoke the next morning, she uncovered her hands and found that they were perfectly cured, neither was there the least trace of wart or wound. She was amazed, and so were all the nuns as soon as they heard it, particularly as the piece of scapular which had effected the wonderful cure was found not to have the least mark of blood upon it. The same day she was able to enter the kitchen and serve her turn.

No less miraculous was what happened to a nephew of the two lay sisters, Frances and Giacinta. The poor youth had a cataract in his eye, and Sister Giacinta, considering it incurable, sent him in a phial some water in which Veronica had washed her hands. With this the young man bathed his eye, which was immediately restored to its natural state. The healing water was sent back to the convent, and the nuns observed that it emitted a delicious fragrance.

But it is scarcely necessary to recount individual instances, when we recollect that her whole life was one perpetual miracle of the most stupendous order. We do not speak of the supernatural character of her virtues and holiness, but such things as are considered miraculous in temporal matters, such as the unheard-of penances with which she macerated her body, the rigorous fasts which she observed, the way in which she deprived herself of sleep, her incessant labours of the most fatiguing description, the frequent and horrible attacks which she endured from the demons, the wound inflicted on her heart, the sacred stigmata, her frequent participation in the chalice, the scourging, the crowning with thorns, and all the sufferings of the divine Passion, including the crucifixion itself. To all this must be added the almost continual transports of her love of God; her frequent ecstasies and raptures, which give assistance and comfort to the soul, in proportion as they enfeeble the body. Neither must we forget her constant infirmities and dangerous illnesses ; and yet, in the midst of it all, she spent fifty years in religion, and attained to the age of sixty-seven. Surely the mere fact of her living on as she did was a miracle, and her whole life was a chain of supernatural events of the most marvellous order. Such was the opinion of her companions in the cloister, and of the medical attendants who investigated her case.

In conclusion, we will relate two miraculous circumstances which came under our own observation. The first was the striking conversion of one of our penitents at Rome. We say striking, because, although not publicly known, it was a very remarkable miracle. We suppose our readers to be aware of the teaching of S. Thomas, in common with all the Fathers and theological writers, that the justification of a sinner is the most wonderful of all the works of God *ad extra;* wherefore the Church prays : " O God, Who dost particularly manifest Thy omnipotence by sparing and showing mercy." Now this person, who had committed enormous crimes, and lived for some year or more in a state of despair, was recommended by us to seek deliverance from his miserable condition through the intercession of Veronica, the writing of whose life had inspired us with great confidence in her. One day, when he least expected it, he felt himself changed at heart, and filled once more with confidence in God, so that he made a generous and devout confession, and lived peacefully ever afterwards, with no sorrow concerning his past life, except the thought of the grievous wrong he had done to

God, more by distrust of His infinite mercy than by any other sin.

The other circumstance occurred to ourselves. We had for a long time desired a spiritual favour, which we have reasons for not describing more particularly, but which was equivalent to a great miracle. As our confidence and devotion towards Veronica increased in proportion as we proceeded with her life, we used to recommend this favour to her, and when we least deserved it, on the 17th of March, 1801, to our unspeakable joy we received the desired grace. Therefore, as a perpetual remembrance of our gratitude to our great benefactress, we mention it in these pages, and we beg all who shall in future reprint our book, not to omit these miracles, in order that all who read of them may be animated to confide in the infinite mercy of God, and in the powerful intercession of this great Saint.

NOTE.

UPON the death of S. Veronica, the bishop began to collect evidence of her holy life. The process was solemnly opened by him on the 6th of December, 1727, and completed by his successor on the 13th of January, 1735. After the usual preliminary examinations, the introduction of the cause at Rome was signed by Pope Benedict XIV., on the 7th of July, 1745. The virtues of the servant of God were approved by Pope Pius VI., on the 24th of April, 1796, and two of her miracles on Whit-Monday, the 7th of June, 1802, by Pope Pius VII., who, on the 12th of

September in the same year, issued the decree of her beatification. Further miracles, which occurred in 1815 and 1818, were approved by the Sacred Congregation of Rites, and, on the feast of S. Philip Neri, May 26th, 1831, Pope Gregory XVI. decided that her canonization could be safely proceeded with. She was solemnly canonized by the same Pope on Trinity Sunday, May 26th, 1839, in the Vatican Basilica, together with S. Alphonso Liguori, S. Francis di Girolamo, S. John Joseph of the Cross, and S. Pacificus of San Severino.

THE SPIRITUAL LIFE

OF

THE BLESSED BATTISTA VARANI,

RELIGIOUS OF

THE ORDER OF S. CLARE.

HISTORICAL NOTICE.

LEANDER ALBERT, in his description of Italy, includes Camerino among the most important towns of Umbria. He says that the sovereignty of this town belonged for a long time to the illustrious family of Varani, of which he gives a brief history. One of the most celebrated of them was Gentilis Varani, renowned for his valour and prudence. His son Rudolph espoused successively two wives, leaving two sons by each. The elder brothers assassinated the two younger, and the town revolted against the criminals. The elder was put to death, and the younger having fled, was killed at Tolentino, but the popular vengeance fell upon his five sons, who were all beheaded.

This frightful tragedy occurred in 1433, after which the citizens maintained their independence for ten years. At the end of this period a return of affection for the family of Varani made them recall Rudolph and Julius Cæsar, the sons of one of the murdered brothers.

Julius was a great warrior, and commanded the troops of the Holy See, under the two Popes, Nicholas V. and Sixtus IV. He afterwards entered the service of the Venetian Republic in the same capacity, then that of Matthias Corvinus, King of Hungary, and everywhere acquired much honour. His brother Rudolph dying without issue, he inherited his sovereignty, and returned to his domains. Under his reign Camerino became a beautiful and powerful city. He constructed several fine buildings, among which the church of S. Mary was remarkable. He rebuilt the walls, and provided for the defence of his territory by the construction of strong castles.

This prince espoused Joanna Malatesta, daughter of Sigismund, Prince of Rimini, and from this marriage sprung Battista Varani, who was born on the 9th April, 1458. She was baptized Camilla, but took the name of Battista on entering religion. History gives us no information regarding her until she was ten years old, and her humility knew so well how to conceal the favours which God bestowed on her during the twenty-three last years of her life, that we are equally ignorant concerning that period, and had it not been for a circumstance for which we cannot thank God too much, we should have been equally uninformed regarding the twenty intermediate years; but our Heavenly Father permitted her to be assailed with such violent temptations from the devil, that for three years she suffered a sort of martyrdom. The confessor who then directed her had known her only six months, and it was necessary that he should be made acquainted with her previous life. He consequently required from her a history of herself, and enjoined her to write unreservedly everything that had occurred to her for the last twenty years. She did so, and to this we are indebted for the treasure of edification which her holy life offers to us. The fragments of it do not form a regular history, and Pascucci, to supply the deficiency, gives a chronological table of the principal events of her life, until the end of the fifteenth century. We place it here, in order that the narrative may not be interrupted afterwards.

LIFE OF BATTISTA IN THE WORLD, IN ITS CHRONOLOGICAL ORDER.

1. She was born on the 9th of April, 1458.
2. Ten years later, in 1468, her heart began to burn with love for the Passion of her Lord.
3. After a general confession made in Lent, 1477, she felt ·herself strongly drawn towards a religious life; but instead of surrendering herself to the call of grace, she struggled against it for a whole year.
4. Vanquished by the goodness of God, she at last resolved to obey, and declared her determination to her father about Easter, 1478.
5. The prince refused his consent, and continued his opposition during two years and a half.
6. In the month of November, 1481, he at length permitted her to follow her vocation, and give herself to God. From this moment she was inundated with graces, and conceived such an ardent desire of suffering that God was moved by it to satisfy her. He sent her a severe illness, so that for a short time she was in great danger, and it left her in a weak state of health for thirteen years.

LIFE OF BATTISTA IN RELIGION.

1. On the 14th of November, 1481, she received the habit of S. Clare in the Convent of Urbino, and, instead of Camilla, took the name of Battista.
2. Five months before her profession she wrote a letter under the dictation of Jesus Christ.

3. Difficulties of which we have no record prolonged her noviciate beyond the ordinary period, so that she was not professed until some time in the year 1483.

4. Her father built a convent at Camerino in the same year, and this was the occasion of many bitter trials to her.

5. She took possession of this convent with some nuns on the 4th of January, 1484, and having made anew a general confession to Father Peter Moliano, Provincial of the Franciscans, she recovered her peace of mind. It was then that her celestial favours became frequent: first S. Clare appeared to her, afterwards she was conducted into a place where Jesus was crucified, and there she remained two whole months. Then the fire of seraphic love burned within her for three months. At last she obtained weekly communion, which she enjoyed during two years.

6. It was during the summer of 1487 that she received the order to write, and that she wrote her Treatise on the Interior Sorrows of Jesus Christ.

7. In the month of August following, while she was enjoying profound peace, God permitted her to be deceived by the demons, in order to prove her still more.

8. On the 11th of October following they began to afflict her with grievous temptations, which she endured for three years without disclosing them to any one.

9. After the death of Father Moliano on the 25th of July, 1490, she took another confessor, from whom she hoped to receive some solace for her pain, but her hopes were disappointed, for he was obliged to quit Camerino two months after.

10. It appears that this new director at once re-

quired from her a written history of her former life, which she completed in the month of March following. He had then left Camerino, but it was forwarded to him. The additional letters were written immediately afterwards.

11. This entire opening of her heart brought back peace to her soul, but only for a short period, for soon after temptations assailed her with redoubled violence, and this tempest lasted about two years. It ceased entirely towards the middle of October, 1492.

12. Wishing to explain to one of her spiritual children the trials through which God makes the souls of His beloved pass, she gave herself as an example, as if she were speaking of a third person, and she thus related the tribulations which she had suffered for five years. "The person of whom I speak," she said, "was forced to call upon God continually, and to invoke His aid, saying, 'Lord, come to my assistance; O Lord, make haste to help me. I have lifted up my eyes to Thee, Who dwellest in heaven. I have lifted up my eyes to the mountains, from whence help shall come to me; all my hope is in the Lord. O my God! help me, and abandon me not in this extreme peril. O God! my strength has gone from me, sustain me with Thy powerful Arm. I can no longer stand, stretch out towards me Thy helping Hand. Thou sleepest, my Jesus, in the frail bark of my soul, and the tempest raised by the demon threatens to overwhelm me. Ah! without Thee the calm will never return.' It was thus that the person of whom I speak fixed her soul on God during this furious tempest, and He never leaves His elect during the time of war. Imitate her, my son, in the temptations which oppress you, and you will soon experience His mercy in your

regard. Act so as to be able to say with the royal prophet, 'The Lord was continually before my eyes, and His divine presence was the object of the meditation of my heart.' You will easily find in the Holy Scriptures many other texts, which prove that the thoughts of the saints were unceasingly fixed on the Lord."

When the Blessed Battista wrote these things, towards the close of the fifteenth century, she had been a nun for eighteen years. Of her spiritual life in religion we know only what she has judged proper to tell. Pascucci has collected some things in the chapters on her virtues in the supplement to this volume. The last twenty-three years of her life are unknown to us. She was never formally beatified, but it is believed that Clement X. authorized the devotions practised in her honour at Camerino, and all authors who have mentioned her since the beginning of the seventeenth century give her the title of Blessed.

PROLOGUE.

My Reverend Father in Jesus Christ,

I must begin by telling you that the whole of this month of February has been to me a season of battle and bitter sorrows, caused by my resistance to a powerful inspiration, of the origin of which I was ignorant. If I had believed it to have come from God, I certainly should not have dared to struggle against it; but I suspected it to be a temptation of the spirit of pride, permitted by God to try me, for the punishment of my sins. Seeing myself destitute of all help, and deprived of all human consolation, I had recourse to prayer, my accustomed resource. I besought the sweet Mother of God, with all the love of which I am capable, to dissipate the darkness into which I saw myself plunged in punishment of my sins, and to cause a ray of light to penetrate my mind, by which I might discern whether it was the Will of God or not. After having, through the whole month, wearied heaven with my cries of distress, without gaining anything but extreme fatigue of spirit, on this second Sunday of Lent, the 20th of February, on retiring from the holy Table, I have resolved to obey the interior inspiration, persuaded that otherwise I shall never regain peace. God grant that this determination be conformable to His Will. I have confidence that it is so; and I believe that it is by His grace that I have made this resolve. However that may be, it is certain that this obedience will cause me nothing but extreme confusion, both before God and before you, and this reason confirms me in my resolution, more than many others which point it out to me as very useful, and even necessary.

This inspiration, my father, makes me anxious about my salvation. I will tell you things which I have never before told to any one, and will discover secrets hitherto carefully hidden in my heart. In a word, I will recount my spiritual life from the beginning until the present time. God is Master: and since He wills it, I will it also. It is true, this is not the first time that I have treated of this matter with you, my father; but what I have hitherto said was so obscure that you could not comprehend it. I must frankly admit that formerly I spoke incoherently; now it will be otherwise, and I will unfold to you, although against my will, that wound which has been hidden for three years at the bottom of my heart, and has pierced it, even as the spear of the soldier pierced the Heart of Jesus. I will tell you all without reserve; deign to listen with an attentive ear.

Oh, my father! have pity on a poor sinner, who, like another Magdalen, prostrating herself at the Feet of Jesus, casts herself at your paternal feet, with tears in her eyes and shame on her forehead, humbly to disclose to you the history of her unfortunate happiness. It seems to me that I may well give it this name, since in punishment of my sins, my infidelities, and my ingratitude, it is changed into bitterness, into wormwood and gall. I conjure you to cast an eye of enlightened compassion on my sad condition, and to judge if there be any sorrow like to mine.

Having to speak of such high matters, for they refer to God and to the divine things, which His merciful grace has deigned to work within me—my spirit is troubled, and with trembling do I undertake to write what you will read, because I know my misery, and recognize that in me there is only falsehood and lies. I implore the Spirit of God, the Lover of truth and purity, with a suppliant and plaintive voice, to assist me in the history I am about to relate. May He grant me the grace to recount simply and without dissimulation, the particular gifts and benefits which I have received, in spite of my unworthiness, from the most clement Father of mercies. On my part, I feel more inclined to curtail than to exaggerate what I have to say. At least, I confide it to you under the seal of confession, and therefore I begin by saying: "I confess to Almighty God, and to you, my father."

NOTE.—The confessor respected her wishes on this point, and communicated the manuscript to no one while she lived. It appears even that he dared not permit himself to divulge it after her death; neither did those whose heritage it afterwards became, so that it remained hidden for nearly a hundred years. But at last, God, by Whose command these wonders had been written, disposed that it should be published for the consolation of devout souls who walk along the way of divine love, in the blood-stained foot-prints of our Redeemer.

CHAPTER I.

HER VOW MADE IN CHILDHOOD RELATIVE TO THE PASSION OF JESUS CHRIST.—HER PROGRESS IN THIS DEVOTION, AND THE PIOUS EXERCISES WHICH IT SUGGESTED TO HER.

BE it known to you, my father, that by the grace of God, it is you, and you only, who have given the first impulse to my spiritual life. I can well imagine your surprise, perhaps even your incredulity, because I know you have no knowledge of the fact I declare to you: for, as it was connected with the favours God has bestowed on me, I had determined never to divulge it, and would not have broken my resolution had I not been compelled to do so. However, your astonishment will cease when you have heard my story, and you will agree with me that all is possible with God. The last time you preached at Camerino, I was about eight years old, or ten at most—calculate yourself, my father, and you will discover the exact time; I am now thirty-three years old, having been born on the 9th of April, 1458. It was on Good Friday that you preached your last sermon, and of my own accord I went to hear you. In truth I heard you, not only with attention, which of itself was a grace of the Holy Spirit, but in an abstraction of the senses, like a person who listens for the first time to something of the deepest interest. I remember very well that the things you spoke of seemed to me future, and not past, which will prove to you that I had still the simplicity and purity of youth. You represented Jesus Christ before Herod, who would release Him if He would only speak. I felt an excessive compassion for Him, and began to pray to God thus: " O Lord, grant that my Jesus may speak, that He may answer Herod, and not be carried away to die." When I heard you declare that He would not break silence, I was deeply afflicted, and I said in my heart, to soften the pain I felt, " Why will He not speak? it seems to me that He consents to His own death." It was so, my good Jesus, it was so; but I did not understand it then. I tell you all this, my father, to show you how young I must have been when this sweet Saviour deigned to take possession of my heart, and establish His dwelling there.

In ending your discourse, you made a touching appeal to your audience to weep for Jesus, and to retain the remembrance of His sufferings. "Make at least every Friday," you said, " a short meditation on His sufferings, and shed one tear for His love. It is but little that I ask from you, and yet I assure you that this will please God more, and be more useful to you, than any other work, however good it may be." It was the Holy Ghost who dictated these words to you, for, in spite of my youth, my heart was penetrated to the quick, and they made on me an ineffaceable impression. When I grew a little older, they constantly came into my mind, and I meditated on them with particular satisfaction. One day I was so deeply touched by them that I bound myself by vow to give to my Jesus every Friday this tear which you had asked, and this was the commencement of my spiritual life, as you will clearly see in the course of my history. It is to you then, my father, that I owe my introduction into this life, and, instead of being surprised, you will unite with me in giving thanks to our Creator, from Whom all good things proceed.

After having made this vow, I did all in my power to be faithful to it, in spite of the many difficulties I had to contend with. It was necessary for me every Friday to put my heart to the torture to elicit this tear which I desired. This came from a sort of aversion for spiritual things, so that I could neither read them, nor bear to hear them read. When, by the special favour of God, I have been able to shed my first tear, do not suppose, my father, I waited for a second; on the contrary, I rose in all haste, and immediately ran away. Sometimes in following the impulse of my natural vivacity I laughed so loud, and diverted myself with so little discretion, that when the time for weeping came, I could not draw from my eyes this blessed tear. Then becoming impatient, I went away, but with a saddened heart, believing that some evil would happen to me for this infidelity, and remorse of conscience would torment me for the whole week.

When Lent arrived, I went to confession to Brother Pacifico of Urbino, and declared to him all my sins as well as I could. He asked me many questions, and, among others, whether I had contracted any obligation by vow. Without thinking, I replied in the negative, but immediately correcting myself, I said, "I have indeed made a vow, but I cannot fulfil it, although I really desire to do so." The good father asked what it was, but because I knew it was a good thing, I was ashamed to tell it, and would not at first reply, but it ended by my yielding. When he knew what it was, he said to me, "Do not believe, my daughter, that I will ever dispense you from such a vow; on the contrary, I wish you to observe it, but on this condition, that if, when you have done what you can to accomplish it, you do not succeed, you will be guilty of no sin."

I continued then to fulfil my obligation, but always with the same difficulty, and it was not till after a long time that it diminished, and God came to my assistance with His accustomed goodness. I chanced to find one day a meditation on the Passion of our Lord, which seemed written for a person little accustomed to this holy exercise; it was divided into five points, after each of which an Ave was to be said. The first point pleased me much, and being soon convinced that I should be equally pleased with the others, I kept the book, and resolved to read this meditation every Friday on my knees. I did so for several years, exciting myself to shed a tear at each of the Aves, which I recited as devoutly as I could. It appeared that this devotion was agreeable to my Jesus, for in general I shed many tears, instead of only one. One Friday it happened that I had been much occupied until midnight, when I obtained permission to go to my room. Seeing the night so far advanced, and that my reading would take a long time, I was much tempted to pass it over for once, and it cost me much to make the effort to begin. I struggled long before I could come to any determination; at length, with the help of God, I overcame myself, and performed my accustomed exercise. Oh, my father in Jesus Christ! if you knew the danger I ran that night, an hour after I went to bed, you would be astonished. If you wish to know, I will tell you another time, but now I will not interrupt my history. Oh, how happy that creature is, who, when assailed by temptation, holds fast by her resolution. I say this, for I know it by experience; but to return from this digression.

The ever-increasing pleasure which I felt in reading this, inspired me with the desire of substituting meditation for it. I then began to meditate on the Passion, not only on Fridays, but every day, and that for a considerable time, according to the inspiration which God gave me, without using the book. This practice procured me such an abundance of devout tears, that I could not say a rosary without weeping, even before strangers. This lasted three years before I resolved to give myself to God. I need hardly add, that the devil did his best to make me give up this holy practice. At his instigation, persons whom I could not avoid, because they lived in the house with me, misinterpreted my tears, imputing them to worldly sorrows, or ridiculous affections. Not content with thinking thus, they said it to my face, and I own that these reproaches deeply wounded my heart. Yet, by the grace of God, I came out victorious from all these combats with my resolutions unchanged. "Interpret my conduct as you will," I said to them, turning interiorly to God—" interpret my conduct as you will, I care little for your blame or your praise." And thus passed those three years, during which devotion to the Passion of Jesus Christ inundated my heart.

I fasted every Friday on bread and water, and bound myself by vow to abstain on that day from certain habitual imperfections. Unfortunately I was not always faithful to this engagement. I often scourged every member of my body, one after the other. Every night I interrupted my sleep, and got out of bed to say a chaplet, and when I had neglected this, I said two the next time. Now that I am a nun, I no longer get up for such a purpose, nor do any good thing whatever.

During these three years I fasted two or three days a week together on bread and water, and also on the feasts of Jesus Christ and His holy Mother, but now I do nothing of the kind. I forgot to say that at the end of my meditations on the Passion, which made me shed abundance of tears, I experienced a sort of rapture, during which my soul enjoyed a peace which I cannot express; I only know that in this extraordinary state, which lasted about as long as one or two Ave Marias, my body was without feeling, like a corpse, and my soul was transported into a place of peace and delight. On coming out of this state, I often said to God with my whole heart, "O my Lord! if Thou foreseest that any worldly thing will separate me from Thee by a hair's breadth, prevent this by sending me a thousand misfortunes." Now I understood by separation the loss of the sweetness I tasted in these moments; for at the period of which I speak I had no other way of approaching God than this. The life which I then led presented many hindrances. Can you imagine, my father, that with the exception of the short time I gave to meditation on the Passion, all the rest was sacrificed to dancing, music, promenades, and similar trifles? Reading devout books tired me or made me laugh. I had such an aversion for religious that I could scarcely bear to look at them. Dress and frivolous reading were my delight. In short, during those three years my soul was as a prisoner, and though I struggled in my meditations and multiplied my prayers, I could not obtain the grace of full liberty. Now, my father, listen to the means by which Providence delivered me. How good Thou art, O my God! Thou knowest how to help in a thousand ways the soul that sincerely desires to apply itself to the pursuit of virtue.

CHAPTER II.

SHE RESISTS THE GRACE OF A RELIGIOUS VOCATION FOR A LONG TIME, BUT ENDS BY FOLLOWING IT WITH GENEROSITY.

GOD, in His infinite mercy, willed that my eyes, so long blinded by the profound darkness of the world, should at last open to the light of truth. Father Francis of Urbino (whose words and teaching seemed to shake my soul like thunder and lightning) came to preach the Lent at Camerino. During the whole season, he repeated those terrible words, "Fear God, fear God!" Now I felt this holy fear, for I perceived the greatness of the offences I had committed against His Majesty, and experienced such a dread of the flames of hell, that had I not known despair to be of all sins the most displeasing to God, I firmly believe that I should have despaired of His mercy. It alone was all my consolation and all my support, for I spoke to no one of what was passing in my heart. I wept night and day over my infidelities and ingratitude, and applied myself with great contrition to meditation on the Passion of my Saviour. giving a long time to this exercise, both morning and evening. Feeling also more than ever the necessity of penance, on Fridays I only took three or four mouthfuls of bread and a glass of water. Sometimes even the whole day passed without my eating anything. I spent the night without going to bed, sleeping so little, and so lightly, that I could say with truth, "I sleep, but my heart wakes."

In this life of prayer, upon which fear made me enter, I began to hear at intervals a voice unknown to me, a voice which seemed to come from afar, but not so far but that the words were quite intelligible: it said to me, that if I would escape the pains of hell, of which I had such fear, I must renounce the world and become a nun. My mind at the same time was enlightened by a light from heaven, which made me see clearly that unless I quitted the world I should be lost. Now these words were very bitter, and this light very insupportable, because I had not yet shaken off the chains of my evil nature, and, accustomed as I was to the pleasures of the world, I was very unwilling to renounce them. I alleged to myself many strong and persuasive reasons, but they made no impression on me, because of my ill-regulated affections, from which it is necessary to be free before we can listen to such inspirations.

During these miserable combats, I was very unhappy, and had I been abandoned to myself, I have no doubt nature would have triumphed, but my Redeemer, the true and only Friend of souls, would not permit it. Touched with compassion, He put into my mind a good thought, which I carried out without repugnance, and, if it did not procure me a complete victory, it at least contributed largely to my conversion. It was this: one day that grace spoke to my heart more strongly than usual, without being able to vanquish my repugnance, it seemed to me that God bid me write to the father who preached; I did so immediately, without telling any one, and without hoping for a reply. It is true that I did not deserve one, for my obedience to the inspiration was far from sincere. I excited his zeal to labour for the soul of one who was a stranger to me, telling him not one word of my personal wants. But I added a postscript to my letter, "Remember me, my father, in the peaceful elevation of your mind." I said this in the persuasion that every servant of God experienced at the end of his meditations that supernatural peace which I experienced, and this good father more than others, because I considered him a saint, almost an angel from heaven. He deigned to reply to me, and sent me by a sure and secret channel the following answer: "I will undertake the affair you recommend to me, and will omit nothing to make it succeed, whether in my public or private instructions. As for you, my daughter, I recommend you to guard carefully the purity of both body and heart, after the example of S. Cecilia and many other virgins, until the moment when God will dispose of you according to His gracious designs. Be careful not to yield to the sensual temptations which assail you; on the contrary, overcome yourself in all things with a holy generosity. Farewell." The reading of these lines produced in me profound affliction; for it was evident that these words were so many arrows shot by the Hand of God at my poor heart. It was very evident that He had made known to the father what was passing within me, since I had never revealed it to any one, and yet he appeared acquainted with the captivity of my heart.

As soon as I recovered from my vexation, I exclaimed, "It is Thou, O my God, Who speakest to me by the ministry of Thy servant, for he could not otherwise have known my combats, and yet he says to me, 'Overcome yourself if you would be perfectly free.' Well then, my God, I will do what is commanded." Will you believe it, my father, scarcely had I made the sacrifice of two or three satisfactions of the eyes, than I was delivered from this evil passion. I then conceived for Father Francis an affection which may have been too strong perhaps, but which was nevertheless necessary for changing the profane love which occupied my heart into a holy and spiritual love. Besides, I owed something to a servant of God who had rendered me such an important service.

After having delivered me from the slavery of Pharao, God pressed me still more strongly to withdraw into the desert, and sacrifice to Him there; that is to say, to shut myself up in a convent, where I should be occupied in His service; but restrained by my perverse nature, I turned a deaf ear to His call; my determination not to quit the world became stronger and stronger, and, fool that I was, I dared to oppose to grace the most frivolous excuses to justify myself. For instance, I said to myself, "My father loves me too much to permit me to go into a convent, and he is too powerful for any one to dare to contradict him by withdrawing me from his hands." I really believed this, and regarded the thing as impossible, even had it been my most sincere desire.

O my God! my God! what had I then done to deserve the interest Thou didst take in me, being as I am a false and sinful creature? What need hadst Thou of my services, O my sweet Jesus, to seek me with so much eagerness? I remember very well all the means He suggested to me for withdrawing myself from my father; but their remembrance pierces my heart too deeply for me to tell them.

This Master, so patient and wise, seeing the hardness of my heart, and yet unable to resolve to abandon me, changed His treatment, and inspired Father Francis to preach a sermon the day before the Annunciation of the Blessed Virgin, on the ardent love which the angelical salutation enkindled in her heart. Never had I heard him preach with so much fervour. I believed, while listening to him, that I heard a seraph rather than a man. He affirmed, among other things, that in one single spark of this divine love which consumed the heart of Mary, there was more sweetness than in all the pleasures of the world combined. This made so strong an impression on me, that all my resistance yielded at once. When the sermon was over, I approached one of the altars, and, throwing myself on my knees, made a vow to the Queen of Virgins, to preserve all my senses immaculate until God made me know His Will. I made one condition, however, which was that the divine Mother would share with me a spark of that fire which burned in her heart at the moment of the Annunciation. From that time this desire and promise occupied my mind day and night, and I prayed, with all the fervour in my power, for this precious spark of love; but because He could not place such a rich treasure in an unclean vessel, God willed to purify my heart in the manner I am about to relate.

The preacher determined to preach on Holy Saturday, though this was contrary to custom, as well as to the wishes of the canons, who objected, on account of the long offices in the cathedral on that day. His audience was very limited, because the public were inclined to follow the general custom; but the grace which God intended this sermon to bestow failed not. The good father began by asking pardon of his audience for this unaccustomed sermon, excusing himself by pleading an inspiration from God, Who required from him that he should prepare them to make a good Easter Communion on the morrow. He then went on to speak of the circumstances which might render this sacrilegious, and dwelt long on the subject. I followed him with great attention, and was struck by the following words : " Whoever has received absolution, without the firm determination to give up all that is or that leads to mortal sin, is forbidden to communicate." " Miserable being that I am !" said I to myself, " it is thus that I have always communicated, for I have never had the firm purpose to renounce all vanity and folly, at least until now; but I will go this evening to confession, and declare specially these sins, with the firm resolution never again to yield to them." And so I did.

[Our readers may be surprised at this declaration, if they take it literally. It is certain that the vanity of which she speaks did not extend to mortal sin, for vanity in itself is not such. To render it mortal, circumstances of scandal must accompany it, and this the whole of her life contradicts. It might be suspected that she had committed grave faults of sensuality; yet we find afterwards that she had always preserved her heart and body pure. It is incredible that so scrupulous a soul should have taken so little care about examination and contrition as to make her confessions invalid. What, then, must we think of the manner in which she judges herself? We must believe it to have been dictated by excessive humility. "It is the peculiarity of pious souls," says S. Gregory, "to see sins where there are none, and to find gravity in matters of little weight." When preachers reproach the guilty, in order to move their consciences and convert them, these good souls take to themselves all that is said, because, by divine light, they see clearly the heinousness of sins which others think lightly of, as the ray of sunshine entering into a chamber shows the dust hitherto concealed. But to return to our story.]

My confessor, Father Olivieri, inquired for how long a time I had communicated in this manner; and, on my replying, "Almost always," he said : "Certainly, my daughter, I will not allow you to approach the holy table. Examine yourself during these days as seriously as you can, and return in a week to make a general confession." The following day, when all rose to approach the altar, I continued sitting in my place, covered with shame and confusion, because I thought every one would notice this humiliating exception. "Well," I said to myself, "the proverb is true which says, 'He who gives not what he can, never receives what he wishes.' This is my bitter experience to-day."

After having made my general confession, God gave me the grace to preserve during Paschal time the sorrow to which it had given birth. As for my confession, it was still very defective. My elastic conscience and my want of light prevented my discovering the faults I see clearly now; but what I did not say then, I said afterwards, as you may imagine; and if my confession was imperfect, it was at least sincere. It was on the eve of Low Sunday, in S. Peter's church, that Father Olivieri heard my confession, and gave me Paschal Communion.

On the same day, I had an interview for the first time with the pious Father Francis of Urbino. He asked me if I thought of entering religion. On my replying in the negative, an air of sadness overspread his countenance, and he said, "You are now whole; sin no more, go in peace." I returned home joyful and happy.

My soul being purified in the manner I have stated, the divine goodness began to knock more loudly at the door of my heart. Its voice made itself heard, not in the distance as heretofore, but within me, and in a manner so clear and distinct that I could not stifle it. I often shut my ears, but it was useless, because it spoke not to my body, but to my soul. When I began to pray, it seemed as if I were going to the war, for then I fought incessantly against God; and there is no war so painful as that. However, I never interrupted the course of my daily prayers. It happened sometimes, that, fatigued with my resistance to grace, God would say to me, "I am He Whom thou desirest, and yet the more I call, the more deaf do thy ears become. The more I press thee, the more thou resistest My love for thee. Well, then, my daughter, go into the world where thy folly leads thee; there thou wilt find no satisfaction for thy desires." Consider, my dear father, that my mind did not assent to these words; I turned them over and over, but found no rest, nor could I resolve to enter religion. Nevertheless, instead of shortening my prayer, I repeated it because it was Friday, and it seemed that some one drew near to assist me. I have never been subjected to such a shock of contending feelings: at one moment willing to obey the call of grace, the next, revolting against it. But at last my free will, which in the midst of the conflict had remained neutral, erected itself into a judge, and decided in favour of the Spirit of God.

The submission was prompt. I determined, with all the affection of my soul, to serve the Lord as He wished, and was ready, if necessary, to suffer martyrdom, rather than continue to resist grace, or even to oppose it by sinful delays. I felt, at the same moment, a lively desire to go to Urbino, something whispering to me interiorly that it was only there that I could serve God with a tranquil heart. The determination was to my soul, exhausted by such painful agitations, what a soft bed of flowers would have been to a body exhausted with fatigue. Since that day I have ever enjoyed profound peace, and great spiritual joy.

CHAPTER III.

SPIRITUAL FAVOURS WHICH FOLLOWED HER ENTIRE CONVERSION.

It is now, O my God, that I feel more than ever in need of Thy assistance, having to recount things more angelic than human. Assist me, then, O Lord, I beseech Thee; grant me the grace worthily to recount Thy admirable benefits, those benefits with which Thou hast loaded Thine unworthy creature for her own shame and confusion. And you, my father, while listening to me, say not once, but a thousand times, " I am no longer astonished at your great trials, but only that God has been so lenient towards you, ungrateful creature that you are ; for what could He have done for you that He has not done ? and how have you corresponded to His adorable goodness ?" In saying this, my father, you would say but the truth. In fact, as soon as I had conformed my will to His adorable Will, all the cataracts of heaven seemed to open upon me, and my sinful soul was absorbed in the abyss of the divine mercies. This God of goodness came to meet His prodigal child ; He received her in His Arms, and pressed her to His Heart ; He bestowed on her the sweetest caresses, and gave her, not once, but many times, with His divine Mouth, the kiss of peace. O my heart, harder than the very stones, how is it that thou dost not break with love ? What art thou doing ? Why art thou so slow in showing thy gratitude ?" And yet the sovereign goodness continued to treat my unfaithful soul as the mother who cannot caress her child sufficiently ; and this covered me with confusion. Oh, how often have I besought, with true humility, this loving Father to cease caressing me, for I was so unworthy ! How often have I withdrawn from prayer in order to escape from His divine Arms ! But this means, which might have been sufficient to save me from His justice, could not tear me from the embraces of His love. It frequently happened that on leaving my prayer my soul required a certain time to return to herself. Often I heard within me words of inexpressible sweetness, words full of manna and honey, of gladness and joy. But what am I doing? Do I pretend that I am writing all? I cannot, and if I could I would not, because of the words of the prophet: "Thy words have I in my heart, that I may not sin against Thee." I will only say with the Spouse in the Canticles: "My soul melted when He spoke," and with the Psalmist: "How sweet are Thy words to my palate, more than honey to my mouth. Thy word is exceedingly refined, and Thy servant hath loved it."

I saw clearly within me the accomplishment of this word of the prophet Ezechiel, "In what day soever he shall turn from his wickedness, I will not remember all his iniquities that he hath done." God did still more for me, He effaced them from my own remembrance. I could not, indeed, remember any of my former sins, and I no longer felt any fear; and therefore I plunged into, and submerged myself in an ocean of love. Such was the fruit of my conversion, which made me understand how the beginning of wisdom (that is, the first taste of the divine sweetness) is the fear of the Lord; and because this taste is strongly felt, in proportion to the strength of the previous fear, it was without measure, as my former fear had been.

For many previous years my heart had experienced a strong necessity to love, and because my affections leant towards creatures, I restrained them with the rein of discretion, for fear of compromising myself, but when they inclined towards God, I slackened the reins, and allowed them to rush forth impetuously towards my sweet Saviour, Who, not content with calling me, showed Himself to me, sometimes under the form of a Father, sometimes under the form of a

Friend, sometimes (and that the most frequently) under the form of a loving Spouse. When He deigns to enter into a soul in this way, I believe, from my own little experience, that He gives birth there to a feeling of divine love, so sweet and delicious, that there is nothing in this life with which it can be compared. If this feeling had not been transitory, I should have wished never to quit this mortal life, because I felt as if I were already in possession of eternal life. In truth, I cannot imagine any difference between this bliss and the joys of paradise, except that which exists between an uncertain and fleeting happiness and a certain and everlasting joy. But, alas! this difference is not small; I would say rather it is sovereign and infinite!

Beholding myself now, on the one hand so tenderly loved, and on the other so guilty and vicious—I could not see myself otherwise; for when the Sun of justice enters into a soul, she finds herself enlightened with marvellous light—I sometimes exclaimed, full of wonder, "O my Lord! if the demons dared to utter such a blasphemy, it seems to me they must regard Thee as the friend of vice. I beseech Thee, my Jesus, I conjure Thee not to permit them to give Thee a name so odious. I say they might call Thee so, for I am but iniquity, and yet Thou lovest me with incredible love. O my Jesus, again I beseech Thee, suffer not the demons to dishonour Thee because of Thy love for me." One day while I was speaking thus, I heard this loving God reply: "Know, my daughter, that I am far from being the friend of vice. I can well rejoice in thee without loving iniquity, since thou hast until now preserved thy innocence. This is what I love and what I enjoy in thee." Now my ignorance of spiritual language caused me not to understand this word innocence. After searching for a long time, I found in a book the following sentence, but it left me as much in the dark as ever: "If thou continuest faithful to Me, I will restore to thee thy first innocence." This only excited my curiosity more, but I was not long in having it satisfied. A devout friend called on me one day, to whom I explained my difficulty, and this is the reply which I received: "God promised to that soul to remit her sins, not only with regard to the guilt, but also to the punishment." I need not say how agreeable this was to me; could it be otherwise, when I had received the assurance that God had granted me this favour?

I understood then what my Jesus meant by speaking of my innocence, but I did not understand what He had added, and I would not ask this person in case it might be discovered that it referred to myself. I then addressed myself to my Jesus, and said to Him: "What joy, my Saviour, what delectation, and what object of love, canst Thou find in my innocence?" He deigned to reply: "When I take delight in thy innocence, I take delight in Myself, and not in thee; for this innocence is My work, and My property; when then I rejoice in it, and love it, it is Myself that I love and rejoice in." I understood by this explanation that God desires and loves Himself alone, in heaven as well as on earth; that He loves His creatures the more, in proportion as He has communicated Himself more abundantly to them, and that there are none worthy of love in themselves. He left me, after having given me this grand lesson of humility, of which I stood much in need, being in danger of becoming proud of His favours.

But let me break off the subject, my father, for the

more I say of it, the more there remains for me to say; and when I shall have said all, certainly I shall have said nothing. You know enough now to understand what must have been my peace, my tranquillity, my sweetness, my delight, my confidence, and my familiarity, in the embraces of my divine Spouse, in the sweet intercourse with His Father, in the graces and the consolations of the Holy Ghost.

O happy time! full of joy and delight! how hast thou given place to the tempest, to darkness and sorrow? O peace which surpasseth all understanding, how is it that the horrors of war have succeeded thy sweetness? O unspeakable delights! by what fatality are you changed into wormwood and gall? O love, which almost took away life! what cruel hatred hast Thou left behind thee! O divine friendship! O intimacy, which cannot be understood, still less explained, to what enmities, to what discord hast thou given place! O Arm of my Spouse, after having embraced me with so much love, how hast thou let me fall from such a height into the abyss? Alas! what a heavy fall! It would not be surprising, O my poor soul, if all thy bones were broken! Well mayest thou now lament, and sigh, and say: "The spouse of the King of kings is plunged in sorrow, and her tears are on her cheeks; there is none to comfort her." All my friends have left me, and made me desolate, wasted with sorrow all the day long. Oh! who will give water to my head, and a fountain of tears to my eyes, that I may weep for my sad bereavement? Alas! my crown has fallen from my brow, because I have not been faithful to my Spouse, and now I am reduced to spend my life in tears. Let the heavens and the earth weep over me, let all creatures endowed with reason join their lamentations to mine. And you, my father, weep for me, if you have a heart that can feel for your desolate daughter!

This is the wound which has torn and still tears my bleeding heart; I discover it to you now, because it is no longer possible to hide it. Apply a remedy if you can; or, if you cannot, give me at least your pity; it will always be some solace to my woe. O patience! O help! how I desire you! Sorrow consumes me, so that I am ready to faint; I am distracted with anguish and bitterness, knowing neither what I say or do. Pardon me, then, if any unbecoming words escape me. But enough of my sorrows; let me continue my narrative. I will recount, according to promise, all the course of my spiritual life, until the time of my desolation, and I hope, through the grace of God, to do so with all truth and simplicity.

He who is the Flower of the fields, the Lily of the valleys, and who feeds among the lilies, wished to leave in me marks of His passage, and ornamented my soul with three lilies of exquisite perfume; the first was such an aversion for the world, that if God had said to me, "Mount the throne of the Cæsars, with the certainty of being saved, or enter a convent and run the risk of being lost," I would not have hesitated a moment in giving the preference to the religious state. Because of the hatred I bore to the world, I saw nothing in it that could please me: its pomps and its pleasures filled me with disgust, for I saw in them neither pomp nor glory, but only a temporary hell, the earnest of an eternal hell. Behold what they are in reality; I say it to the shame of those who think differently. The second lily was a profound humility, which made me sincerely believe and confess that the earth bore not on her surface a greater sinner than myself, a creature deserving to be condemned by His justice, and saved only by pure mercy. The more He showered His benefits upon me, the more unworthy I believed myself to be; I therefore considered His graces, not so much as gifts, but as deposits which He confided to my care, or rather as funds with which I should traffic for His benefit. Oh how worthy of love are these truths! Oh what gratitude do I owe Him for such precious instructions! The third lily was 'an ardent desire of suffering. Such in fact was my inclination, that if it had been proposed to me to mount to heaven by any other road than by Calvary, I should have refused the invitation. I sometimes said to Him, with all the affection of my soul, "If the good things with which Thou honourest me, my Lord, proceed really from a sincere heart, wilt Thou give me proof of it, by associating me to the sufferings of Thy beloved Son?" He promised that He would, and He kept His promise, for since then I have drunk at least four times the chalice of bitterness even to satiety.

Soon after this I fell ill of a sickness, from which I have suffered for thirteen years. I have always borne it with inconceivable joy, except for this last year, when it seemed that I could bear it no longer. I do not glory in this, my father, but I return all glory to the Lord, for I know that patience is one of His gifts. After the first seven months (during which time I was every minute at the point of death), I was able to leave my bed. It was then that Father Gregory, who now (if we may trust the universal belief) reigns in heaven, taught me to meditate on the Passion of our Lord, by reciting the chaplet of His holy Mother, which occupied me three hours every day. This devotion procured me unspeakable sweetness, and inexhaustible consolations. One day in particular, whilst I contemplated the glorious mystery of the Transfiguration, I received such heavenly promises, that I cannot now hear it mentioned without my heart palpitating with joy. There is nothing more true than the words of the prophet: "Taste and see." I know it by my own experience, for as soon as I had tasted, I saw that God alone deserved to be loved. From that moment I experienced a burning desire to behold the beauty of His countenance, and my prayers were all more or less languishing desires of love. All creatures seemed to invite me to contemplate this divine Lover. The sight of a blade of grass, or of a flower, was sufficient to recall to me His sovereign beauty, and inflame my heart. Each time I turned my eyes towards the heavens, the psalm " Cœli enarrant " came into my mind, and I cried, "O my Jesus ! if Thy works are so beautiful, what then must be the splendour of Thy Face ? Show Thyself to me, I beseech Thee, my good Master, show Thyself to me—show Thyself to me ! What pleasure canst Thou take in seeing me languish for so long a time ? Thou alone art my life and my hope; Thou alone art all my love. Why, then, dost Thou hide Thyself ? Why dost Thou deprive me of the sight of Thy fair countenance ?" During the time of which I speak, I did not fly from Him as I had done before ; on the contrary, I pursued Him saying, " I run after Thee to the odour of Thy ointments, so superior to all perfumes. Show Thyself to me and I shall be content. Oh that thou would'st kiss me with a kiss of Thy Mouth."

When I had passed six months in the agitation and suffering of these desires, it pleased God to hear my vows in such a manner, that instead of showing me His Face, He turned away from me, saying, " Write these words, my daughter, ' My Jesus grants me indirectly that which I have asked of Him. It is truly in an indirect manner that He now listens to me and hears me, and yet my desires are directly accomplished. I feel it, for now my soul is happy and tranquil.' "

But it is necessary for me, my father, to give you a more detailed account of this apparition. One day, when I was at prayer, I recognized by certain signs that He was present in my soul. When He was about to withdraw, He said to me : " If thou desirest to see Me, raise thy head." I looked, and saw Him retiring, as one man would leave another, turning round, and continuing His way. When I first saw Him, He was already more than six paces off, and traversing with slow steps a large hall, at the extremity of which there was a small door, like the door of a cupboard. I could observe Him at leisure, until He reached this door, when, stooping because of His great height, He passed through it, and disappeared. At the same moment the hall and the little door both vanished, and I saw my own room as before. If I was not happy enough to behold His Face, I at least remarked His vestments. He was clad in a robe of dazzling whiteness, which descended to His Feet. It was embroidered with a border of golden letters, which swept the ground; and this border was about the breadth of a finger's length. I could not read the letters, as much because of the distance as of the continual movement of the robe; not that

His steps were quick, for on the contrary they were slow, but He walked without ever stopping. His waist was very thin, and girt with a golden band, about the breadth of two fingers. He was taller than any man I had ever seen, by a head and shoulders. His golden hair, which was slightly crisp, floated over His shoulders and reached to His girdle. Something adorned His Head, but I cannot say whether it was a crown or diadem, or a simple circlet of roses and other flowers. I am inclined to believe, as He was arrayed with the magnificence of a heavenly King, that I was considered unworthy to behold Him. I could never describe the effect of His golden hair, mingled with the dazzling whiteness of His robe, as it floated over His broad shoulders. All that I can say is, that, enchanted with the richness of His apparel, and still more by His majesty and grace, I remained stupefied with admiration.

During the two years and a half that I continued in the world after my conversion, preparing for the complete sacrifice I wished to make of myself to God, He gave me many other graces and gifts, of which I will say nothing, as it is better to be silent than to speak of such extraordinary things at the risk of interrupting the peace which my heart enjoys. I ought, however, to tell you, that during this time of tranquillity God showed me all the trials to which I should be subjected at a later period. His intention was doubtless to enable me to support them with as much prudence as resignation; but, alas! my father, I cannot conceal it, I have neither done one nor the other. I have acted quite contrary to what a faithful sheep would have done, and now I am condemned to weep for my folly: "O all ye who pass by the way of divine love, attend and see if there be any sorrow like to mine."* My soul, once the spouse of the Lord, initiated into His secrets, and brought up in scarlet, is now reduced to dwell on a dunghill, because she allowed herself to be seduced by the deceits of the devil. [It is needless to add that it is her humility which makes her speak thus, for nothing in her conduct would justify this lamentation.]

There is a time for everything. The moment of afflictions and trials arrived, to prove whether my virtue was gold or lead, and I had much to suffer both in body and soul. Besides the illnesses with which God afflicted me, I was the object of a very painful persecution, the author of which I am not at liberty to name.

[Pascucci, the historian of her life, explains it thus: Her father, who became sovereign of Camerino by the death of his nephew, Nicholas Varani, was not satisfied with being named general-in-chief of the troops of the Venetian republic, but, wishing to increase the splendour of his family by a rich alliance, he did all in his power to force his daughter into a certain marriage, as we shall presently see.]

Every temptation was employed to overcome me; at first promises and flatteries, then threats, which ended in my being imprisoned; but, by the grace of God, caresses made no impression on my heart, nor promises either. Threats excited in me a strong desire to see them fulfilled, and imprisonment only rendered my determination more fixed. At length all this ended, like the Egyptian captivity. God withdrew me from the hands of the powerful Pharao, whose hardness of heart lasted two years and a half,

* Lament. i. 12.

and who ended by saying to me with his own mouth: "I yield to the Lord, Whose vengeance I dread. The fear of drawing upon myself His vengeance, alone forces me to restore your liberty. Otherwise you never would have obtained my consent to become a nun."

I escaped then from Egypt, where a yoke of iron had crushed me for so long, and I came out laden with spiritual riches. I passed the Red Sea dry-shod. I understand by the Red Sea the purple and honour of sovereignty, brilliant chimeras, which seduce mankind, but which conceal much misery, and end in smoke. When safe across, I turned my head to look back, and saw Pharao and his host overwhelmed in the waves; that is to say, the devil with all his stratagems, all his sins and vices. After having returned thanks to God my Deliverer, I plunged into the desert which was to lead me to the promised land; that is, to speak without figure, I went to the monastery of Urbino, where you, my father, were witness to my joy, which forced me to cry with Mary, the sister of Moses, "Let us sing to the Lord, for He is gloriously magnified; the horse and his rider He hath thrown into the sea."* You might find others, my father, who renounced the world as willingly, and with as much pleasure as myself, but not with more joy and heartiness. You have perhaps been surprised by my comparing myself to the children of Israel, but I cannot find a more striking comparison; for God loaded me with especial graces, as He did them, and like them, I have resisted His goodness with invincible hardness of heart.

[Perhaps the reader may wish to know why Bat-

* Exod. xv. 1.

tista, in quitting the world, preferred the monastery of Urbino. Pascucci gives the following reasons: A short time before, the Princess Battista Malatesta, the wife of Guido of Montefeltre, since known as Sister Jerome, had entered this convent. It was also in this monastery that her relation, Elizabeth, widow of Peter Gentilis Varani, had lived. This princess, after the murder of her husband, became a nun at Foligno, but the hatred of the enemies of her family pursued her into her retreat. They persuaded Pope Nicholas V. that her profession was but a feint to cover the design of bringing the town again under the domination of her family; and, in consequence, she received an order to depart. Thanks to the intervention of some Italian princes, the Pontiff gave her the monastery of Monteluce, where twenty-one nuns from Foligno followed her. Seven years afterwards, at the request of the Duke of Urbino, Pope Calixtus III. gave her orders to found a monastery in that town. She did so, and governed it with as much wisdom as edification. Her daughter, Francesca Varani, lived there also with her relation, Euphrasia Chiavelli of Fabriano, Emerentiana Colonna, Clara Cappelli, Bernardina Baglioni, and several other ladies of illustrious birth. The Blessed Battista entered the convent on the 14th of November, 1481.]

CHAPTER IV.

WHAT SHE HAD TO SUFFER DURING HER NOVICIATE. —HER RETURN TO CAMERINO, WHERE SHE RECEIVED GREAT FAVOURS FROM HEAVEN, AND, AMONG OTHERS, A VISIT FROM S. CLARE.

UNTIL now, my father, I have been giving you the history of my spiritual life, during the time that the glorious Virgin Mary, touched by my prayers, communicated to me a spark of divine love. It was, indeed, but a spark, detached from that furnace which burns in eternity; yet it kindled such a fire in my heart, that I could scarcely support the delightful heat, which often compelled me to cry out, "No more, Lord, no more." I will now tell you what occurred to me when I was clothed with the habit of S. Francis. An old writer says that we must retire into solitude to hear the singing of birds, to breathe the perfume of flowers, to contemplate their brilliant colours, and to discover the hidden dwelling-places of animals. Scarcely had I entered the sacred monastery of Urbino, than I found there similar pleasures; the harmonious chant of the divine praises, the beauty of edifying example, and, if I dare say so, the dwelling-place of graces and celestial gifts. Powerfully moved and urged by the Holy Spirit, I felt within me a burning desire to penetrate into the centre of the desert; that is to say, into the depths of the Heart of my most sweet Jesus, and to discover there His most hidden griefs. I renounced, therefore, as much as possible, the manna of heavenly sweetnesses; not that I was tired of them, as the ungrateful Jewish people were, but because I had a profound feeling of my own unworthiness, and feared besides that these anticipated payments were drawn from the capital of my future happiness in heaven. I therefore besought my God, with a pure and sincere heart, to nourish, to satiate, and to fill me with the sorrowful pain which my Jesus had endured in His cruel Passion, and to let me drink long draughts from His bitter chalice. This was, indeed, the only want which my soul felt, and her only desire; so that I could say with the Spouse in the Canticles, "A bundle of myrrh is my beloved to me; he shall abide between my breasts."*

I resolved then to employ my whole time of prayer in meditation on the Passion of Jesus Christ, not wishing to occupy myself with aught else, in order to plunge with all the vigour and impetuosity of my soul, into the sea of bitterness which inundated His Sacred Heart. And how could I not desire, O my beloved Jesus, to penetrate into Thy loving Heart, where I knew my name was written in letters of gold, ever since the manifestation Thou didst deign to make to me! Oh! how bright they appeared on the crimson of Thy divine Heart, those large golden letters, "I love thee, Camilla." Thou didst grant me this favour, O my good Jesus! because I could not understand that Thou hadst for me such a tender love. "How is it," I once said to Thee—"how is it that Thou canst love such a wicked creature?" "I cannot do otherwise," Thou didst reply, " for thy name is written in My Heart!" and then lifting Thy glorified Arm, Thou madest me read the words across the Wound of Thy Heart. O my soul, why dost thou not take courage and confidence at the remembrance of this

* Cant. i. 12.

goodness, this love of thy beloved Jesus? Thou wilt say to me, I know, that it is not possible. Alas! it is too true, that this remembrance, instead of encouraging me, pierces my heart, and forces me to cry out in lamentation, "O all ye who pass by the way of divine love, attend and see if there be any sorrow like to mine."

But to return. After having persevered during two years in meditation on the Passion of Christ, with the desire of partaking of His sufferings, I was introduced by an admirable grace of the Holy Spirit, into the sacred bed of His divine Heart, which contains an ocean of bitterness, of which neither man nor angel can measure the depth. How often should I have been submerged in this ocean, if God had not sustained me by His powerful Arm: for I had much more difficulty in supporting the bitterness of my sorrows than the sweetness of His love. Therefore I often said with all the fervour of my soul, "No more, my Lord, no more; if I plunge deeper in this ocean, I shall be swallowed up, for it has neither bottom nor shore." Then my God would appear to me no longer as a paradise, but as a hell. And indeed, in my simplicity, I often gave Him this name; for no other seemed to suit Him so well. I will say nothing further on this subject now, as I intend to recur to it again, but there is one observation I believe I ought to make, namely, that although my interior pains were as dreadful as it was possible for my soul, assisted by the Holy Spirit, to bear, they were to the sufferings of my Jesus but as a grain of sand to heaven and earth.

During these two years, which I spent in the monastery of Urbino, before returning to my own country, my soul was fertilized by benign influences of the Sun of Justice, and produced different flowers, agreeable to her beloved, so that she could say with the spouse in the Canticles, "Winter is now past, the flowers have appeared in our land."* Among them was the lily, planted in the barren soil of my soul at the beginning of my conversion, namely, the desire of suffering. This desire, in particular, was cultivated by the royal hand of the true Assuerus, my blessed Jesus, and largely bedewed with the waters of His interior sorrows. But although often reduced almost to death, I ceased not to say to the Lord, "But when, O my God! wilt Thou conduct me into the rich pastures and delicious gardens of Thy sufferings, where Thou nourishest Thy elect and beloved sheep? O my Jesus! Thou deferrest the accomplishment of Thy promises for a long time; fulfil them, I beseech Thee, without delay; yes, immediately, my Jesus, immediately! for I can wait no longer. Let not my numerous sins make Thee repent of the promises Thou hast made me? Ah! Lord, I beseech Thee, deprive me not of so great a benefit."

About this time my calamitous profession approached; I call it thus, because of the horrible tempest of which it was the cause, a tempest which agitated not my monastery only, but the whole order, and also some seculars. I believe I ought not to give details of this event, and I would even desire that no guess should be made on the subject. What I can say is, that if my profession was the cause of trouble on earth, it was a subject of joy to the angels, and the occasion of a solemn festival in heaven. Be assured of this. It is not on the report of others that I affirm

* Cant. ii. 11, 12.

it, but on the clear knowledge I had of it myself: and would to God that all sinners were as certain of their salvation as I am of the truth of this fact. Is it that I glory in it? Certainly not, for I could never believe that the angels would rejoice in this manner over me, but over the great advantages which my monastery would after a time derive from my profession, and over the acquisition of a soul, withdrawn by grace from the world. Now this double event which rejoiced the angels, could not fail to displease the devil; therefore he avenged himself by raising the tempest of which I speak.

You, my father, were elected this same year vicar of your order in this province, a charge which you had not had for a long time before, and which since then has not been imposed on you. Am I deceived in believing that heaven arranged it thus, in order that he who had been the instrument of my conversion should continue and terminate the work? You continued it, indeed, by sustaining me in this great trial; and you finished it by re-establishing me in the peace which I have enjoyed since September, and the sweetness of which I still taste. It is true that you have had much to suffer from this tempest, which agitated every house of the order in the province, and even seculars of all ranks; but was it not fitting that it should be so, since you had been the cause of so much good? Besides, I know that the trouble which this affair cost you has not been without its reward, for though this monastery was the cause of much vexation to you, yet you have shared in the good which it has done, and still continues to do. And although you opposed the selection of this site, God changed your opinion, and it was you yourself, who by your authority enclosed us here, and thus instituted this holy monastery. Fly, if you will, from this house of Camerino. You have nowhere else done so much good as at Camerino. Therefore the devil, who knows how much harm you have done him, causes you to dislike the place. I say this to you, my father, with filial confidence.*

When I had, with my companions, taken possession of the monastery in virtue of the Apostolic rescript, I had no scruple on the subject of my transfer, for God had made known to me, in a special manner, that it was agreeable to His Majesty. Yet it pleased His goodness to give me for my consolation a still more manifest sign of His Will in this matter. The second Friday after our entrance, Sister Constance, whom you know well, was spinning beside me, while I was sewing; she began to sing the hymn, "Anima benedetta dall' alto Creatore," &c.—" O soul, blessed by the Most High Creator," &c. When she had finished the first verse I sang the second, and so we continued alternately until we came to the words, " Ris-

* The origin of this monastery is thus described by the historian Wading: "Julius Cæsar Varani, wishing to give his daughter a convent at Camerino, besought the Roman pontiff to give up to him the monastery of S. Constance, which was falling into ruins, and contained only one old nun, that with the materials he might build another in a more convenient place for the daughters of S. Clare, under the invocation of S. Maria Nuova, and the direction of the fathers of S. Francis. The Pope granted his request on the following conditions:—1st. That the church of the ancient monastery should be preserved and repaired. 2nd. That the new community should give a pension for life to the old nun, which was accordingly done. It was into this convent that Battista entered, with seven other nuns of S. Clare, on the 4th of January, 1484."

guarda quelle mani, risguarda quelli piedi, risguarda quel costato"—" Behold these Hands, behold these Feet, behold this Side," when sorrow rendered me mute, and I fell into the arms of my sister. She at first believed that this proceeded merely from physical causes, but my distress was purely spiritual. My soul was enraptured by the contemplation of the afflicted Mother, when she received into her arms the dead body of her adorable Son. I heard most distinctly the mournful voice of the most holy Mother; I heard the loving and afflicted Mary Magdalen crying out, " O my Master !" The plaintive voice of the beloved disciple John also sounded in my ear, saying in a low voice : " My Father ! my Brother ! and my Master !" I heard also the lamentations of the other beloved Maries. I remained in this state from the hour of compline until the second hour of the night, and it would have lasted much longer, had I not made a great effort to recall my spirit, and relieve the sorrow of my sisters ; for I sometimes heard them weeping, although I was in the state of rapture, and their affliction made the tears flow from my eyes. At other times, when I heard the voice of the glorious Virgin Mary, my soul seemed to have left my body, and I perceived none of the things of this world. When I came to myself, I experienced such excessive exhaustion and sorrow, that for more than a fortnight afterwards I looked like a corpse risen from the grave.

Before this event the mystery of Mary with the Body of her Son in her arms had never presented itself to my mind. When I had applied myself to meditate on the Passion, it was either the agony of my Saviour in the Garden of Olives, or His crucifixion, which absorbed my attention ; but from this moment I became so much affected by this devout mystery, that for more than two years I could not look at a pair of pincers, a ladder, a hammer, or a nail, although in my ecstasy I had seen none of them. It was thus that it pleased God to show His approval of my return to Camerino; for if He had been displeased with this step, He would not have granted me such a favour, which I could not look upon otherwise than as a singular mark of His love. "O all ye who pass by the way of divine love, attend and see if there be any sorrow like to mine!" God willed formerly that the Hebrew people should be baptized, as the apostle says, in water and in fire; and thus it pleased Him to treat me, for after having washed my soul in the tears of contrition and devotion, He willed also to baptize it in divine and seraphic fire. You can easily understand what was His design in this; I had without doubt committed many faults during the time of my tribulations, and He wished to purify my heart in the fire of His love, to render me fit to receive the new favours He had in store for me.

At length this year of tribulation came to an end; a year that had brought me so many bitter sorrows, which the Lord had permitted to embellish my crown, and not to punish me; for you know, my father, it was love of my vocation which excited against me this violent tempest. I wished to establish this new monastery under the title and the rule of the Poor Clares. This project displeased many persons, who neglected nothing to bring it to naught, but without success, for my wishes were accomplished, as you see. During this time Father Peter de Moliano was elected our vicar, a glorious and holy soul, now manifestly blessed, on account of the miracles which he worked during his life, and continues to work now. He came from time to time to our monastery. One day he asked me, in presence of my sisters, "Are you not Sister Battista Varani?" On my replying in the affirmative, he said, "Prepare your confession, my daughter, for I wish to hear it before I go." "I have no need to confess, my father," I replied. "It is by inspiration that I ask this of you, my daughter," he said; "you must expiate your sins; I know you have need of it." "I have not, my father," I answered; but he insisted, saying, "Send away your sisters and confess, for God wills it." Seeing that I still resisted, he said again, "Why do you refuse to make your confession?" I answered that I refused because it was not necessary. This reply seemed to displease him, and he said, "Away with you! you had better reconsider the matter." Oh, my father, you were too good to such an ungrateful creature!

He departed, and I was not sorry; but the next day I was tormented by remorse of conscience, and ashamed of myself, saying, "I have behaved very ill to this good father. Certainly when he returns I will confess to him as he desires." In the meantime I wrote to him to ask his pardon. Some days afterwards I felt an extraordinary desire to confess to him. The Lord shed upon me the light of His grace, and I perceived in myself many things which negligence in my examinations had hitherto prevented me from discovering and confessing. From that moment I had no repose, and I wrote to him letter upon letter, beseeching him to have pity on my soul, and hasten as much as possible his return to Camerino; but, like a skilful physician, he rather delayed, in order to render my desire more ardent still, as he acknowledged afterwards. I had to wait until the feast of the stigmata of S. Francis, but the grace of God knew how to render this a profitable time to me. Never did I shed such abundant and bitter tears over my sins, as well those I had confessed as those I had not. The sorrow I felt for having offended the infinite goodness of God, inspired me with such hatred of myself, that I earnestly desired to become an object of detestation to the good father; but God promised me that, on the contrary, I should be more loved than before, when I should have made known to him all my miseries. In reality, on hearing my general confession, he was so much consoled and pleased by my frankness and repentance, that he bestowed on me his holy friendship, and preferred me afterwards to all his spiritual daughters. I can assure you that after this confession of all the sins of my past life, I was filled with greater consolation and joy than he was, and since then I have been in constant tranquillity.

Some days after this, not only while I was praying, but nearly always, I had a vision of a religious of my own order, of the most ravishing beauty, and in the black veil like one of ourselves; I saw her more distinctly than if I had seen her with my bodily eyes, and with a pleasure which the sight of no creature had ever inspired. She followed me everywhere, and showed her love for me by smiling with the most gracious and caressing air; and my joy was so intense, that I was continually in a state bordering on ecstasy. I tried to guess who she could be, which seemed to please her exceedingly; and I thought I heard her say, "Do you not know me?" Each time that she appeared to me (for I did not enjoy her continual presence), I knelt before her instinctively, whether I was at the grate, or at table, or occupied in work. In vain would she sign to me to rise; I persisted in retaining the posture I thought fitting towards such a venerable personage. The more I contemplated her beauty, the more I was ravished by it, and I could not comprehend how she could love such a creature as me. These apparitions were often repeated during fifteen days, but I have never had them since that period. I forgot to mention that she appeared to be about forty years old.

I was far from suspecting that this nun was S. Clare, our own glorious mother. This thought never came into my mind, for I had never had the desire to see her, except in heaven; but if you wish to know what I thought, my father, I will tell you in all simplicity. Until then I had always refused to receive nuns from other convents who asked admission, in which I was actuated by a right zeal. I accordingly thought that God wished to introduce here this person whom I saw, and that He showed her to me beforehand to propitiate me in her favour; and this made me say interiorly, "I will willingly receive such a religious, for her aspect alone is enough to fill us with consolation." It was not until these visions had ceased, that it came into my mind that perhaps it might be our glorious mother, and the thought inspired me with the most tender devotion towards her. Now I have no doubt that it was she, and if ever I attain to heaven (which, through the merits of the Blood of Christ, I hope to do), I shall recognize her without difficulty in the midst of all the glorious host, and I will embrace her fondly, saying, " O. my most sweet mother! it is you who didst deign to visit me during my weary exile." But, alas! what have I been, and what am I now?

O all ye who pass by the way of divine love, attend and see if there be any sorrow like to mine.

CHAPTER V.

OTHER DIVINE FAVOURS ACCORDED TO BATTISTA: THEY ARE FOLLOWED BY NEW TRIBULATIONS.

"THY testimonies are wonderful, O Lord, and to the soul who seeks Thee, exceedingly credible." Now what I have to say is Thy testimony; how then should I conceal it from my venerable father, who seeks Thee in truth? No; I will recount to him Thy praises without disguise, and I will recount them for Thy glory, and my own confusion. O ye angelic spirits, who are no strangers to what I am about to say, assist me, I beseech you, that I may speak the whole truth. It was but a few days after our holy mother S. Clare had withdrawn from me her beloved presence, that two angels appeared to me, clothed in robes of dazzling white, and with golden wings. They took my soul in their hands, and carried it on high, where they placed it at the Feet of Jesus crucified. They retained it there during more than two months, so that in the interval, whether I wished to walk, speak, or act, it seemed to me that I had no soul, and that my body only took part in these different movements. When this period had elapsed, they restored my soul, but burning with love and devotion for the seraphim to such a degree that I spoke of them incessantly, and prayed with the most tender affection to have one of them sent to me, as had been done to the prophet Isaias.

After having made this prayer continually for several days, without obtaining what I asked, one morning before prime I addressed myself to the Mother of God, and said to her with holy impatience: "O most sweet Mary! O Queen of incomparable goodness, I know that thou reignest over the angels, and that they all are eager to fulfil thy will. Command then, I beseech thee, one of the seraphim to fly towards me, as one did towards the prophet Isaias; thou knowest, O my most holy Mother, with what ardour I desire this grace." I was still speaking, when the Mother of God, touched by my prayer, promised of her own accord what I wished, which caused me to feel extraordinary joy. Some days after, having said matins at night, I continued to pray, and it came into my mind to meditate on the greatness of the love of God for His creatures. This method of prayer was not usual with me, yet I followed it, because my mind is accustomed to follow the attraction which comes from God. I began, therefore, to search for this love in the smallest and most abject things, but was soon transported in an ineffable manner to the contemplation of the most sublime and most divine things; that is to say, I plunged into so vast and so deep a sea, that more than once I desired to withdraw, but could not. What passed within me was neither reasoning nor vision, but a certain light, which is altogether inexplicable. I will relate only three things for your consolation.

The first is, that those who contemplate the great

and innumerable benefits with which the most bountiful and most clement God has favoured them, immediately recognize themselves to be burdened with two debts, which they can never pay : I mean the love with which He has first loved us, and the Passion He has willed to endure for us. What indeed can we do to acknowledge suitably these immense benefits? The second is, that all our love for God might be called hatred; all our praises, maledictions; all our thanksgivings, blasphemies; so remote are these sentiments from the sublime degree in which they ought to be found in us. The third thing which I perceived very clearly was, that the august Mary, the Mother of God herself, together with all men and all angels, could not return adequate thanks for even the production of the smallest flower, because there is an infinite difference between the excellence of the Creator and the lowness of His creatures.

Now, my father, you can easily understand the abyss into which I saw myself descending in contemplating the immense benefits I had received from my God. Then I really despaired of myself, and all my best works seemed as nothing. I renounced from my heart all spiritual joy, from the fear of adding debt to debt, ingratitude to ingratitude; so that had Jesus Christ appeared to me then, I should have closed my eyes firmly not to see Him. Prostrating myself with my face to the ground, I besought my God to keep me constantly attached to the Feet of Jesus crucified until my last hour, and to punish me afterwards for all the time I had passed there, as if I had employed it in blaspheming and betraying Him, persuaded that if I did not employ it thus, it would be entirely owing to His mercy. In short, I besought Him to place me after my death in the position most conformable to His good pleasure, declaring to Him that I was ready to descend into hell if He willed it, because His holy Will was the only object of my desires, and that I wished no other reward, no other beatitude, no other glory than that.

At the sight of the immense love with which God embraces all His creatures, a love which appeared to me without bounds, I could not hinder myself from reproaching Him by saying, "O folly! O folly!" It seemed indeed that I could not otherwise qualify such a love. The Feet of my Saviour were given up to me according to my prayer, so that during five years I never ceased to see them and to occupy myself with them, which gave me inexpressible happiness and peace. Now that this favour has been withdrawn from me, and I am deprived of so great a blessing, which was the treasure of my heart, I am inconsolable, and continually cry, "O sacred Feet! O only hope of my soul! how can I live without you, who were my heart and my life? O my Jesus! give them to me but for one hour of the day, and cast me into hell if Thou wilt, for with this consolation I should find it endurable. My sojourn there would not be long, for I would shed so many tears, I would embrace Thy Wounds with such continued ardour, that my heart would break, and this body of sin would be destroyed. O sacred Feet! I would, for love of you, see, touch, and kiss the feet of every creature. O most sweet Feet! where are the tears of love and devotion which you caused me to shed? Alas! bitterness has replaced these delights of my heart. O beloved Feet! I could not have believed that I should be torn from a place where adulterous and dishonoured women found an asylum; for was it not at the Feet of my Jesus that the sinners of the gospel came to seek their pardon? and now what was granted to them is refused to me. I am, then, more severely punished and more unfortunate than other sinners. O most clement Feet! if I did not fear to tire him who reads these lines, I would employ the whole day in writing my lamentations." This need not astonish you, my father, for the pain I experience is so bitter, that all other sorrows seem nothing in comparison. I have, doubtless, enjoyed this favour longer than others, but because of this, my harp, accustomed to give forth notes of confidence, is now turned to mourning. But I wander from my subject while I speak of the Feet of my Saviour; I will return, and the recital which I have begun by the inspiration of God, I will finish by the help of His grace.

When this light, of which I have just spoken, had vanished, it left such a fire in my soul, that, if I may dare say so, my soul became in it what iron becomes in material fire. If I remember correctly, this fire continued to burn me during three months; but I must explain to you its nature. It was a desire to quit the body and enjoy Jesus Christ, but a desire so lively and so ardent, that if I were to try to express it, I fear I should not be believed. Yet God knows I wish to speak only the truth. The flame of this desire was so burning, that during all the summer I seemed to suffer the pains of hell; pains which made me look for death as a blessing, as a feast, as the day of my nuptials with the Beloved of my heart; so that I would say with the apostle, "Oh, how I desire that my body should be dissolved, that I might go to be for ever with Jesus Christ;" and with the prophet: "Bring my soul out of prison, that I may praise Thy Name." This sacred fire with which I burned, made me understand that a seraph had flown towards me, to accomplish the promise made by my sweet Empress, the most holy Mother of God.

In the meantime, I was tormented interiorly and exteriorly by this most ardent desire, to an extent I cannot describe, and shed inexhaustible torrents of tears, sobbing and praying night and day to my God to withdraw me from the world and call me to Himself. One day when during my prayer I besought this grace with more than usual earnestness, my blessed Jesus manifested Himself to me with an air of great compassion, and embracing my soul with His left Arm, He drew her to His Breast, and wiping away her tears with His right Hand, said repeatedly, "Weep no more." This was a weeping of the soul, and not of the body, though I also shed many bodily tears. These sweet words ought to have lessened my grief, but, on the contrary, I wept more abundantly, and my prayer to obtain the end of my captivity became all the more ardent. He replied, "I cannot yet." "But Lord," said I, "art not Thou almighty?" "Behold," said He to me, showing me His divine Hands, "they are firmly bound." I could not understand this, but He added: "These bonds are the prayers which your brethren and sisters, the Franciscans, address to Me, to have your life prolonged; be then patient."

I know not whether that which I am about to recount took place before or after what I have already related. Once, when I felt such a heat that I could not bear it, I turned in a dying state towards the seraphim, and said to them, complaining, and almost reproaching myself for having asked their aid: "O most sweet spirits, if I have asked with so much fervour that you might come to me, it was because I believed that being so near to God, your presence would be paradise; how is it, then, that since you have come to me I suffer the pains of hell? indeed, I understand not what you have brought with you." Then these sublime spirits, entering into familiar conversation with me, as with a friend, replied: "That which afflicts you is precisely that which renders us happy. Being unable to enjoy God while you are captive in the prison of your body, you are reduced to form desires which torment you in proportion to their strength. With us, on the contrary, desire being always united to the presence of the Beloved Object, the more ardent it is, the more it augments our felicity." After these words, they told me that their intimate presence with God was such that God could not be a single instant without them, nor they without Him. They told me, moreover, that there exists such an intimate union between the seraphim and cherubim, that one could not be in a soul without the other. "Sometimes," they said, "it is the cherubim who hold the first place in a soul, sometimes the seraphim; but it is we seraphim who enjoy the pre-eminence in your soul. Because of this, our seraphic fire prevails in you above the light of the cherubim." This accorded exactly with my own experience, for, though the light which I had seen was really incomprehensible by reason of its intensity, nevertheless, in comparison with it the fire was thrice as strong. On this occasion I learned that the two angels who held my soul during three months at the Feet of Jesus, were one from each choir. This is that fire in which I was baptized and purified, after my general confession to Father Peter Moliano.

The Sacrament of the Eucharist is really the Bread of angels: I say this, my father, because after the visit of the angels I felt a hunger for this divine sacrament which I could not assuage. This made me begin the custom of communicating every Sunday, which I continued for two years; but it was too seldom to satisfy the desires of my soul. I would have wished to communicate every day, and when I considered the long abstinence through the week, I became weak and faint with sorrow; but otherwise, during the three years preceding my great tribulation, I lived happily in the possession of profound and truly angelic peace. Then all the ways of Sion were opened to me, and seemed to my eyes equally smooth and agreeable; I no longer walked; I ran quickly, and met with no obstacle, because my desires and pious prayers removed every hindrance from my way. I had then, or at least I believed I had, an angelic and celestial heart rather than a human one, for there never rose within it any sentiment of pride, unless it be pride that dictates to me what I now say. In short, I was in such a state, that had any one told me I should ever be in the condition in which you now see me, I should have believed it absolutely impossible. I think that this disposition was not pure pride; at least, my conscience reproached me with no sentiment of the kind. It was at this time that, by a singular gift of the Holy Ghost, I resolved never to meditate on any other subject than the Passion of my divine Master, desiring to make every day a Good Friday for myself, that I might weep to my heart's content over the sufferings of my sweet Jesus, persuaded that if I employed my life in weeping for Him, He would make me taste at my death the joy of His glorious resurrection. From that time there was no difference for me between Easter and Christmas, between the joyful and sorrowful feasts of holy Church. Even Fridays produced no change for me, for I only performed my accustomed devotions on those days. It is true that my thoughts turned towards the mysteries which the different feasts recalled, but it was in spite of myself, for my firm resolution was to think of nothing but the sorrowful Passion of my good Master. Thus, my father, the spiritual life to which your sermon on Good Friday had given birth, ended by becoming a continual Good Friday for me. So true it is that in nature there are things in which the beginning and the end meet; *sic respondent ultima primis.*

I was then traversing the desert of this world, flowing with delights, leaning on my Beloved, separated from Him bodily, but united to Him spiritually by continual meditation on His sufferings. I was far from anticipating the misfortunes which threatened me. He Who knows everything future had fully predicted them to me, but my extreme ignorance would not permit me to understand. And yet the time foretold was approaching, that deplorable time which was to witness my spiritual ruin. One day, when I had just begun my prayers, I heard a voice say to me, "Arise quickly, and write My interior sorrows, which I will make known to you." I made an excuse, saying, "Lord, I am so incapable of doing what Thou biddest me, that I know not even how to begin; how then could I resolve to relate the favours Thou hast granted me?" The voice repeated the command, and bid me begin my recital as if it referred to a third person. I immediately began, and my words flowed so rapidly that I had no need to study how I should write. What happened to me then, happens to me now; I always take up my pen with extreme reluctance, but immediately things present themselves to me with greater rapidity than I can express them. When I received the command, I assuredly did not foresee the consequences; and yet I refused to obey, as if I had known it would turn to my detriment. Listen to what God seemed to say to me : " I foresee that the vase of thy soul will contract stains, and such stains that it will be no longer worthy to contain the balm of My interior sorrows. It is, therefore, necessary that thou shouldest pour it into others; besides, it can no longer be useful to thee, because of thy infection." Oh how I fear that what I am writing now will produce in me a similar result. I seem to hear the voice of God saying : " Vomit from thy mouth all the benefits I have filled thee with, because I am ready to vomit thee from Mine." Deliver me from this terrible sentence, O my God!

In the month of August following I found myself engaged in a serious combat, which at first gave me no fear, because I enjoyed profound interior peace, and was totally ignorant of the snares of the demon, so that I suspected no danger. My blindness was even so profound that I saw nothing but good in his machinations. This lasted for two months; when at length, on the octave of S. Francis, God opened my eyes a little, and I saw myself, as it were, in the midst of a vast plain, delivered up to a terrible combat, and surrounded by mighty enemies, out of whose hands God alone could rescue me. Overwhelmed with hopeless sorrow, and not knowing what to do, I passed the octave day of S. Francis fasting on bread and water, and ceasing not to implore the help of the Most High, and conjuring this great saint to grant me his powerful protection. The following night, instead of my deliverance, God showed me in a dream all the labours and afflictions which awaited me. This was the signal for my greatest trial. Then the pit of the abyss, which had been shut for ten years, was opened, and the dragon came forth, roaring against me, and assailing me with such fury that it seemed as if he would devour me alive; but the powerful Hand of God, which never abandons a soul that trusts in Him, drew me unhurt from the jaws of this monster. You already know the circumstances, my father, but I repeat it, that the glory may be given to God alone, to whose goodness it was owing, and not to any virtue or prudence in me. Nevertheless, this cruel enemy despoiled me of my precious garments; he took from me the light which enlightened my eyes, and cut off the hair of my spiritual strength, and "having wounded me went away, leaving me half dead."

I remained two years in this state of affliction, and during those two wretched years I was deprived of all help and consolation, with the exception of speaking three times to Brother Peter Moliano, my holy and glorious father. It was at this time that he became vicar, which gave me much joy; for I said to myself, "Provided I can consult with him, the demon will be defeated in his enterprise, for he will give me the means to come out victorious from this sad combat." O my holy father, after the journey which obtained for me these visits from you, you returned again to these parts, but your beloved daughter could not converse with you, for death snatched you from her. Oh!

how bitter for me was this death! I lost all courage at seeing myself deprived of your help, and in my despair I made a firm resolution to speak of my pain to none, at least till God obliged me to give my confidence to a new father, by His grace showing him to me as an instrument of His choosing. O my good father, I did not then comprehend the good you were to do me, I was ignorant that you left me an orphan, only because it was expedient for my salvation; but I was not long in receiving the proof of it. Immediately on your death, you took from my enemies all their power, and brought me back again into the path of truth. This was not the only service which you rendered me; for I cannot doubt that your charity obtained for me the inspiration to give my confidence to the father who directs me, and to disclose to him all my tribulation. This inspiration was anything but agreeable to me at first. I experienced extreme repugnance to manifest to a new director that which passed within me, but God made me see that this openness was necessary to my salvation, and nothing could be more true, as you, my father, to whom I write, well know. Whence, then, came this repugnance to open my heart? Doubtless from the demon; for since I have frankly told you everything, I find in myself such consolation and peace, that I cease not to bless heaven for having inspired me with confidence in your fatherly care, and I say with truth and without flattery, I would not have taken any other than you to be the confidant of my sorrows.

CHAPTER VI.

BATTISTA ADDRESSES TO HER SPIRITUAL FATHER PARTICULARS SUPPLEMENTARY TO THE HISTORY OF HER LIFE.

It was on the 3rd of March, in the year 1491, that the Blessed Battista finished the writing we have just given to the reader. It ended thus: After having faithfully retraced all my spiritual life, in obedience to the divine inspiration, I finish my work to the praise of my glorious Saviour Jesus Christ. I will now write, according to the order in which I have received them, the lights He gave me on His interior sorrows. When you read what follows, my father, you will perceive that I attribute the revelations to a sister of the convent of Urbino, to prevent their being supposed to be mine. If, then, I speak in the third person, it is to avoid the honour which might accrue to me, and when I speak of this soul as holy and blessed, it is only the better to conceal myself.

[It appears that the Blessed Battista wrote the foregoing important treatise in a separate packet, which she kept beside her in order to show it to her spiritual father, when he came to Camerino. While she was waiting for him, she wrote three other letters in obedience to the inspiration given her. This is one of them:]

My Reverend and much-loved Father,—After the hard battle which I had sustained for two years, I had hoped to obtain peace, or at least a truce, but this hope, which seems to me so legitimate, is vain.

Scarcely had you quitted Camerino, when I had to endure still more horrible temptations than before. I revolted, to a certain degree, against God, imputing to Him my faults, my sins, my errors. I dared to call Him to account for His conduct; I accused Him of falsehood in several things He said in the Scriptures; accusations which rendered me guilty of heinous sin.

[The reader will see in this but a new proof of her humility, for it is certain that these horrible thoughts were entirely involuntary.]

I did other things besides, which I pass over in silence. I am sure, my father, that in reading this sad story, you will think that my poor soul lived in hell, during the six months you have been absent from her; and certainly you are right, for to speak the truth, it seems to me that I have become altogether infernal and devilish; but what renders my torment more insupportable, and almost breaks my heart, is that I have no person to whom I can communicate my pain, and that I cannot receive the slightest consolation in my pressing necessity. Into what country of the world have you fled, my father? I have been so unhappy, and your absence leaves me without counsel and without support. Oh! how cruel has this privation seemed to me, and how long! I can do nothing but groan in penning this dolorous history, and repeat the sad lamentation: O all ye who pass by the way of divine love, attend and see if there be any sorrow like to mine. If I had a voice sufficiently strong to reach to the ends of the world, I would cry aloud and say, "Servants of God, who aspire to the perfection of love, humble yourselves, and let my example be a warning to you, for had you been admitted to the conversation of angels and saints, of the Virgin Mary, and of God Himself, you might yet, like me, fall from your high estate into the abyss of mortal sin. Oh! let my unfortunate and most miserable soul serve you for an example. She had happily entered the immense ocean of divine love and spiritual sweetness, and then a terrible tempest overwhelmed her, and made her descend even to hell." Farewell, my father, &c.

[She thought she had fallen into the abyss, because she took for mortal sins all the bad thoughts that came into her head, but she did not consent to them, for her will had never ceased to be unalterably attached to God; she had some difficulty in separating these two things, because of the violence of her temptations, as we see in the following letter, which was dictated to His servant by Jesus Christ, to fortify her against the temptations of which we have already spoken, and to enlighten her on certain things connected with this trial.]

" My Sister,—You have often spoken of the promise made to you by God at the beginning of your conversion, that He would make you pass through heavy trials, and on this occasion you manifest to Me the fear of forgetting this promise when the trials come, and, in consequence, of falling into discouragement, perhaps even into despair.' For this reason I have resolved to dictate this letter to you, that it may serve as a memorial to encourage you, and I doubt not that it alone will suffice to sustain your patience in the midst of tribulation. Remember, in the first place, that your vocation has not been the effect of human words, but the call of God against your own will.

Remember, that to the desire of goodness succeeded that of suffering, and that immediately you were attacked by sickness. Remember, that from your earliest infancy I have always drawn you to meditate on My Passion, wishing that you should conform your life to it, as much as the frailty of human nature permitted you to do. Begin by foreseeing in your morning prayer the trials that will overtake you during the day. I beg and beseech you to follow this advice, because you can do nothing more agreeable to Me. Worldlings have more pleasure in contemplating those they love under one habit than under another, and I also, be it known to you, attach a value to certain garments; and when you in a manner clothe yourself with the thought of My suffering, then I find you most according to My heart. Would you wish an example? You will find it in Me, in the Garden of Olives. Whilst I was in prayer, it pleased My Father to discover to Me all the pains which His justice reserved for Me; and despoiling myself of My own Will, I said to Him: 'Fiat voluntas tua'—'Thy Will be done.' Now this was not a vain word, as you well know. I arose from this prayer with a heart burning with charity, so that I could have died in that torment, not for My own interest, but for the honour of My Father and the salvation of souls. You have remarked, doubtless, that on this occasion I returned to My prayer three times, and I would have you and all who desire to please Me, learn from this that a passing prayer is not sufficient to gain My heart, but that it is perseverance in this holy exercise which charms Me, overcomes Me, and conquers Me.

"Remember, that although I, being God, came to

suffer, yet when I saw My Passion approaching, because I was Man as well as God, I was forced to pray and cry out, 'My Father, if it be possible, let this chalice pass from Me!' For this reason I would say to you, My daughter, that although you have often besought Me to give you sufferings, you may well tremble when you see them approach, and then you will say to Me, 'My Father, if it be possible, let this chalice pass from Me!' but provided you add, 'Not my will, but Thine be done,' there is in this neither despair nor anything to displease Me, since it is according to the example I, as Man, have given, for your instruction and that of others. But if, while you persevere in prayer amidst your sufferings, My Father should deign to show you all the pains which still await you, as He showed them to Me; and if this vision should so enkindle you, as to make you willing to suffer them all, not for your own advantage, but for the love of God and the salvation of your neighbour, as I did; your resemblance to Me in this would constrain My Father to love you in the highest degree of true charity.

"Offer Him, then, your heartfelt thanksgivings for the tribulations which He in His bounty has sent you, and weep bitterly for the loss of those which He did prepare for you, but did not send because you had rendered yourself unworthy by your ingratitude and slowness in the spiritual life; for you must know that His love for you is so great, that He would have wished to send you all afflictions, that He might have an opportunity of giving you all blessings. And now, acknowledge in all sincerity that you do not deserve to be conformed to His beloved Son, by walking after Him in the way of His Passion. This is the nuptial robe with which I, your true Spouse, was always clad; and in reality the most precious treasure, next to a good will, which God can give you, is suffering. You can always refuse the cross, as I could have refused it Myself; but know, that in flying the cross, you fly from all good. It was by accepting the bitter chalice out of pure love that I pleased My Father most, and you must do the same if you would render yourself like Me, and therefore agreeable in His Eyes. When I rose from prayer, burning with the fire of charity, I presented Myself before my enemies, and you also will meet your enemies without fear. One of My disciples betrayed Me by a kiss; you will also be deceived and afflicted by those whom you dearly love, and towards whom you feel nothing but kindness and good-will.

"Remember the five points I am about to propose to you: 1st. When any persons offend you, grieve more for the injury done to God than the injury done to yourself. 2nd. Beseech Me with all your heart to pardon them, and to forgive them the chastisement which they merit, as you would beseech Me to spare your own eye or any of your members; for your neighbour is indeed as your eye and a member of your body. 3rd. You must know that you owe more to those who ill-treat you, than to those who treat you well; for the former purify your soul, adorn it, and render it singularly agreeable to Me. 4th. Consider the extent of My charity towards you. It is so great, that even if you had been My enemy by mortal sin, I should still regard all the injuries you receive from others as done to Myself. In like manner your hatred of your enemies should only be to consider the harm which may befall them as your own. 5th. Think that the injuries done you are far from being proportioned to your offences, and that if I permit them to happen to you, it is only for your good; and beware of imputing sin to your enemies, whatever they may do.

"Consider that after I had received the kiss of My perfidious disciple, I asked of the crowd, 'Whom seek ye?' 'We seek Jesus of Nazareth,' they replied; and when I answered, 'I am He,' this word was so powerful that it overthrew them; but at the same time it gave them power to apprehend Me. Because I united My will, as Man, to the Will of God, the soldiers could not touch Me, and it required but a word of My mouth to overthrow them. It is true that afterwards they had the power to seize Me, because My Father gave it to them; but what happened to them at first ought to have taught them that My power was not human, but divine. Thus, My daughter, each time that with an honest heart you deliver your will up to God, saying sincerely that you beseech Him to do His Will—Fiat voluntas tua, Thy Will be done —you will assimilate yourself so closely to Me, that the demons will have no power to touch you until they receive it from on high. Until then they will fail in their enterprises; they will fall before you, and the Will of God alone can raise them up; and, whatever be the power given them, they can never hurt you as much as they did Me. I, the only Son of God, was abandoned and forsaken by the whole world! You, therefore, must rejoice and be thankful in proportion as you participate in My abandonment. I was dragged before different judges, I was loaded with shame and torment by the people I so tenderly loved. You, therefore, must suffer from all sorts of persons, even from those most dear to you. I was suspended on the cross in complete nakedness. I therefore wish you to be stripped on the cross of holy religion, that is, despoiled of all other love. Three nails fixed me to the cross; you must be fixed there by the same number, that is to say, by poverty, obedience, and chastity. I have already said many things to you on this subject, which I will not recall to you now.

"Remember that I gave you a greater token of My love in afflicting you than by pressing you in My paternal Arms. Call to mind, when suffering weighs you down, how often I have lavished upon you the sweet names of sister, daughter, spouse, and that too in accents of tenderness which made you languish with divine love. Remember, poor soul, that in those moments of pain, God has Himself said to you such wonderful things about Himself, that you could not support the sweetness of His communications, but were forced to cry, 'No more, Lord, no more,' and to take to flight from humility.

"Remember that to guard you against the movements of your excessive pride, God told you that it was not because of your merits, but from pure love that He loaded you with these rare favours, explaining this to you by the following comparison: When a physician sees that the state of his patient becomes dangerous, he no longer applies ordinary remedies, but employs energetic and powerful means. It was thus that God, like a wise physician, dealt with you; not because you deserved such treatment, but from simple charity to heal your grave and dangerous infirmity.

"Remember also, that to render you more humble, I clearly showed you that these spiritual sweetnesses could not be obtained naturally, but that God communicates them by His infinite charity alone, to whom and in what measure it pleases Him, according to the counsels of His wisdom, and the necessities of the soul to which He may impart them. Now it pleased Him to give them to you independently of all merit, because He knew your pride, and was well aware that if He had waited to bestow His favours until after your trials, you would not have failed to attribute them to your virtues. Know then, My daughter, that the more sins you avoid, the more good actions you perform, and the more sufferings you endure, so much the more are you indebted to the divine goodness. It is a great gift not to sin; it is a greater one to do good; but the superlative degree is to support affliction for God's sake, or for the love of justice. I call them gifts, because it is certain that you could do none of these things without the grace of God; 'for without Me you can do nothing.' Has not your own experience shown you that there is no evil you would not have committed, if God had not restrained you; no good that you would have performed, if He had not concurred with you in producing it? that you would have come out of no trial without sin, if He had not added His strength to your weakness? What gratitude, then, do you not owe to God, for having given you such heavenly light!

"Know then, and remember, that God has made you clearly see that you would be unable to render Him sufficient thanks for the least of His benefits, even if you had never sinned, and had alone performed more penances than ever were performed by His saints, or had shed as many penitential tears as would have filled the ocean, or had borne as many sufferings as human nature could endure. How then would it be possible for you to make satisfaction for your infinite faults? Say then to the Lord: 'My God, my life, the joy of my heart! since I cannot, either by doing good or by bearing afflictions patiently, thank Thee fittingly for Thy graces, nor satisfy for my numberless and abominable sins, at least grant me this favour, to regard me as one guilty of every crime and destitute of all good, and then let me employ faithfully the short remainder of my life according to Thy holy Will; and at last place me, after my death, wherever I can render Thee most honour. Even though Thou shouldst banish me to hell, I will be content to remain there, because I desire, O my God, that Thy honour may be my glory and my happiness.'

"Remember the promises I have made to you; I will not dictate them to you now, because you know them already. If you remember what I have said to you regarding your tribulations, nothing will seem difficult to you. Everything on earth passes quickly away; calm succeeds the tempest, and after sorrow comes joy. The very moment of tribulation itself will be to thee, in great part, an acceptable time, and a day of salvation. Remember the generosity with which you have sometimes said to Me in prayer, 'Now, Lord, hasten the time, for I can wait no longer; Thou art too long in sending me the trials Thou hast promised. When wilt Thou conduct me into the pasturage of suffering, where I may fatten with Thy faithful sheep?' Remember, when you are on the cross which God designs for you, never to say, 'My God, why hast Thou abandoned me?' I have told you why I forbid this complaint; namely, that the more you are resigned to see yourself abandoned by

Me, the nearer I will be to you. I wish to do with you as my Father did with Me, and to load you with as many sufferings as your weakness will permit you to bear.

"God once said to you that He might permit you to fall into some great error, or deception, or violent temptation, or betrayal; but be not discouraged on this account, for nothing is so displeasing to Him as despair. Be firm in fear and humility, as you have been until now, with sweet confidence, for you must now turn over a new page; and you will seem to yourself as much an object of His hatred and displeasure, as hitherto of His love and favour. Nevertheless, remain constant and immovable, for it is to the conqueror that the crown is reserved. Remember the royal offering you made to your God, when you said you would serve Him, not to avoid hell and gain heaven, but because He is above all infinitely and singularly worthy of love, and, in consequence, deserves to receive from every creature all praise, service, and love; and that you would serve Him purely and with fervour until death, even if you knew your damnation to be certain. God did not reveal these things to you because of your good and holy life. Forget not this; and be confounded in considering, on the one hand, so much wickedness and misery, and on the other, such astonishing goodness.

"I feel sorrow and compassion for you, poor soul, when I see Myself obliged to let you fall into such lamentable desolation, after so many sweet endearments, so many tender words, so many proofs of My excessive love, and after you have felt and tasted how much God is worthy of love, gracious, kind, and gentle above all the rivals who have disputed your heart with Him. Keep yourself, then, in My fear, and no longer say, 'May God preserve me from this, and I will preserve myself from that.' It is for having held such language as this that He has found it necessary to teach you at your own cost, that an ant would have sufficed to make you break your neck, if He had not sustained you by His powerful Arm. Trust no longer in your own strength, even if God should give you power to work miracles every day. I have taught you that when you bear devoutly great sorrow, you pay some portion of your debt. Remember that this exhortation is not dictated by hatred, but on the contrary, by the love I have for you. I will not recompense your merit in this world, as I have already often told you; I wish you to be on the cross, alone and despoiled of all affection that is not for Me. Love and suffering will end in uniting you to Me, and it is only on the cross that our holy and spiritual marriage can be consummated. You have heard what the spouse in the Canticles says, 'My Beloved is mine, and I am His;' but where has she found Him? 'In the midst of the lilies where He feeds;' that is to say, 'in the midst of many sorrows.'"

Behold, my father, what our Lord said to me while I was yet in the world, after having taken the firm and irrevocable resolution to serve God in perpetual enclosure, in the order of the glorious S. Clare. I wrote them under the dictation of Jesus Christ, in the monastery of Urbino, five months before my profession. Glory be to this sweet Saviour, and praise for ever and ever.

[One thing in this letter might surprise the reader, and consequently deserves to be explained. We find that God had permitted the Blessed Battista to become the victim of an error or deception, She believed herself to be in a state of mortal sin, for having given credence to vain apparitions, and opened her heart to false consolations; but this only proves her humility and the delicacy of her conscience; for how could it be possible, that an error, which God promised as a grace, and permitted for her good, could in reality serve to render her guilty? Every person who is conversant with spiritual things, on reading this passage attentively, will allow that the error was in the understanding of this holy soul, and not in her will. Otherwise, the deception could not have been a gift of God, which it nevertheless was, and according to His promise. We see, in short, that this generous soul, desiring to testify to God the excess of her tender love, asked of Him heavy trials, and that God promised to satisfy her; which He did, by delivering her during two months to the delusions of the infernal spirit. We would ask, Is it possible that a prayer dictated by such a love could be answered by the loss of that love? So far from it, rather would we believe that the sorrow produced by this false apprehension of having mortally offended her God, and incurred His anger, would, on the contrary, unite her to Him more and more. This merits particular attention. It cannot be supposed that Jesus Christ, Who is incapable of error, could ever take the sins of men as really His own. Yet having offered Himself to support the punishment of them, He felt grief and confusion for them before His Father, as if He Himself had committed them, and became, in a certain sense, as our representative, the object of the divine hatred and indignation, whilst at this very time His Father delighted in Him as much as ever.

Our Saint reproaches herself, above all, for certain words that had escaped her in the course of her tribulations, and we have seen that she looked upon them as blasphemies, which overwhelmed her with sorrow; but does it not seem as if God had taken upon Himself to prove her innocence, by preserving her tongue from corruption after her death? Truly, when we consider this prodigy, we could imagine we heard God say to His servant, as He said to holy Job, "Sister Battista sinned not by her lips, nor spoke she any foolish thing against God." If any reader should find these reasons insufficient, let him read with attention the following prayer composed by the Saint, and committed to writing by her at the end of her three years' trial.]

"O God, most gracious and full of goodness, Father of infinite mercies, I am that sheep from among the hundred, who had quitted Thy fold, to seek bad pasturage, where I have fed on bitter herbs and poisonous husks. After three years passed in this sad wandering, I desire with all my heart to return to Thee. O God of sweetness and clemency, only source of true peace, receive me, then, with charity, take me on Thy merciful shoulders. O generous and faithful Shepherd, Who hast given Thy life for Thy sheep, bring me back into Thy dear fold, and turn not Thy Face away from me. O my sweet Jesus, do not permit me to be shipwrecked in the very port of religion, after having struggled so hard to withdraw from the stormy ocean of the world. Remember, O my Jesus, the price I have cost Thee. Remember, O my Redeemer, all the Blood Thou hast shed on the cross to redeem my poor soul. Remember, O my Well-beloved, not what I have done, but what I have wished to do, for Thy honour. My Jesus, I am the poor publican spoken of in the gospel; shame for my sins hinders me from raising my head, and the confusion caused by them makes me not dare to look up to heaven. Like him, I cast my eyes on the ground and strike my breast, saying: 'O God, be merciful to me a sinner.'

"O most clement Lord, receive into Thine open Arms a prodigal daughter, who has wandered far to dissipate her goods, by not living in uprightness. My divine Master, I am not worthy to be called Thy servant, nor even Thy slave, because I have persecuted the souls purchased by Thy Precious Blood. Come to me, notwithstanding, O my Jesus, come with Thy grace. Press my afflicted soul in Thine Arms, and visit her as Thou wert accustomed to do in happier times. O my good Father, refuse not this kiss of peace which my heart desires. Put an end to this cruel war, from which I have suffered so much for the last three years. If I do not deserve it in any other way, I would willingly give my life to obtain peace. O my Beloved, call me from this exile, and from the darkness of this world. Deliver me from this loathsome prison of my miserable body. Draw me towards Thee, my God, draw me to Thee, and leave me no longer to languish in this valley of tears. I cannot remain longer here. Infirmities, demons, other creatures, and interior tribulations cry to me, 'Fly, fly from this earth. You have dwelt long enough here; a longer sojourn is forbidden you.' Receive me to Thyself, my sweet Jesus, receive me; I am ready to depart, with a joy I cannot express. Banish me whithersoever Thy honour may require it until the judgment-day, provided I be not separated from Thee eternally as I have deserved, and I will bless Thy great mercy. Glory be to Thee, O Lord. Amen."

CHAPTER VII.

FIRST PAIN.—SORROW FOR THE SUFFERINGS OF THE LOST AND THE ELECT.

"There was a devout soul who hungered after the food of the Passion of our most sweet Jesus, and who after many years employed in her own spiritual reformation, was at length admitted by a special favour to communication with the interior sufferings which afflicted His Heart. It is from her that I heard all I am about to relate.

"After having prayed long to be introduced into, and submerged in the sea of His interior sufferings, this good Master, through pity, mercy, and grace, consented to plunge her into this ocean without bottom and without shore, where she was soon obliged to cry aloud in her distress, 'No more, Lord, no more; my weakness is unable to support the overwhelming weight of Thy sorrows.' I find no difficulty in believing this, for I know how abundantly He gives to those who know how to solicit these sort of favours humbly and perseveringly.

"One day that this devout soul was at prayer, she said to Him with great anxiety of heart, 'I entreat Thee, O Lord, to permit me to enter the sacred bed of Thy interior sorrows. Submerge me in that ocean of bitterness; there I would wish to die, O sweet life of my soul. Tell me, Jesus, my hope, how cruel were the pains that afflicted Thy sacred Heart?' 'Since thou art ignorant, My daughter,' this good Master replied, 'of the greatness of My sufferings, I will tell thee that they were equally great with the love which I bore to My Father, and to creatures.' Now this devout soul told me that at another time long before God had made her understand the complacency He took in His love for His creatures, and she communicated to me many beautiful and devout thoughts, which are too long for me to relate. I will therefore proceed to speak of the sorrows of my good Master. On hearing Jesus give His love for man as the measure of His sufferings, and knowing before the grandeur and immensity of this love, her senses failed her, and she was obliged to support her head, because of the distress of her heart and the weakness of her whole body. When she had recovered a little, she began to say, 'O my God, since Thou hast told me how great Thy sufferings were, make known to me the greatness of the pains which crushed Thy sacred Heart.'

"Jesus replied with sweetness, 'Know, My daughter, that the pains I bore in My Heart were innumerable and infinite ; for innumerable and infinite are the souls, my members, who tear themselves from Me by mortal sin, for each soul separates itself from Me, its Head and source of life, as often as it sins mortally.

"'This pain My Heart felt most cruelly and deeply. Imagine to yourself what are the sufferings of a criminal on the rack when his members are dislocated by violence, and you will have some idea of My martyrdom at the tearing away of as many souls as would be lost for ever, and indeed the tearing away of every member, when it commits mortal sin. The suffering caused by tearing off a spiritual member is as much greater than the suffering a corporeal member would cause, as the soul is superior to the body. Neither you, nor any one living, can understand how great is this superiority; I alone, Who created both, can appreciate the nobleness of the soul and the baseness of the body. Therefore, neither you, nor any other creature, can comprehend the severity and bitterness of My pain. I speak now only of the damned. As mortal sins are not all equally heinous, and as there are different manners of committing them, accordingly the separations were more or less painful; hence arose the quality and quantity of My pains. On the one hand, because the will of the lost remains eternally perverse, their sufferings also are eternal; while on the other, according to the number and gravity of the sins of each, they will be more or less tormented.

"'The thought that these innumerable members were torn from Me for ever was terrible and insupportable, and it is also this fatal *for ever* which is and will be the greatest torment of these lost souls throughout eternity. In the overwhelming sorrow produced by the thought of this fatal *for ever*, I would willingly have consented to suffer, not once, but an infinite number of times, these cruel separations, with their different lacerations, to recover but one of these souls, and see it again united to My living members, that is, to My elect who live eternally in the Holy Spirit, by the life which comes from Me, Who am the living life, that is, the life of all living creatures. You may judge by all that I have said, how inexpressibly dear a human soul is to Me. It is also necessary you should know that this terrible *for ever* afflicts lost souls to such a degree, because of My justice, that there is not one who would not willingly suffer various and infinite pains to recover the hope of being re-united to Me at any period, however distant; but as they never can, this is the most frightful of their sufferings. Consider what pain I suffered mentally in my Heart for all the lost, and that too until the moment of My death.'

"After this discourse, the devout soul to whom it was addressed felt an ardent desire to propose to Jesus a certain doubt. In consequence, she ventured to say to Him, with respect and fear, and also with the greatest confidence and simplicity : ' O sweet and sorrowful Jesus ! I have often heard it said that Thou hast endured all the pains of the damned ; and I would wish to know, provided my curiosity does not displease Thee, if Thou hast experienced the different pains caused in these wretched souls by cold, heat, fire, gnashing of teeth, and other torments which they endure in hell. Tell me, then, my Jesus, if Thou didst feel these things.' This question appeared not to displease Him, and He replied : 'I have not felt, My daughter, the different torments of the damned in the manner in which you understand them ; that could not have been, because their sufferings are the sufferings of members, dead, and separated from Me, their Head and Body. I will explain this to you by the following comparison. If one of your members were diseased, you would feel keen agony until the surgeon had cut it off from your body ; but once removed, it might be submitted to the action of fire, or ice, or thrown to dogs or wolves without your soul experiencing any of those different torments, because it is dead, and entirely separated from the head. But yet you would not be insensible to the ill-treatment of a member which had once been yours, and the more it was tormented, the more, doubtless. your heart would feel for it. In the same way, when mortal sin tore these members from My Body, the pain was terrible, and because they retained, during their life on earth, the power to be re-united to Me, I felt unspeakable and infinite pains; but after their death I felt this pain no more; but yet I experienced another unspeakable and incomprehensible pain, in considering that they had been My true and real members, and nevertheless were now fallen under the power of the infernal spirits, and would suffer divers other torments for all eternity.

" 'Another sorrow which pierced My Heart was caused by My elect themselves; for you must know that all those among them who have sinned, or who will sin mortally, have done Me the same injury by their separation from Me as those who are lost, since they also are members whom sin has torn from My Body. As great as the love which I was to have for them, and they for Me, for ever, and as great as the degradation to which they fell by sin, is the pain which I felt in all these My members. In this it differed from that inflicted by the lost, that after their death the latter was felt no more, whereas I endured all the bitterness and pain from which the elect suffer in life and after death—namely, the martyrdoms of all martyrs, the temptations of all the tempted, the infirmities of all the sick; the persecutions, discredits, journeyings—in a word, all the afflictions, great and small, of every one of the elect, and that as keenly as you would feel a blow on your eye, your hand, and any other of your members. Now consider the number of the martyrs, and the various tortures which each of them suffered. Add to this the sufferings of all the elect, their number and variety, and then make your calculation. If you had a thousand eyes, hands, feet, and other members, and in each member a thousand different pains, how exquisite would not such a torture be to you? But My members are not counted by thousands or millions—they are innumerable; nor is it possible to count the sufferings of martyrs, of confessors, of virgins, and all the other elect; they would reach almost to infinity. You may then conclude, that as no one can comprehend the glory and blessedness prepared for My elect in heaven, so no one can comprehend the number and greatness of the mental pains which I suffered for them.

"'But I was not satisfied with feeling all the afflictions of their lives; I felt equally the diversity and number of the torments which remained for them to suffer in purgatory, according to the quality and number of their sins; for their souls are not dead members, separated from Me like those of the damned; but they are My living members, spiritually united to Me, all of whose sufferings I consequently endure. There is no difference between the pains of hell and of purgatory, only that the first are eternal, while the latter endure but for a time; and the souls in purgatory remain there willingly, resigned and contented, suffering in peace, and returning thanks to the justice of God. But I have said enough of this pain.'

"Now this soul, comprehending how much her sins had displeased God, and what suffering she had caused to her beloved Jesus, was inconsolable, and in her anguish said such touching things, that I would fain recount them, but they have escaped my memory. I only recollect that she said to her Saviour—'O my God! I have made Thee suffer much, whether I be saved or damned. Ah! I never could have believed that sin produced such frightful effects; for had I known it, I certainly never would have committed sin with such facility. Nevertheless, Lord, pay no regard to my words, for if Thy beneficent Hand do not restrain me, I shall do even worse things than before. O Jesus! my true Lover, sweet to my heart are all these pains of which Thou hast told me!'"

SECOND PAIN.—THE SORROWS OF CHRIST FOR THE SUFFERINGS OF HIS MOTHER, S. MARY MAGDALEN, AND HIS DISCIPLES.

"The most loving Saviour continued His recital thus: 'Hearken, hearken, My daughter. Do not yet speak thus. I have still to recount other most bitter pains. First, that sharp sword which pierced My Soul, the suffering, I mean, of My pure and innocent Mother; for no one felt so deeply as she did the death and Passion of her Son. She well deserved that We should exalt her in the heavens, and crown her Queen of angels and of men. The more any creature is humiliated and afflicted in this world for love of Me, the more they are exalted, glorified, and recompensed in the kingdom of heaven by the rule of God's justice. Now, as no one on earth suffered so much for Me as this most sweet and afflicted Mother, no one has equalled her in glory, and because she was to Me another self in My Passion and sorrows, she is in heaven another self by power and glory, excepting only in divinity, in which she does not participate, for it belongs to Us Three alone—Father, Son, and Holy Ghost. But be it known to you, that I, the Incarnate God, have suffered no sorrow during My mortal life that My beloved Mother has not shared. Only I suffered in a higher and more perfect degree, because I was Man-God, while My Mother was but a pure and simple creature. I would willingly have spared her this suffering, and taken her pains upon Myself. It would have been a solace for Me, an inexpressible consolation; but as I was not to feel any solace in My cruel martyrdom, this favour was not granted Me, although with filial reverence I besought it many times, and with abundance of tears.'

"At these words, that soul was penetrated with such a lively compassion for the glorious Virgin-Mother, that she almost fainted, and in the excess of her grief she could only pronounce these words: 'O Mother of God! men should no longer call you Mother of God, but Mother of Dolours, Mother of afflictions and pains, since you have suffered so many sorrows that it is impossible to understand or enumerate them. If it has been a hell for thy Son, it has also been a hell for thee. What other name can I give it that would be suitable?—O my Lord, no more, no more on the sorrows of Thy blessed Mother; speak no more to me of them, I can bear no more. What Thou hast already told me is enough for my whole life, were it to last a thousand years.'

"Jesus seeing that she was overpowered with compassion, went on to say: 'If you only knew, my daughter, how much I had to suffer from the affliction of My beloved disciple, the tender Magdalen! But it is a mystery which neither you nor any other can comprehend; because it is in her and in Me that all holy and spiritual loves that have ever been have found their beginning and foundation. Those who have the active and passive experience of holy and spiritual love, can form some idea of My perfection as a loving Master, and of the love and goodness of My beloved disciple; but in practice no one can attain to it. Never did such a Master meet with such a disciple, and there never has been, or will be, another Magdalen. Next to My Mother, Magdalen felt most compassion for My Passion and death. It was for this reason that after My resurrection she received My first visit, which could not have happened had any other surpassed her in sorrow; but because she was the most afflicted after My Mother, she was also the first, after her, who deserved to be consoled.

"' When My most beloved John rested on My bosom during the Last Supper, I made him see clearly My resurrection, and the abundant fruit that would result from My sufferings and death. Nevertheless, he felt My sufferings more keenly than any other disciple, but not more than My loving Magdalen, who was not capable of receiving such high and sublime communications as he did. If John had been able to prevent My Passion, he certainly would not have done it, knowing the immense benefits that would result from it. It was not thus with My dear Magdalen; she knew no other good but Me alone. So that when she saw Me draw My last breath, she believed she had lost everything in heaven and on earth, because in Me was all her hope, her love, her peace, her consolation; and then her sorrow was without measure. Therefore I cordially carried her in My soul, and I received from her all the tenderness of which a holy and spiritual love is capable.

"'If you desire to understand better what I have said, observe the difference that existed between My disciples and this sinner, who detached herself from everything that was not Me. After My death they returned to their nets, but she did not return to her luxurious life. Burning and inflamed with holy desires, she sought Me incessantly, and having no hope of possessing Me alive, she would at least possess Me dead, feeling that without her dear Master, living or dead, there was no consolation for her on earth. So true was this, that she left the company of My dear Mother, who was all that was most amiable, most delectable, most desirable in the world after Me, in order to seek My Body. She thought nothing of the sweet conversation of the angels ; she was so occupied with Me, she could neither see nor listen to any one else. In short her sufferings were so great, that she would have died of grief, had not My supreme power miraculously preserved her life. I was much afflicted for her, but I did not permit her to die, because I desired to make her, as I did afterwards, the apostle of My apostles, for she announced My resurrection to them, as they afterwards announced it to the world. I wished to make her the mirror, the example, and the model of all contemplation and holy life, by her thirty-three years' retreat in the desert, where she lived unknown to the world, and where she tasted and felt all that is most delicious in divine love, that can be tasted in this mortal life. This then is the pain caused Me by My beloved disciple Magdalen.

"'Another sorrow which pierced My soul was the fixed and unceasing thought of what would happen to My apostles at the time of My Passion and death. They were the pillars of heaven, and the foundations of My church militant on earth, and I saw them dispersed as sheep without a shepherd ; I thought of all they would have to suffer for love of Me ; I beheld all their torments and their martyrdom. Then you must consider, My daughter, that no father ever had for his children, no brother for his brethren, no master for his disciples, a love so tender and cordial as that which I bore these My beloved brethren and disciples, these blessed apostles. Although I have ever loved all creatures with an infinite love, still I had a special predilection for those with whom I lived on earth. Therefore when I exclaimed, "My soul is sorrowful even unto death," it was less from the consideration of My own sufferings, than of the sufferings of those who were about to be left without Me, their Head, Master, and Father; and this abandonment was so painful to Me, that it seemed another death. Whoever meditates upon the last discourse that I addressed to them cannot but be moved to tears, however insensible he may be, because every word is full of compassion, and flowed from the depth of My Heart, which seemed bursting with love of them.

" 'I saw, moreover, how for love of Me one would be crucified, another beheaded, another flayed; I saw, in short, by what sort of martyrdom each one of them would finish his life. Judge from that the pain My soul experienced. If you were closely united to a person by the ties of holy love, and you saw him insulted, tortured, suffering because of you, how wretched would you be to see yourself the cause of his sufferings. Yes, your deep distress would be all the greater, that you would wish, on the contrary, to procure him all sorts of good things, honours, and consolations. Now it was I, My daughter, who was to be the cause of the misfortunes of My apostles. What more is necessary to explain to you My sorrows, and to make you comprehend how deserving they are of your compassion?'"

THIRD PAIN.—THE SORROWS OF CHRIST FOR THE INGRATITUDE OF THE JEWISH PEOPLE, AND OF ALL CREATURES; HIS ESPECIAL SORROW IN THE GARDEN.

"'Another sorrow, which pierced My Heart continually, like a three-edged and poisoned blade, was the impiety and ingratitude of Judas, first My beloved disciple, then My wicked betrayer; the hardness and perverse ingratitude of the Jewish people whom I chose; and the evil blindness and ingratitude of all creatures who have been, are, and will be. Consider first the ingratitude of Judas, whom I chose for one of My apostles, whose sins I forgave, upon whom I conferred the power of working miracles, and whom I made the dispenser of the offerings made to Me. When I saw the design of betraying Me forming in his heart, I redoubled the proofs of My tenderness, to turn him from his criminal thoughts, but it was of no avail; nothing would touch his wicked heart. On the contrary, the more affection I showed him, the more he was hardened in his perfidious resolution. When, at the Last Supper, I performed the humble and touching ceremony of washing My disciples' feet, My Heart could not contain itself; but I wept bitterly, and watered his polluted feet with My tears, for I said within Myself: "O Judas! what have I then done to you, that you should betray Me thus? O unhappy disciple! is this to be the last proof I shall ever be able to give of My love for you? O son of perdition! why dost thou leave Thy Father and Master? O Judas, if you would have thirty pieces of silver, why not go and ask them from My Mother and thine; she would sell herself to free thee and

Me from danger and death. Ah! ungrateful disciple, to-day I wash thy feet, and kiss them with so much love, and in a few hours thou wilt kiss My Face, to deliver Me up to My enemies. O dear and beloved son, what a return thou makest to One who weeps the loss of thee more than His own Passion and death, because for this He came into this world."

"'While My Heart was speaking thus, My tears watered his feet, but he saw them not, because I was kneeling before him, My Head bent down, and My long hair falling about My Face, so that he could not see My tearful countenance. But John, my beloved disciple, to whom I had revealed all the mysteries of My Passion during this sad Supper, observed My every action, saw My tears flow on the feet of the traitor, and understood that they proceeded from the tenderness of My love. When a father sees his only son about to die, he is eager to serve him, and says in his heart, " Farewell, my son, this is the last service I shall be able to render you." Thus did I act towards Judas, when I washed and kissed his feet. When I caressed and kissed them with tender compassion, John, perceiving with his eagle eye all My gestures and actions, was more dead than alive with wonder and admiration. When at length I approached to wash his feet, for his humility had made him take the last place, on seeing me stoop he could no longer contain himself, but as I knelt he threw his arms round My neck, and held me fast in a long embrace as if fainting, weeping and sobbing and saying in his heart, without uttering a sound, " O my dear Master! my Brother, my Lord and my God! how hast Thou had the courage to wash and kiss with Thy sacred Mouth the cursed feet of this infamous traitor? O my Jesus! what a perfect example of charity dost Thou leave us! but how shall we follow it when we shall no longer have Thee Who art all our good? And Thy sorrowful Mother, what will become of her, when I recount to her this act of humility? And now, that my heart may break, Thou desirest to wash my vile feet, and apply to them Thy sacred Mouth. O my God! each new proof of Thy love serves but to increase my grief." After these and similar words, all full of tenderness enough to soften a heart of stone, he took off his sandals, and with great modesty presented Me his feet to wash. I tell you all this, My daughter, that you may know how much My Heart had to suffer on this occasion from a disciple who seemed to be determined to show Me as much hatred and ingratitude as I had shown him love.

" ' The obstinate hatred of the Jewish nation was also a grievous wound to My Heart, and you will understand this intolerable pain if you consider the nature of their ingratitude. I had made of the Jews a holy people, a priestly nation. I had chosen them from among all the nations of the earth to be the portion of My inheritance. I had delivered them from Egyptian bondage, and from the hands of Pharao. I had brought them through the Red Sea dry-shod, I had cared for them in the desert, nourished them with miraculous food, enlightened their march during the night by a column of fire, and protected them from the sun by day by a cloud. I gave them the old law on the heights of Mount Sinai, and when the fulness of time had come, I announced the new law to them with My own Mouth. I chose to be born of their race, I dwelt thirty-three years in the midst of them, to give them an example of all virtue.

With how many benefits did I not load them during the last three years of My life, giving sight to the blind, hearing to the deaf, speech to the dumb, health to the sick, and life to the dead. When I heard them cry with inconceivable rage, "We will not have this Man: crucify Him, and give us Barabbas," My Heart seemed to be rent asunder. None but they who have had experience of its bitterness know what it is to meet with all kinds of illtreatment from those we have loaded with all sorts of favours. But there is something still more revolting, to hear a whole people cry out against a just and innocent Man, " Let Him die, let Him die !" and for the vilest of criminals, " Let him be delivered, let him be delivered !" These are things which can be felt rather than spoken.'

" These words inspired this holy soul with such deep sentiments of humility, that she confessed in all sincerity to God and the whole court of heaven that she had received more gifts and more graces than Judas and the Jewish people, but had nevertheless betrayed and crucified her divine Master. In this persuasion she descended in thought to hell, and placing herself under the feet of Judas, she cried with a plaintive and touching voice, 'O my Lord, full of goodness, what return can I make Thee for having borne with me, I who am a thousand times more criminal than the traitor Judas? Thou didst only choose him to be Thy disciple, but Thou hast adopted me for Thy daughter and Thy spouse. Thou didst pardon his sins, and Thou hast also pardoned mine. Thou didst confide to him the dispensation of Thy earthly goods, but Thou hast confided Thy spiritual riches to me; for it is from Thy treasures that I have received so many favours, so many valuable gifts. Thou didst place in his hands the power of working miracles, but Thou hast performed for me the greatest of all, in withdrawing me from the world, and placing me where I now am. And, after so many graces, O my Jesus! I have betrayed and sold Thee, not once, like Thy perfidious disciple, but times without number.

"'Ah! if the ingratitude of the Jews seems to Thee so black and insupportable, what must mine appear? for I have certainly treated Thee worse than they, after having received from Thy liberality many more benefits. Yes, it is Thou, my most sweet Jesus, Who hast delivered me from the Egyptian bondage of my sins, and from the hands of that cruel Pharao who ruled my poor soul at his pleasure. It was Thou Who didst open up a path for me through the sea of the world, and introduced me into the desert of religion. Scarcely had I entered it, when Thou madest a delicious manna to rain upon me, which partook of every taste I could desire. I would speak, Lord, of Thy spiritual consolations, which rendered the pleasures of the world insipid to me; pleasures, which altogether are not to be compared with one of the least of Thine. It was Thou Who gavest me on the Sinai of holy meditation Thy spiritual law, engraven by the finger of Thy mercy on the stony table of my heart. It was Thou Who didst protect me against the vehemence of my passions, and gavest me the victory over them. Thou wert born in my heart by grace, and Thou didst show me by Thy divine light the path I should follow to arrive at Thee, the true Paradise. Thou hast made me see, speak, hear, and walk; for I was indeed blind, dumb, deaf, paralyzed in mind, and incapable of all spiritual things. What more can I say, O my God! Was it possible that Thou couldest have done more for me? Yet who has scourged Thee? I. Who has crowned Thee with thorns? I. Who has given Thee gall and vinegar to drink? I. Who has crucified Thee? I.

"'O my God! Thou knowest why I say that I have done all these things. It is because I have seen light in Thy light, and I know that my sins have caused Thee more pain than all Thy corporal sufferings. Speak no more to me, then, of the ingratitude of men. I know enough of it, since Thou hast given me grace to see, at least in some degree, my own, and that is sufficient to make me comprehend the affliction Thou didst feel at the ingratitude of all mankind. When I consider by Thy light the evil that I and so many others have done Thee, I am lost in wonder at the patience Thou hast shown to such ungrateful creatures, and the charity with which Thou hast unceasingly provided for all our temporal and spiritual wants. To understand fully, O my God, all the depths of my ingratitude, would be as difficult as to number all the marvels Thou hast wrought for Thy ungrateful creatures in heaven and on earth, in the water and every other element. There is but Thee, Lord, I confess and believe, there is but Thee, to Whom it is known. Thou alone canst know the number and extent of Thy benefits, and Thou alone canst appreciate the enormity of our ingratitude, and know the horrible evil Thy creatures have done against Thee. Yes, my Jesus, I confess this truth in my own name, and in that of all Thy creatures, who are not one moment in existence without abusing Thy benefits, and rendering ourselves continually guilty of the blackest ingratitude; an ingratitude which I feel was one of Thy most cruel and insupportable torments.'

" I finish this writing, to the praise and glory of my Jesus, this Friday, the 12th of September of the year 1488.

" What I am now about to write was revealed to me one day that I was meditating on the sorrowful agony of my divine Master. When the sun is in the sign of Leo, its heat is greater than at any other time of the year, because it has entered on its own proper domain. In like manner, when Jesus prayed in the Garden of Olives, His mental sorrows became more intense than they had been during all His previous life, because He had then arrived at the most elevated point of His suffering love. The sign of the Lion was, then, for this glorious Sun, the culminating point of His agony.

" It was shown me, in the revelation of which I speak, that there is the same difference between a soul which meditates on the mental sorrows of Jesus, and another which stops at the crucifixion of His sacred Humanity, as between honey or balsam enclosed in a vessel, and that which exudes from it exteriorly. He, then, who wishes to nourish himself on the Passion of the Saviour, should not confine himself to simply tasting the edge of the vessel; by which I mean His admirable Wounds, and the Blood which flowed from His most holy Body; for in this way he will never appease the hunger which devours him. Let him enter into the vessel itself, that is to say, into the Sacred Heart, and he will find there more than enough to satisfy him.

" I would not insert this revelation in my manuscript, for fear of injuring the devotion of those who stop at the contemplation of His Humanity, and find there sufficient nourishment. It is not for every one to sail on this sea, especially for women, since our capacity is limited. Nevertheless God gives the power to all who ask it of Him in truth.

"O my father! you cannot tell what I have suffered in writing these things. Verily as the sea is my contrition."

[It appears that this postscript was added by the Blessed Battista three years later, in 1491, when she copied out the original document, in order to send it, with a narrative of her life, to her spiritual director.]

SUPPLEMENT TO THE

LIFE OF THE

BLESSED BATTISTA VARANI.*

CHAPTER I.

HER HUMILITY.

IT is truly admirable to see the length to which the zeal of this blessed soul went for the honour of God. Her desire to promote His glory was as great as her horror of everything that could possibly diminish it. Thus, for example, her humility persuaded her that she was the most wicked and ungrateful of creatures, and she regarded the graces and favours which God granted her as misplaced in her heart, which she conceived to be the vilest place in the world; and from this conviction she believed herself obliged to hide them with the greatest care. She would often devise some excuse or other to withdraw from the spiritual

---

* This supplement is a collection from different letters of this servant of God to a priest whose name is unknown, and who was, probably, one of her confessors. It appears that Father Pascucci only edited this collection, changing the order, the better to exhibit each of the virtues of the Saint. The reader must not forget, that it is she who speaks in the third person, to conceal herself as much as possible.

reading made in common, fearing lest something might escape her which would make those present imagine she had received some favour from God. For the same reason she warned the reader not to go on reading about the Passion while the sisters were at meals, for that they could not eat comfortably when listening to that history of love. She did this lest any one should observe her own conduct during the reading, or take note of any outward sign she might then give of her feelings. She also came seldom to the refectory, principally for the same reason.

I disclose these things to you, my son and my father in Jesus Christ, that you may learn from this soul to hide the graces and the spirit which God gives you, until it pleases Him to command you to do otherwise. Oh, how happy is the soul who desires no other witness of her spiritual operations than her Creator. You cannot imagine how many difficulties this thy mother had to overcome for this reason; how many attacks, presumptuous judgments, rash and false testimonies to bear. How often has it happened to her to be reproved and humbled before her sisters and brothers, for things worthy of praise in the eyes of God and man; but in the midst of these tempests she remained firm, constant, and immovable in her resolutions, with the sure confidence that her faithful Spouse would take sword in hand on her behalf, and when the fitting time came would justify her, after her faith and patience had been sufficiently tried. This soul, on her part, manifested much uprightness of heart, seeking to please God alone, heeding not the judgments of men, and caring little to find herself covered with confusion, provided she could save the honour of her Master. Be careful, my son, never to rob God of anything; I would not have you attached to anything here below. If your heart retained the slightest earthly affection, it would be a disgrace to your spiritual mother, and to yourself a much greater injury. Show yourself, on the contrary, faithful in all things. Fear, love, honour God. Whatsoever the Lord pleased, He has done in heaven, in earth, in the sea, and in all the deeps.

This devout soul, in her profound humility, besought God with all her heart to transfer the graces and favours with which He loaded her, to some one else more worthy of pleasing Him, and more capable of honouring Him for His benefits. She could not, indeed, persuade herself that there was another creature in the world more unworthy of His heavenly favours. Nothing would have consoled her more than to obtain this, because she sought the honour of God more than her own interest. It is to a soul such as this, if I mistake not, that the words of Christ apply—"Well done, good and faithful servant, because thou hast been faithful over a few things, I will place thee over many things; enter thou into the joy of thy Lord." To such a soul as this, it is said in the Apocalypse, "Be faithful unto death, and I will give thee a crown of life." It is not enough to be faithful during ten or twenty years, it is necessary to be so unto death. He is a truly faithful servant, who, in dying, remits intact to his Lord the deposit confided to him. Be careful, my son, never to steal what belongs to God, else He will cause you to be hung by the neck, not caring that you are a priest and a doctor, in no way inferior to others who hold those dignities. Of such persons is it said, "Serve ye the Lord with fear; and rejoice unto Him with trembling."

Your mother, fearing lest she should rob God of the love due to Him, from her entrance into religion until this hour, has always taken care never to give her whole self to any one, nor to suffer others to give their whole selves to her; but she strove to love all with a general love that she might not be loved unduly in return. Although very affectionate by nature, she has avoided all occasions of loving any one, or of exciting love in others towards herself. If she sometimes observed that any one loved her more than others, she was deeply grieved, and besought God with abundance of tears to temper the affection of this person for her, or to extinguish it entirely. At other times, to relieve herself of this importunate love, she sought to turn it in another direction, towards some one she believed to be more deserving than herself. She did all this that she might not withdraw from her Creator that love which He alone merits. In short, I affirm that no creature ever took so much pleasure, joy, and consolation in seeing itself loved, as she found annoyance, sorrow, and displeasure in the affection of which she was the object, when she saw it was not according to God; and over this she would shed bitter tears.

There is a wonderful revelation, my son, which you must ask God to disclose to you: it is to make you see clearly what you are, what you are capable of, what you know, and what you deserve. Without this revelation none can attain perfection; it is a secret which one man cannot learn from another, for it is laid up in the Sacred Heart of Jesus Christ, who does not discover it to all, but only to a few, and that not equally, for He says more to one, and less to another, according to the different degrees of perfection to which each is called. I believe the secret cannot be entirely understood in this miserable life, but only in the future, when we shall fully and truly comprehend our vileness, our frailty, and our folly. Now it is from this revelation that humility of heart comes, which does not strike the eyes of men, but which God beholds and looks on with satisfaction. Your spiritual mother would never desire any other revelation than the knowledge of God, and of herself. And yet the Dispenser of graces, always generous and bountiful, has added many others, and not denied her that one.

Several years ago, my son, this soul, while praying before a crucifix, was divinely enlightened on this precious truth, that she could not arrive at perfection without knowing another trinity besides the divine Trinity. Just as to be a Christian it is necessary to believe and confess one Most Holy Trinity, Father, Son, and Holy Ghost; so in like manner to become perfect, it is necessary to believe this triple verity—namely, that before God we are but nothing, all foolish, and all detestable. O Most Blessed Trinity! Thou art neither known, valued, nor believed by ignorant spiritual persons. O my God, said she, rather take from me my bodily life than the knowledge of this loving truth. Reduce my bones to powder rather than permit this doctrine of eternal wisdom to depart from my mind. I cannot glory in my power, since my power is nothing; nor in my wisdom, since I am but a fool; nor in my merits, since I am a creature vile and abominable in the eyes of the Lord, more to be hated than hatred itself.

He who commits sin, becomes the servant of sin; this is of faith. And since sin is nothing, in committing sin, as I have often done, I have become the slave of a nothing; I am then less than nothing, since I am as much below this nothing as thes ervant is below his master. That sin is nothing may be gathered from the property it possesses of annihilating in us the image of God, by Whom, says S. John, all things were made.

Hence when the soul feels in herself the power of doing good, she may be sure that it is the Person of the Eternal Father who comes to aid her nullity. In the same manner, when she sees that she can speak and instruct others in the spiritual life, she ought to recognize that the wisdom of the Son makes her folly wise. Again, when the soul perceives that she loves God, and is beloved by Him, she may well believe that it is the Holy Spirit who loves her, and renders her hatefulness lovable. By favour of this light, this soul refers to God all that she has of good, and is free from the pride which the angel expelled from Paradise; so that she can say and sing with the Prophet, "Lord, my heart is not exalted, nor are my eyes lofty." This person held it for a certain truth, that if a soul, however spiritual, did not obtain this light, this knowledge, this necessary revelation, she could never sincerely and cordially humble herself before God and before men.

Know that she is reverent in her exterior actions, and an irreconcilable enemy to shameful hypocrisy. Nevertheless, not only in private, but in public, she often kisses the pavement of the church which her sisters have trod on, believing herself unworthy to be able to put her mouth on the footprints of these pure virgins. I write this with tears in my eyes, because it costs me much to disclose secrets long shut up in my heart, but I cannot resist the force of your devotion and your prayers. Consider, O blessed soul, that she would prefer to humble herself under the feet of all, were she not prevented by the respect she owes to her charge and her position. For this reason, whenever another pays her external reverence, she never fails reverently to incline herself, and never has it come into her mind to say, I am above her. It even happens frequently that she is the first to salute the least of the sisters, apparently in playfulness, but in reality from her heart, seeing in this sister the spouse of Christ.

And you, also, my dear son, endeavour to be humble of heart, kind, compassionate, gentle, and agreeable, looking into the most pure Heart of Jesus as into a beautiful mirror, to see the feelings it contains, and conforming yourself to them as much as possible, if you would have a share in His love and His honourable friendship.

It was from that divine Heart, from that sacred Side, that your mother derived all her interior and exterior adornment. His most loving Heart was her school; she was learned only because it was there that she studied. In this divine book you read nothing but truth, kindness, sweetness, benignity, peace of conscience, and true joy. We find nothing there but love—love for God and charity for men. O Divine Heart! I cannot help naming Thee, since she saw herself written conspicuously in Thee in beautiful letters of gold. Enter into this Divine Heart, my son, if you desire to become soon perfect; it is the short, hidden, sure, and infallible way, that your mother has always followed. Follow it, for conformity begets and preserves love.

In short, my son, turn towards God, and say to Him, "I beseech Thee, O Lord, to give me this revelation, for without this I can never be perfect; and yet my priestly office demands perfection." Say this to Him with a heart full of confidence; He will certainly give you this grace, for He showers graces on the just and on the wicked, even when they ask them not, out of the fulness of His mercy. Therefore this soul whom you love will sing throughout eternity the mercies of the Lord.

I would wish you to serve the Lord, not as a slave, from the fear of temporal and eternal chastisements; neither as a sinner, who looks for a reward; but as a noble child, who gives to his good Father love for love, blood for blood, life for life. Behold these hidden paths, short as they are, which escape human eyes, but which are perfectly known to God, to Whom all is open. What I speak of is a movement of affection; and, if it be pure, God waits not for the soul to take the first step, but opens at once to her the treasures of His immense wisdom; He waits not for her to knock at the door of His divine mercy to come to her aid; she receives, before she asks it, more than she can desire—more than she knows how to ask. Our merciful and loving Jesus is extremely liberal towards those who conform themselves to Him, and open to Him a generous and magnanimous heart; but He will never dwell in a straitened and base heart, because He is great, and "high above all gods" (Exod. xviii. 11). Leave then, beloved soul, leave this deceitful and perfidious world, not from the fear of hell as a slave, nor from the hope of a recompense as a sinner, but as a loving daughter and spouse, from pure love for your crucified Jesus. Press Him in the arms of your most tender affections. Your mother has given you the example; for she grieved for what she had not and was not, and that she could not give up more for the love of Jesus crucified, whom she loved with a pure heart and perfect intention.

As it is necessary for the soul who would attain this point to keep her mind fixed on God, as much as her frailty and divine grace will permit, she can do nothing more useful than this. This attention to God sanctifies the soul, inflames her affections, enlightens her understanding, and preserves her from venial sins; it sweeps away her vices, and is the best preparation for prayer and meditation. Many persons pray all day without keeping God before their minds, and feel dry, indevout, and full of dislike for this holy exercise, and they tell you, I have not the grace of prayer. But it is not so. The reason is that they take no pains to fit themselves for it, by directing their thoughts to God. Those who consider how to do so best, arrive at the desired end without delay, and obtain the grace of tears, compunction, sweetness, and devotion. This was shown to your mother by the Holy Spirit, that her soul might be more ardent for this angelic exercise; and in truth she possesses the grace of invoking her Redeemer in her heart, and keeping the remembrance of Him within her.

Such is the method which truly wise and spiritual men follow, and which they will continue to follow for ever in the glory of heaven. There is no better sign by which to know if any one is written in the Book of Life. Know for certain, my son, that the more you think of God, the more He will think of you. Many strive to attain purity of heart by a way as long as it is painful, in watchings, fastings, scourgings, lying on the bare ground, enduring cold and heat, mortifying their body in other ways, because they know that interior purity will elevate them to the summit of perfection. But your mother is sure that by thinking frequently on God we arrive at the same end without any difficulty, and much more quickly; and if this be so, how can you do better than imitate her? Would a traveller be wise, who, being able to go to Rome with ease in one day, chose a more difficult road four times as long? Choose then, my son, this short, easy, safe, and secret way, which will lead you to Paradise. Embrace Christ, and you will make your fortune without any one knowing how you trade. When a man is constantly occupied with God, God dwells in him; and is not he rich who possesses God by grace? Take care that God be the object of all your thoughts, and the aim of all your intentions, without attaching yourself to creatures. Thus, for example, when you exercise charity towards your neighbour, although you would do well to consider him as your neighbour, you would do much better to consider him only as a member of Jesus Christ, for the more noble one intention is than the other, the more meritorious is it.

Do not sleep in sloth and negligence, for the kingdom of heaven suffereth violence, and the violent bear it away. The Holy Ghost has imprinted this word of the gospel so deeply in the heart of your mother, that, sleeping or waking, she calls it to mind. You must guard continually against this fatal sleep to which too many religious persons abandon themselves, who, forgetful of their first fervour, perform all their works without attention. You know the habit of goats—when one leaps over a fence all the rest follow. Thus these religious observe their rules and ceremonies. They see what others do, and follow them, but without considering why they act thus. Such souls are like asses, which are sometimes employed by their masters to carry wines, and yet only drink water. Now this is exactly what happens to religious persons who have this spirit of slumber; they carry burdens which cause them great fatigue, and derive from them but little fruit. As matter without form is neither useful nor beautiful, so likewise good works performed without a definite intention are little pleasing to God or beneficial to the doer. The work may be praiseworthy in itself, but the want of an intention deprives it of form, and renders it fruitless; so that they are but fools who act in this manner. In place of imitating their folly, strive, my son, to follow the example of the wise and prudent, who consider God alone in their works, whether they be great or small, doing everything to please Him, and suffering everything for love of Him. For the love of God make your prayer or spiritual reading, sing the divine office, sweep the house, wash the dishes, clean vegetables, do works of charity; for believe me, my son, if you are faithful in saying to God, whenever you remember it, that you wish to act only for His love, you will come at last to say it even without thinking.

Such has always been the practice of your mother. It is true that she has rarely been able to apply herself to such works, because of her weak health and long infirmities, but it may be said of her for your edification, that she has done more than she had strength to do. Always have an ardent desire to do penance, but be prudent in the outward practice of this virtue. If, instead of following your own will in this, you follow the direction of your fathers, you will merit much before the Most Holy Trinity, who considers only the heart. Take care that your heart be constantly inflamed with charity, for while oil is boiling, flies will not approach it, but when it begins to cool, then they come, sink into it, and spoil it. In the same way, when a soul is burning with divine love, she has nothing to fear from the demons nor from evil thoughts; but if she becomes lukewarm, then the flies of vanity and useless thoughts approach her and fall upon her, and thus the fatal sleep of negligence is born in that negligent soul. Hence it comes to pass that so many souls sleep in holy religion, and dream that they are advancing in perfection; but at the hour of death, they see the fallacy of all these dreams, for they find their hands full of the illusions of the spirit of deceit and lies. Open then your eyes, my dear son, while it is time, and lose none of the few days yet remaining to you. Be watchful and fervent, according to the grace given to you, that you may be able to say with the apostle, "His grace in me hath not been void," for "to Thee do I watch at break of day." If you follow this method, be sure that you will advance quickly in the way of perfection.

CHAPTER II.

HER CHARITY TOWARDS HER NEIGHBOUR, MANIFESTED IN THE WARNINGS SHE GIVES HER DISCIPLE.

I DESIRE, my dear son in Jesus Christ, that you be at the same time liberal and avaricious; very liberal towards your neighbour, and very avaricious towards yourself, which is precisely the opposite of what is done by the world. In truth, worldlings are very prodigal towards themselves, very attentive to provide for all their own wants; but they act very differently in regard to their neighbour. They will see their brother in want of a hundred things before they will make up their minds to give him one. O excessive blindness! O deplorable calamity! The Lord gives generously; He is liberal without measure, and from Him are all things, for the Psalmist says, "The earth is the Lord's and the fulness thereof," while man has nothing he can call his own; he must leave the world naked as when he entered it. He is but the steward and the dispenser of God's riches, and yet he is parsimonious, avaricious, without mercy, cruel to his brother and his neighbour. O Most High Trinity! O Most Holy Trinity! I return Thee infinite thanks. O power of my powerlessness! O wisdom of my folly! O most clement love of my hatefulness! I return Thee thanks for me and my poor nature, as much as my impotence can, as much as my folly is capable of, as much as my hatefulness can please. I thank Thee that by Thy power, Thy wisdom, and boundless clemency, Thou hast found means to reduce human pride to what it is—to nothing; for in reality we are nothing, and return to nothing. What sweet joy my heart feels, when I consider on the one hand Thy power and wisdom, and on the other human misery: when I see that Thou alone art and wilt be eternally what Thou hast ever been, while sinners, who, in their pride, would be masters of the earth and all its riches, and who refuse to exercise mercy towards their neighbours, will soon return into dust and nothingness. Mounted on the unbridled desire of always possessing more, I see them falling under the powerful Hand of God; and not falling to the ground only, but into the very depths of hell, because of their accursed avarice.

Alas! that this detestable vice should insinuate itself into holy religion. It is not uncommon to see religious persons, who have given up great riches for the love of God, so tempted by the demon, that they grudge giving a morsel of bread or a lettuce to the hungry, or a little wine to the thirsty. How shameful that the servants of God should be still subject to such a detestable vice! What displeasure for Him, and what an affliction for His Heart! How can such a liberal Master bear such avaricious servants? I wish, then, reverend father and dear son in Jesus Christ, that you should act differently from worldly persons. I wish that if you want four things, one alone should content you, abandoning the care of your body to the Providence of God, Who, provided you trust implicitly in Him, will inspire some one to provide for all your necessities, so that you will want nothing. Such has always been the faith of your mother, and God has inspired so many to provide for her necessities, both temporal and spiritual, that she has had nothing more to desire. Also, I do not believe she ever asked from her superiors anything for herself; on the contrary, she refused such things when offered, saying, "Mother, I do not require this, will you give it to one of my sisters who needs it more than I do?"

But it is not enough that you be avaricious towards yourself, you must also be very liberal towards others, even giving four times as much as they ask. God was pleased to draw your mother to the contemplation of His generosity and love. He made her see the heavens adorned with the sun and moon and stars, the earth covered with plants, flowers, and fruits, enriched with the fragrance of a thousand perfumes, and abundantly furnished with medicinal herbs. What multitudes of fishes in the water ; what variety of birds in the air ; what hosts of beasts feed in the woods, and on the mountains. All this, and more, has God made for our poor bodies. He has bestowed on them, besides, rich harvests of corn, of wine, and oil. But if this great God has shown Himself so liberal towards our bodies, what has He not prepared for our soul, which is created in His image and likeness? What variety of glory, what diverse beatitudes, what incomprehensible joys, what inestimable delights she will find at last in the holy and triumphant Jerusalem! O city of God, glorious things are said of thee! Thy open gates are adorned with precious pearls. Thy walls and streets are of pure gold. Thither are admitted those who have been found worthy to suffer for the Name of Jesus Christ. O blessed Jerusalem! thou art the vision of peace, the place of true happiness, the fruition of eternal glory.

Why has God created so many great things in heaven and earth, in the sea, and in all the elements, if not to manifest to us mortals His bountiful charity and His infinite mercy? He is so generous, so good, so gracious, and so indulgent, that after having loaded us with His riches, He gives Himself to us in the most Holy Sacrament. O most gracious God! how is it that the sinner refuses to give to his brother the least thing? It was from this consideration, my son, that your mother learned to become generous, although from her infancy she had shown a tendency to this virtue. Now she takes more pleasure in giving than in receiving, and she feels this grace daily growing more and more. And you also enlarge your charity, if you would become conformed to God, for He loves nothing else in us but Himself, His image and likeness.

This doctrine your mother learnt in the school of divine wisdom. If it seems to you obscure, ask and you will find that God is worthy of love in all things, and that all things out of Him are hateful. None is good but God alone, He is compassionate and merciful, and His mercy is without end. Glory and praise be to Him for ever. Amen.

I do not speak here of the tender charity of the same servant of God, which rendered her so compassionate to the weakness and imperfections of her neighbour, because it is not always expedient to open the eyes of the blind. I only declare to you that your mother, even while in the world, was instructed by God on this subject; but as she was then ignorant of all spiritual things, she neither understood the importance of this teaching, nor its deep meaning. When, however, she entered into religion, the Holy Spirit gave her on this subject such abundant light, that during eighteen years, neither as subject nor superior, did she ever speak ill of any creature.

If God permits for the increase of your crown of glory that any one should speak evil of you, leave to no one the care of punishing them, but take vengeance yourself by praising all your brethren to the Visitors, without accusing those of whom you have to complain, that you may not open in your heart a way to hatred or indignation; for these two vices would render your service and your homage abominable in the eyes of the Lord. Now in order to act according to this advice, two things are necessary :—the knowledge of yourself, and the habit of thinking of God. By these means, you become blind to the faults of others, and can say with truth that your brethren seem to you like angels incarnate. Your mother had this grace, for when the

Visitors came to the monastery, she had nothing to report, and the very novices could say more than she could on the faults of the other sisters. If sometimes others spoke of them before her, she said to herself that if they had been real she must necessarily have observed them.

God discovered to her another device of Satan, which deceives many, even very perfect persons, wherefore I will tell it you, because I love you from my heart. Know then, my son, that the backbitings and criticisms which you hear in religious houses are inspired by the demon, who fails not to veil them under an appearance of good, so that his subtle snare is undetected. It is like a leech which attaches itself to religious, and sucks out all their toil and labour. It is the leprosy of Mary, the sister of Moses, whom her gift of prophecy could not save from punishment. She was struck with a painful and pestilential leprosy; and if Moses, against whom she had murmured, had not interceded for her, this terrible malady would have conducted her in a few days to the tomb. O noble example, given us by the Holy Spirit in the Old Testament, at the sight of which those spiritual persons who detract others ought to tremble!

But this doctrine is little thought of, and still less understood; so that I would dare to say that any religious who is entirely free from this leprosy possesses a sure sign of predestination. This is why your mother had so much pity for detractors, and envied those who were the objects of their backbitings; because to those who love God, all things work together for good.

It is the property of leprosy, not only to consume the flesh of the wretched sufferer, but to defile others by its touch. Because of this, the Lord commanded Mary to be put out of the camp; but he who backbites does not sin more in speaking than others do in listening. These last are even more guilty; for if there were no one to listen, no one would backbite. One demon sits on the tongue of him who speaks, and another in the ear of him who listens; and these demons rejoice, and mock both him who speaks and him who listens. Be wise, my son, and carefully avoid both these faults; if you show to him who detracts another that you are vexed, you will do two good things at once; you will put to flight the devil on the tongue and the devil at the ear. I will conclude this long digression, into which, perhaps, your prayers have led me, by saying that I desire you should detract no one under any pretext or reason whatsoever, either for good or evil. Never forget this, and beware of transgressing, for I do not speak without cause. Remember what S. James has said in his canonical epistle, "If any man think himself to be religious, not bridling his tongue, this man's religion is vain."

Every time that the Visitor enters a monastery, the demon fails not to spread his subtle snares. He is not ignorant that the best works, if they want the foundation of charity, are unfruitful and hateful to God. Therefore he employs all his industry to make us say to the Father Visitor a number of useless things, which, fully considered, are only rash suspicions and ill-founded judgments. Hence it follows that the bond of peace is broken, charity grows cold and is extinguished, the demons triumph, and with reason. They care not for our obedience, poverty, chastity, modesty, our penances, and all our good works, for all these are nothing without charity, which alone renders the others agreeable to God, and opens the gates of heaven. Therefore the demon holds his bow bent, and aims his poisoned arrows against the root of brotherly charity, and does his best to destroy it. He insinuates rash judgments and detractions; during the visitation, he fills us with suspicions; lastly, he sows cockle in the hearts of others, and destroys our zeal for the honour of our order, that our tongue may take occasion to say and report things which it should not.

Alas! alas! how much good is lost by souls whom their own malice blinds! how many labours are rendered unfruitful! what disquiet of conscience springs from it! These poor religious are so troubled, that they scarcely know what is right. If they engage in prayer, they have no longer any taste for it, and they are incapable of spiritual joy; and it is the tongue which has produced this evil. Silence then, silence about things with which we have no concern. A prophet has said that he refrained even from saying what was good. Behold, my son, the rule you should follow, as your mother has done; from it she has derived an interior peace, which can scarcely be expressed in words, but which I pray that you also may enjoy.

This religious whose secrets I disclose to you had received from God many graces and spiritual gifts; and her divine Spouse took pleasure in giving her daily proofs of His love and benevolence. Nevertheless, in the midst of this abundance, there remained one desire, for the accomplishment of which she ceased not to beseech God; it was the desire of loving her enemies with sincere love, and even with love superior to that she felt for her benefactors. "O my God," she would often exclaim in her devout prayers, "O my most clement Lord! if Thou didst reveal to me the most hidden secrets of Thy Divine Heart; if Thou didst manifest to me daily the angelic hierarchies; if Thou didst grant me the power of raising the dead at will, this would not be enough to convince me that Thou lovest me with an indefectible love. But that I may have this assurance, Thou must grant me the grace of a sincere heart, that I may love those who hate me, that I may speak well of those who speak ill of me, and that I may praise, without requiring to do violence to myself, those who persecute and unjustly calumniate me. Then, O eternal and most merciful Father, I shall possess an infallible sign of Thy love for me; then I shall no longer doubt I am indeed Thy daughter. Then I can comfort myself by the example of Thy beloved Son Jesus, the only good of my soul, Who in dying on the cross obtained grace for His murderers."

Thanks to the goodness of God, this soul reaped the fruit of her prayer; for when any one did her an injury or spoke against her, she felt in her heart no sentiment of aversion from them as others do; and yet she had often to suffer much in this way. I do not tell you how; but it is known to God and her persecutors. It is only their sins which afflict her; and she prays to God with her whole heart that He may pardon them. To say or do anything that may gratify them is one of her greatest pleasures. She often says a Pater and Ave for them. I wish you to do the same, my son, that you may tread in the steps of your mother, who loves you so much that she writes these things for your edification.

I have confidence in God and your prudence that you will profit by the counsels I give you. Never divide into two years that which can be done in one. Walk, run, fly in the path of God. The just walk, the wise run, the loving fly towards the enjoyment of the divine Majesty. You will be wrong to walk if you can run, and to run if you can fly; because time is short. You ought always to advance in the paths of holiness, and never to fall back. If we do not add wood to the fire, it will soon go out. The same thing happens to the soul if it does not grow in virtue. It begins by "I believe in God," and will end by "The resurrection of the body," that is, the cares of this world. I pray God to preserve you and every Christian soul from going along a road like this. If, however, you wish to make great progress, fear God, and love your enemies. It is this which I try to instil into you in this letter. How few there are who ardently desire to attain this evangelical perfection which our divine Saviour preached so touchingly by His example, as well as by His words; few who arrive at that true perfection, which consists in loving their enemies.

I finish here, my reverend father and beloved son, these salutary warnings, which, I trust, you will make use of with the same charity which has dictated them. I have wished to console you by making known to you the spiritual life of your mother; nor has this been difficult to me, because I am convinced that the examples and lessons it contains will contribute to your advantage and consolation. You will find no special advice on your principal obligations, such as poverty, obedience, and chastity, and that for two reasons:—
1st. Because if you follow the counsels contained in what I have written, it is impossible you can be otherwise than obedient, poor, and chaste. 2nd. Because I know you are already so well disposed towards these

virtues, that all exhortations on these subjects seem to me unnecessary. I will add only these few words to confirm your good-will. You cannot offer to God a more agreeable sacrifice than to submit your will to holy obedience; for it is He Who has said, "I desire obedience more than sacrifice." As to poverty, I would that you possessed nothing but Jesus crucified, in whom you will find all true riches. Oh! how poor is he who seeks aught else but God! How rich is he who has nought but God! As to chastity, it is because God has ornamented your body with this precious pearl, and embellished it with this angelic splendour, that I have confided to you your handmaid's secrets, that they may be laid up and preserved in you. As to prayer, I will add but this one word. When you cannot reap, take with violence ; that is, pray at least with your lips, when you cannot with your heart.

CHAPTER III.

HER VIRTUE IS TRIED BY THE GOOD AND EVIL FORTUNE OF HER FAMILY.—SHE ESTABLISHES A MONASTERY AT FERMO, AND RETURNS TO CAMERINO, WHERE SHE IS RAISED TO THE DIGNITY OF ABBESS.

THREE years had scarcely elapsed since she addressed the foregoing instruction to her disciple, when dreadful misfortunes befell her family, which furnished her with occasions of exercising heroic charity towards her enemies. Her father, Julius Cæsar Varani, after having governed Camerino during fifty years, was deprived of his power, and in the year 1502 died a tragical death, of which Leander Albert gives the following account in his description of Italy:—"When the inhabitants of Camerino made themselves over of their own accord to Pope Alexander VI., Cæsar Borgia, Duke of Valencia, imprisoned Julius in the citadel of Pergola with his sons Venantius, Peter, and Hannibal, and put them all to death most cruelly. John Mary, the youngest of the children of Julius, alone escaped, his father having sent him to Venice with his treasures at the beginning of the war." This good fortune was probably due to the merits and prayers of his sister Battista. Alexander VI. dying in the following year, it was easy for John Mary with a troop of Venetian soldiers to reconquer the town; and, accompanied by Muzio Colonna, Toparch of Matelica, he entered Camerino amidst the acclamations of the inhabitants. We may believe his return gave pleasure to his holy sister; but her consolation was soon followed by a new affliction; for in 1508 she lost her mother, Joanna Malatesta, who had become, some time before this, a religious of the third order of S. Francis.

In the interval which elapsed between the return of her brother and the death of her pious mother, Battista was chosen by Pope Julius II. to establish a monastery of her order at Fermo. After a year's absence she returned to Camerino, where, under her brother's protection, she succeeded in making her monastery one of the largest and most illustrious of the country. The mother abbess being dead, her sisters elected her to that office. This is proved by the signature of a letter addressed by her to a monk of S. Francis named John of Fano:—"Your unworthy daughter, Battista Varani, abbess and useless servant of the monastery of Jesus Christ."

she calls him son at the end of the letter, we may presume that it was he to whom the foregoing instructions were addressed.

CHAPTER IV.

FRIENDSHIP OF BATTISTA WITH JOHN OF FANO.—BEGINNING OF THE CONGREGATION OF CAPUCHINS.—DEATH OF BATTISTA AND VENERATION OF HER BODY.

AMONG other letters which Battista wrote to this holy man is one in Latin, which we will give entire, as it is not without interest in her own history.

"JESUS.—Upon the rivers of Babylon, there we sat and wept: when we remembered Sion. These words, dictated to the Psalmist by the Holy Spirit for the consolation of the afflicted, suit well, it seems to me, the state of persecution and tribulation in which your reverence finds yourself. The elect seat themselves and repose upon the rivers of Babylon, while the impious and sinful sink and disappear under their waves. You, therefore, who are of the number of the elect, are seated on the banks of the rivers of Babylon, that is, by the waters of affliction, in the hope of the resurrection of your virtue and innocence. You have rested in God your Saviour, Who is the defender of the innocence of His elect. You see your defamers carried away by the waves of their loquacity, losing themselves in the depths of shame and confusion. You know, my beloved father, that the darkness of night precedes the dawn, and the richest countries are hidden behind mountains. The heavenly Physician,

Who has come to die on the cross for the salvation of the human race, after having permitted the waves of persecution and tribulation to cover His elect, gives them joy and consolation; and they learn the smile of angels in the school of the crucified Humanity of Christ. Although the sick man knits his brows at the taste of a bitter medicine, he soon rejoices over his returning health. This loving and compassionate Master sheds bitterness over all that surrounds us, in order that He alone may seem sweet and worthy of love. O most sweet Jesus! O unspeakable love! how sweet and delightful are Thy works to the soul which seeks Thee, to the soul which loves Thee without fraud or dissimulation, to the soul which affectionately reposes in the Heart of Thy crucified Humanity, 'where the fulness of Thy Godhead corporally dwells' (Col. ii. 9).

"Rejoice and be glad, O daughter of Sion, O soul loving and beloved of God! Thy detractors, unknown to themselves, have placed a crown of precious stones on thy head. They thought to despoil thee of thy honour, and, on the contrary, they have woven for thee in this life a robe of immortality; for gold, tried in the fire, comes out purer than before. You, my reverend father, before this trial, were a precious, but a closed lily, but now you are a full-blown lily, whose delicious perfume embalms all the houses of the province you have governed for three years with so much wisdom and prudence. While you were seated upon the rivers of Babylon, we, your daughters, wept at the remembrance of your sweetness and goodness. Now we exult, and render eternal thanks to Almighty God, who has saved John, the son of His handmaid. He has shown me a token for good, that those who hate me may see and be confounded, because Thou, O Lord, hast helped him, and comforted me. I have written these foolish words in feminine fashion, to engage your fatherly prayers, to which I humbly and devoutly recommend myself, begging your blessing for her who will always be your servant and your daughter. Farewell in Him who is the salvation of all those who hope in Him.

"From the Monastery of S. Maria Nuova, of Camerino, this 20th of April, 1521."

It was this same John of Fano who, when elected anew vicar provincial of La Marca in 1525, treated so harshly Brother Matthew of Bassio, the first Capuchin, who, after having been chamberlain to Julius Cæsar, the father of Battista, entered the order of Friars Minor of the Observance, where he became an able and zealous preacher. This friar sought to introduce a change in the shape of the cowl of his order, and went to Rome for this purpose. On his return the provincial rebuked him in the provincial chapter at Matelica, treated him as an apostate, and threw him into prison. The Duchess of Camerino, who had a great devotion to Brother Matthew, having heard of this, was very angry. She first wrote a threatening letter to the provincial; she next summoned him to the palace with the father guardian, and spoke with such force that he was obliged to release Brother Matthew, who immediately on leaving prison, set out for Rome, where he obtained leave from Pope Clement VII. to live as a hermit in the habit he had adopted.

In the following year Brothers Louis and Raphael, led by the same spirit as Matthew, took the same habit, without, however, associating themselves with him, and obtained from the Pope a similar approbation. Having afterwards gone to Camerino, the duke and duchess received them provisionally into their palace, until a fitting place was prepared for them and others who joined them.

The provincial looked with an evil eye on the protection given by a prince of such prudence to what he called a new order, and he wrote the duke a pressing letter to urge him to send away these contumacious brothers, and to compel them to return to their obedience. He wrote a similar letter to the duchess, and a third to the Blessed Battista, begging her to aid him with her relations. The replies to these three letters not being satisfactory, he came in person to Camerino, hoping to gain by his eloquence that which his letters had failed to obtain; but the wisdom of man and all his counsels can do nothing against the Lord. The event showed the wisdom of the advice of Gamaliel:—"If this counsel or this work be of men, it will come to nought; but if it be of God, you cannot overthrow it."* Such was the reply of Battista to the father provincial; for at that time she knew not whether to approve or disapprove of this novelty, and grant or refuse her protection to Matthew and his brothers. But at last she and the provincial acknowledged that it was God who had inclined the hearts of the people of Camerino to protect the Capuchins. Then the provincial not only ceased to persecute them, but contemplated embracing their reform himself; and Battista, whom he consulted, as he usually did in cases of importance, gave him every encouragement to do so, assuring him that the thought came from God.

It is believed that Battista died on the Feast of

* Acts v. 38, 39.

Corpus Christi, the 31st of May, 1527, when she had entered upon the sixty-ninth year of her age. There can be no doubt her death was holy as her life, but no particulars of it have been preserved.

The nuns buried her in their choir, in order to have a memorial ever present of their foundress, and a pledge of the protection they hoped from her in heaven. Thirty years later the nuns would not allow the precious body to continue hidden in the earth, and disinterred it with the greatest respect. Great was their joy when they saw it in a state of perfect preservation, the eyes bright as in life, and the countenance lit up rather than pale, as if she were saluting them. They wished to preserve the holy body in a better place, where it would be more honoured, but their confessor was opposed to this, and insisted that it should be buried again; he even, with great indiscretion, caused the sacred body to be placed between two boards, and, when a quantity of earth had been shovelled in, and water poured over it, he made his companion tread it down.

The strict obedience which these holy women observed hindered them from opposing the strange zeal of this religious, and still more from withdrawing the holy body from the grave in which he had placed it. It rested there until the year 1593, when the necessity of making a new vault obliged the nuns to reopen the grave. The elder nuns, who knew the place exactly, told the workmen to dig with all possible precaution, which they did. When they reached a certain depth they found a board, on removing which a delicious odour made it evident at once that it was the one which covered the holy body. Immediately all the nuns came running together, and shed abundance of tears, not doubting that this heavenly odour was a sign of the glory enjoyed by the Saint in heaven.

Another circumstance occurred to increase their wonder. Her flesh was reduced to dust (according to the wish she had expressed to God), but her tongue remained fresh, moist, and red. The confessor of the convent, Brother Evangelist of Fabriano, who was present, was moved to tears at the sight of this miracle, and testified his admiration in the words of S. Bonaventure at the sight of the incorrupt tongue of S. Antony of Padua: "O precious tongue, which hast always blessed the Lord, and taught others to bless Him, it is now manifest how great thy service of God has been!" When the nuns had satisfied their tender devotion, they placed the holy body in a marble tomb, which they had previously caused to be constructed in the choir; but the tongue was enclosed in a precious reliquary apart.

INDEX.

Abstinence of the Saint, 116
Agony suffered by the Saint, 147
Albizzini, Mary Gertrude, abbess, 46
Alexandra, a servant of the Giuliani, 6
Alva, Peter of, 140
Ambroni, the Canon, confessor of the Saint, 10
Ambrose, Saint, saying of, 301
Angelucci, Luc' Antonio, 176
Antony, Sister, charity of the Saint to, 212
Apostles, the, our Lord's sorrow for, 373
Avarice, 395
Azzi, degli, Sister Mary Angelica, 111
Backbiting, 399
Bastianelli, Father Girolamo, 216
Battistelli, Father, confessor of the Saint, 234
Blood, tears of, shed by the Saint, 216, 217, 239
Bordiga, Gian Francesco, 176, summoned at the last illness of the Saint, 181
Borghese, Don Giovan-Antonio, baptized the Saint, 4
Boscaini, Don Domenico, Prior of S. Sisto, 216
Boscaini, Sister Mary Magdalen, 74, 111, 120, 158, 175, 184, 275 ; appointed sacristan by the Saint, 179 ; testifies to the Saint's shedding tears of blood, 216
Brozzi, Sister Gabriella, death of, foretold by the Saint, 179
Cappelletti, Sister Catherine, 281
Cappelletti, Father Ubaldo Antonio, director of the Saint, 19 ; narrates a vision of the Saint, 75 ; prophesies the enlargement of the Saint's convent, 80 ; tests the miraculous state of the Saint, 158, 168, 178 ; diary of, 196, 199 ; orders the nuns to pour water on the hands of the Saint in ecstasy, 209 ; testimony of the Saint's humility, 254
Capuchins, the, annals of, 111 ; troubles of, 406
Casoni, Father, S.J., 232
Catherine, S., of Siena, 88, 100, 103, 106, 107, 140, 174
Catherine, S., Ricci, 174
Cavamazza, Father, confessor of the Saint, 62
Cecilia, S., prayer of, 134
Ceoli, Sister Florida, 20, 120, 173, 264, 273 ; treads on the Saint's foot, 72 ; dower of, how spent, 80 ; sees on the Saint's head the marks of the crown of thorns, 97 ; had the gift of prophecy, 112 ; holy death of, 207 ; saw the Saint shed tears of blood, 217

INDEX.

Chalice, the, seen in vision by the Saint, 86, 232
Cherubim, 343
Christina, Blessed, 140
Cicerbola, the, 265
Città di Castello, monastery of Capuchin nuns in, 42
Clare, Blessed, of Monte Falco, 174
Clare, S., 144, 187; appears to the Blessed Battista Varani, 335
Clare, Sister, companion of the Saint, 216
Clement XI., 224
Codebò, Mgr. Alexander, 176, 181, 251, 272, 275, 280; prophecy of the Saint concerning, 277
Communion, Holy, the Saint's joy in, 114; miraculous, of the Saint, 211
Confessions of the Saint, once made difficult, 185
Constance, Sister, of Camerino, 331
Constance, Sister, 227
Conversion of a sinner obtained by the Saint, 284
Corvinus, Matthias, 289
Cosmo III., Grand Duke of Tuscany, 81
Crivelli, Father Giovan Maria, S.J., 164, 261; tries the spirit of the Saint, 165, 168. 247; preaches a sermon to idolaters before the nuns, 204; testimony of, to the Saint's zeal for the conversion of sinners, 215; and to her humility, 250; seen by the Saint in a vision, 251; death of, 252; prophecy of the Saint, concerning, 278
Cross, the, impression of, on the heart of the Saint, 63
Cross, pectoral, of the Bishop, 186
Cures, miraculous, wrought by the Saint, 280
Cybo, Cardinal, 151
Dereliction, divine, of the Saint, 91
Devils, the Saint assaulted by, 90
Dionysius, the Carthusian, 160
Directors, openness of the Saint with her, 47
Dying, the, charity of the Saint to, 213
Elect, the, sins of, a sorrow to our Lord, 368
Enemies, love of, 403
Epiphanius, S., Bishop of Ticino, 190
Espousals, spiritual, of the Saint, 99
Eustachj, Mons. Luc' Antonio, 97, 275; sanctions the use of the mysterious liquid, 120; tests, the spirit of the Saint, 150, 164; witness of her mystical state, 173; his severity to the Saint, 243; testimony of, to the Saint's humility, 245.
Ever, for, 366
Exercises, the spiritual, 130
Fabbri, Domenico, the Chancellor, 176, 251
Fabbri, the physician, 231
Falconi, Don Giovanni, 176
Fast, the great, of the Saint, 115, 122, 246
Fasting of Blessed Battista Varani, 303
Felicia, Sister Clare, unjustly blamed, 238

414 INDEX.

Felix, Sister Clare, 42
Food, miraculously multiplied, 66; the Saint mortified in her, 117, 231
Frances, Sister, helps the Saint in the kitchen, 65; death of, in the odour of sanctity, 111; placed in authority over the Saint, 248; rough in her ways, 261
Francis, Father, of Urbino, preaching of, 304, 308; letter of, to the Blessed Battisti Varani, 336; the Blessed Battista converses with, 311
Francis, S., of Assisi, 140, 143, 187
Francis, S., Xavier, 255
Fucci, Sister Mary, 282
Gaetana, Sister Mary, 224
Gasparini, Mgr. 277
Gellini, Don Giacomo, 176
Gentili, Giovan Francisco, surgeon, 160, 163, 176
Gertrude of Oost, 110, 140
Gertrude, Sister, of Pisa, 111
Gherardi, Mgr., 272
Giacinta, Sister, 111, 120; helped the Saint in her penances, 233
Giannini, Don Cesare, 176
Giuliani, Francesco, father of the Saint, 3; removes to Piacenza, 22; puts difficulties in the way of the Saint's vocation, 31, 32; amends his life, 38; dies, 39
Giuliani, Ursula, changes her name to Veronica, 46, *see* Veronica
God, love of, 72
Good Friday, 298, 345
Gotoloni, Sister Mary Rose, 78, 111
Gregory, Father, 319
Gregory, S., Pope, 259
Gualtieri, Mgr., Bishop of Todi, 251
Guelfi, Father Raniero, 159, 175, 260; deposition of, concerning the instruments of the Passion, 176; sent for in the last illness of the Saint, 181; with the Saint on her deathbed, 183; testifies to the Saint's great knowledge, 204; the last confessor of the Saint, 210; prophecy of the Saint concerning, 278
Habit, the religious, dignity of, 107
Heart, the Sacred, 381, 386, 389
Heart, the, of the Saint, wounds of, 132; marks on, 173, 176, 273
Helena, Blessed, of Hungary, 140
Humility, source of, 387, 388
Ida, Blessed, of Louvain, 140
Ignatius, S., 265
Illusions, safeguards against, 48
Ingratitude, sin of, 214
Innocence, 315, 316
Insults borne by the Saint, 242

INDEX. 415

Intention, effects of, 16
Intercession of the Saint for the Church, 219
Jesus, the Infant, appears to the Saint, 7, 195
Jews, the, ingratitude of, 377, 379
Joanna of the Cross, Blessed, 140
John of Fano, 405
Judas, sin of, 375
Lady, our, presents a chain to the Saint, 88 ; appears to the Saint, 161, 266 ; places the divine Infant in the arms of the Saint, 8, 273 ; sorrows of, the sorrows of our Lord, 370
Leprosy, 399
Letters, written on the heart of the Saint, 176, 177
Lidwine, of Holland, 119, 140
Liquid, the mysterious, 119 ; miracles wrought by, 120
Lomellini, Giacomo, Abate, 255 ; prophecy of the Saint concerning, 278
Love, divine, the Saint's speaking of, 209
Lucy, Blessed, of Narni, 140
Lukewarmness, the true plague of souls, 72
Magdalen, Mary, love of, 372 ; mirror of contemplation, 373
Maggi, Monsignor, 224
Maggi, Sister Maria, 74
Maggio, Sister Mary Joanna, 180, 184, 241, 244
Malatesta, Joanna, 290 ; death of, 405
Mamma mia, 221
Mancini, Benedetta, mother of the Saint, 3 ; last communion of, 11
Margaret, Blessed, of Città di Castello, 174
Martyrdom, the Saint's longing for, 205
Mary Magdalen of Pazzi, S., 174
Massani, medical attendant of the Saint, 98
Matthew, Brother, of Bassio, 405
Meazzoli, Sister Mary Celestine, 184
Meditation, 25, 28
Mercatello, birthplace of the Saint, 3, 17 ; the Saint brought back to, 36 ; three sisters of the Saint's, nuns in, 42
Moliano, Father Peter, 292, 344, 347 ; elected vicar, 333
Mori, Lorenzi Smirli, 251
Mortification, 113 ; of the Saint, 231
Moscani, Sister Angela Mary, 111
Nicholas, S., of Bari, 5
Nicholas V., Pope, 325
Novices, how trained by the Saint, 69
Noviciate, sufferings of the Saint in her, 238
Obedience of the Saint, 48, 259
Olivieri, Donna Julia Albani, 227
Olivieri, Father, 311
Onorati, Monsignor, Bishop of Urbania, 20
Osanna, Blessed, of Mantua, 140
Pacifico, Fr., of Urbino, 350

Passion, the, devotion of the Saint to, 21, 25, 46, 64 ; devotion of B. Battista Varani to, 303, 305
Patience of the Saint, 240
Penances of the Saint, 232
Penna di Billi, della, Sister Margaret Marconi, 212
Persecution, endured by B. Battista Varani, 324
Pesucci, Don Francesco Maria, 176
Piacenza, the Saint taken to, 29 ; the Saint removed from, 36
Piazzini, Sister Mary Anne, 111
Pierleoni, Father Florido, 136
Pius VI., 121
Poor, the, devotion of the Saint to, 12
Poverty, the Saint's love of, 225
Praise, the Saint shrinks from, 257
Prayer, preparation for, 391
Presents made to the nuns, how dealt with by the Saint, 229
Profession of the Saint, 56 ; of the B. Battista Varani, 329
Prophecy, gift of, 275
Purgatory, the threefold, of the Saint, 179, 181, 184 ; pains of, 369
Purity, virtue of, 236
Ranucci, Margaret, prophecy of the Saint concerning, 276
Raynaud, Theophilus, 140
"Religious," meaning of, 143
Ristori, Sister Teresa, mistress of novices, 47
Rodriguez, Father, works of, 73
Rose, S., of Lima, 14, 15, 16, 88, 103, 106
Rules of life given by our Lord to the Saint, 197
Saints seen in vision by S. Veronica, 274
Satan, disguised as the mistress of the novices, speaks to the Saint, 49 ; strikes the Saint, 61 ; assumes the appearance of the Saint, 126 ; assumes the likeness of the bishop, 184 ; assumes the appearance of our Lord, 200 ; attempts to frighten the Saint, 249 ; beats the Saint, 263 ; burns her hand, 264
Sebastiani, Monsignor Giuseppe, bishop of Città di Castello, 42 ; admits the Saint to a monastery, 43 ; prophecy of, on giving the religious habit to the Saint, 46
Segapeli, Father Vincent, 183, 203 ; prophecy of the Saint concerning, 278
Seraphim, 343
Sin, effect of, 387
Slumber, spirit of, 392
Souls, delivered from purgatory by the prayers of the Saint, 221 ; pain of our Lord because of lost, 365
Spada, Cardinal, 152
Spanaciani, Sister Mary Constance, miraculous healing of, saw the ring of espousals on the finger of the Saint, 108
Spanacieri, Signor Giulio, 224
Staphenia Soncinati, Blessed, 140

INDEX.

Stigmata, the, 139, 151; account of, 153; the Saint prayed for the removal of, 258
Suffering, love of, 13; the Saint prays for, 61, 234; great worth of, 63; the Saint's desire of, 115, 235; B. Battista Varani prays for, 358, 365
Sweetness, spiritual, 356
Tassinari, Father, Confessor of the Saint, 68, 120, 221, 251, 253, 260; Confessor of the community for forty years, 78; appointed to test the spirit of the Saint, 152; obtains her intercession for a dying nun, 217
Teresa, S., 174, 235
Tests, physical, of the Saint's supernatural state, 97
Thorns, the crown of, 93
Ticciati, Father, 217
Tommasini, Fr. Antonio, S.J., appears to the Saint, 161
Tommasini, Sister Maria, 171
Tongue, the sins of, 400
Torrigiani, Cardinal, 176
Tosi, Sister Mary Celestine, 184
Trance, the Saint falls into a, 62
Trials, supernatural, of the Saint, 127; severity of her, during her last illness, 181
Trinity, 387
Turks, the defeat of, foretold by the Saint, 221
Urbino, monastery of, the Saint enters the, 312, 324
Ursula, the Saint baptized as, 4
Vallemanni, Sister Mary Teresa, 111, 230
Varani, Camilla, 290; enters the convent of the Poor Clares in Urbino, 291; removes to Camerino, 292; moved to write an account of her inward life, 295; moved by a sermon on Good Friday, 298; makes a vow, 300; devotion of, to the Passion, 302; disliked the sight of religious, 303; resistance of, to her vocation, 307; makes a general confession, 310; conversion of, 314; sees our Lord in a vision, 321; suffers persecution, 322; becomes a nun, 324; prays for suffering, 327; general confession of, 335; sees her own soul in the hands of angels, 337; burning love of God of, 342; writes reluctantly, 346; self-abasement of, 385; her love of her enemies, 403; sent by the Pope to found a monastery in Fermo, 405; death of, 409; incorruption of the tongue of, 411
Varani, Gentilis, 289
Varani, John Mary, recovers Camerino, 405
Varani, Julius Cæsar, 289; becomes lord of Camerino, 290 cruel death of, 405
Varani, Peter Gentilis, 325; widow of, a nun, 325
Varani, Nicholas, 323
Varani, Rudolph, 289; death of, 290
Vecchj, de', Father Giulio, 169; witness of the Saint's mystic state, 170

418 INDEX.

Veil, a, of the Saint stained with tears of blood, 216
Veni Sponsa Christi, 105, 106
Veronica, S., birth and baptism of, 4; infancy of, 5; miraculous speech of, 6; devotion of, to the Infant Jesus, 7, 273; sees the Host shining, 10; her love of suffering, 13, 25; youthful zeal of, 18; confirmation of, 20; trials of, in her father's house, 31; return of, to Mercatello, 36; singular illness of, 36; sees her father in Purgatory, 39; and obtains his deliverance, 40; miraculous knowledge of Latin of, 43; becomes a nun, 44; frankness and obedience of, 47; sees our Lord in a vision, 55; the impression of the cross on the heart of, 63; mistress of novices, 67; humiliations of, 71; severe illness of, 75; elected abbess, 77, 250, 256; begs our Lady to be the abbess, 268; carefulness of, in providing for the needs of the house, 79; vision of the chalice, 86; attacked by devils, 90, 249; vision of the crown of thorns, 93; endures the cruel tests of the surgeons, 97; her preparation for the spiritual espousals, 104; burns the Holy Name into her flesh, 112; abstinence of, 116; miraculously nourished, 120; has leave to live on bread and water, 122; supernatural trials of, 127; her heart is wounded, 132; writes with her own blood, 134; wound in her hand, 138; receives the stigmata, 140, 151; tests of her miraculous state, 166; the Saint undergoes the pains of the Passion, 168—171; and the Dolours of our Lady, 172; commanded to make a picture of the miraculous impressions on her heart, 175; foretells her own death, 179; struck with apoplexy, 180; sufferings of, from the treatment of the physicians, 182; death of, 190; zeal of, for the propagation of the faith, 204; wrote under obedience, 262, 272; miracles of, 264
Visions, not desired by the Saint, 58
Vitale, Father, appointed to test the spirit of the Saint, 152
Vocation, graces of, 107
World, the, hatred of, 318
Wounds, the Sacred, 141, 149
Xavier, S. Francis, appears to the Saint, 161

THE END.

R. WASHBOURNE, PRINTER, 18 PATERNOSTER ROW, LONDON.

Printed in the United States
150842LV00003B/61/A